Peripheral Migrants

Peripheral Migrants

Haitians and Dominican Republic
Sugar Plantations

Samuel Martínez

The University of Tennessee Press / Knoxville

Frontispiece: Haitian cane cutter, Batey "Yerba Buena," Dominican Republic, 1986.
Photograph by the author.

The paper in this book meets the minimum requirements of the
American National Standard for Permanence of Paper for Printed
Library Materials. ∞ The binding materials have been chosen
for strength and durability.

Library of Congress Cataloging-in-Publication Data

Martínez, Samuel, 1959-
    Peripheral migrants : Haitians and Dominican Republic sugar plantations /
Samuel Martínez. — 1st ed.
        p.   cm.
    Includes bibliographical references and index.
    ISBN 0-87049-901-7 (cl.: alk. paper)
    1. Alien labor, Haitian—Dominican Republic. 2. Migrant agricultural
laborers—Haiti. 3. Sugar workers—Dominican Republic.
I. Title.
HD5856.H2M37 1995
331.6'2729407293—dc20   95-4359
                                                                                CIP

Contents

Figures

Maps

Tables

Preface

This book examines the circulation of labor from rural Haiti to sugar estates of the Dominican Republic. It is about Third World migrants who neither move from the country to the city nor emigrate from poor countries to rich, but circulate between distant rural areas in the world's economic periphery. Rural-rural migrants in Third World countries constitute an important but relatively little understood category of labor migrants internationally. One aim of this book is to stimulate greater scholarly interest in the global phenomenon of labor circulation in the periphery.

Among peripheral migrations worldwide, the circulation of Caribbean islanders as cane workers to the Dominican Republic is unusual in having endured for more than a century. No study of it would be complete which ignored this long history. I ground my analysis in the history of an island—Hispaniola, on which Haiti and the Dominican Republic are situated—and of a region—the plantation and postplantation societies of the Caribbean. I believe that the history of labor in the postemancipation Caribbean may contribute much to understanding the origins and continued existence of this migratory labor system, which might seem anomalous if viewed in isolation from its regional historical context.

Above all, this book is about the impact of labor circulation on the lives of the migrants and of the kinfolk they leave at home in Haiti. The economic maneuvers by which migrants and their kin attempt to accommodate labor circulation to their own needs and preferences are the main subject of the book. In common with migrants throughout the Third World, the emigrants who adapt best are those who maintain close ties with their

home areas. Even so, this book is *not* always a story of poor people tri-
umphing over the odds. For these migrants, circulation is not a reliable and
relatively risk-free form of economic attainment. It is, rather, a gamble
fraught with danger. Important as it is to explain how rural Haitians survive under severe poverty and oppression, I think it important also not to
lose sight of the risks they run in crossing the border as cane workers: divided families, hunger, economic insecurity, and, all too often, early death.

My analytical approach owes much to a set of academic perspectives
on migration termed "structural" or "historical-structural." I combine descriptive ethnography, written and oral history, and data from the personal
histories of migrants, returnees, and stay-at-homes to draw a composite
portrait of this migration. The picture of labor circulation that emerges is
not just of a migration stream shaped by host area employers and/or the
international political economy. Rather, my findings suggest that the structural imperatives of the migrant's society of origin also determine the composition, spatial-temporal pattern, and consequences of this migration.
Specifically, among the factors that shape the migrant's behavior, I lay emphasis on the roles s/he plays in a domestic group, in an extended family,
in a gender- and age-based division of occupations, and in local and national wealth and status hierarchies. In short, this book looks at migration
as a phenomenon determined at levels of social organization somewhere
between the individual migrant, on the one hand, and the global political
economy, on the other. It thus seeks to join a growing anthropological tradition of migration studies.

This book is largely the product of extended, firsthand observation of
the migrants' ways of life in the Dominican Republic and Haiti. Community-based fieldwork in the Dominican Republic preceded fieldwork in
Haiti. I spent 12 months, August 1985 to August 1986, in Yerba Buena, a
company compound for cane workers (*batey*) on a state-owned sugar estate, Ingenio Santa Ana. In Haiti, I did community-based fieldwork for six
months, September 1986 to March 1987, in the *commune* of Cayes-Jacmel,
on the country's southern coast, 16 kilometers east of the city of Jacmel. I
divided my time more or less equally between two rural neighborhoods
(*katye*). One, Cabrouette, lies in the alluvial plain surrounding the coastal
town of Cayes-Jacmel. The other, Rocheteau, is situated on the Cap Rouge
Plateau, about eight kilometers north of town.

Surprisingly, doing fieldwork on sugar company property in the Dominican Republic proved in many ways easier than doing fieldwork in village Haiti. Before embarking on my Dominican fieldwork, I anticipated
that getting permission to reside in a *batey* might be difficult, and I was
unsure of how freely I would be permitted to move about and work on

sugar company property. As it turned out, I encountered much less official interference than expected. After consulting with experienced students of *batey* society, it was I, not company administrators, who identified and chose Yerba Buena as my fieldwork site. To my knowledge, no company official ever attempted to restrict my movements or overtly monitored my contacts with Haitian workers. Nor did it seem that Haitians in Yerba Buena and its surrounding *bateyes* were reluctant to discuss abuses they had experienced in the Dominican Republic. Finally, the treatment Haitian *braceros* got in Yerba Buena was similar enough to what earlier investigators have reported from other *bateyes* to allay any suspicion that Yerba Buena had been made over into a "model *batey*." Probably, some company officials expected me to flee the *batey* promptly, and this may have helped me keep a low profile in Yerba Buena. Nine months into my fieldwork, the high-level administrator who approved my residence was surprised to find me still living there. Dominicans regard "*batey*" as practically synonymous with "awful." A young man with whom I spoke in the colonial sector of the Dominican capital city of Santo Domingo needed only these words to justify his desire to emigrate to the United States: "This," flipping a wrist dismissively at his picturesque but run-down surroundings, "is a *batey*."

In Haiti, my fieldwork took place in the year following the overthrow of Haitian president Jean-Claude Duvalier. This was a time of increased uncertainty about the political future of the country. The forced departure of the old regime's agents of repression left a gap in the structure of authority in rural areas. All unfamiliar outsiders, Haitian or foreign, were met with the suspicion that they wished to take advantage of this situation for political or monetary gain. Rumor had it, for instance, that "communist" provocateurs were marching the countryside, gathering information in a manner much like doing a household census. Fear of unfamiliar outsiders, I am convinced, was real. Not long before I began my fieldwork, villagers in other parts of Haiti had chased away development agencies' survey enumerators with sticks and stones. I responded to this difficulty by adopting a cautious, step-by-step approach, piecing together information about households in both *katye* through repeated informal visits. The unfavorable research climate slowed the pace of my work and hindered the collection of quantitative data, particularly concerning the sensitive issue of land tenure. Yet I do not think it diminished the quality of the information I gathered. In particular, people did not seem hesitant to discuss their migration histories. I ultimately felt confident enough to carry out personal history interviews, like those I had done in the Dominican Republic. Any success I had in this regard can be attributed largely to the help of my previous local acquaintances, the people I knew from an earlier visit to Cayes-Jacmel in February-March 1985.

Participant-observation was my main method of inquiry in both the Dominican Republic and Haiti. In both places, I was generally more an "observer" than a "participant." In Yerba Buena, for example, like many other single men in permanent residence, I eventually obtained a room of my own in a company barracks. But I did not work in the cane fields like other men. Naturally, I tried my hand at cutting cane, but about 15 minutes of awkward slashing produced only a pathetic little pile of cane, a painful tendinitis in my right forearm, and a badly bruised ego. Yet, in spite of significant limits to my participation in the host society, my fieldwork strengthened my belief in the value of ethnography in migration studies. On both sides of the border, my visits to homes and workplaces and my chance meetings with neighbors along footpaths and in marketplaces produced a continuous stream of firsthand observations and subtly shaped my perspective on the lives of these people. Like Massey (1987), I am convinced that information drawn from earlier ethnographic fieldwork can help survey researchers formulate situationally appropriate questions for any Third World migrant group with which they might work.

As specific information needs became apparent in the course of fieldwork, I used other more focused and quantitative field surveys and interviews. For brevity's sake, I largely confine discussion of my survey methods and interview techniques to a postscript to this study. Even so, one formal interview technique merits brief mention at the outset, because it, more than any other, shaped my interpretation of the migrants' motivations and behavior. I refer to the personal histories I elicited from 94 Haitian nationals in the Dominican Republic (70 men and 24 women) and 36 returned migrants in Haiti (31 men and 5 women). Personal histories not only produced highly detailed data but tended to get a different *kind* of response than synchronic, standardized questions. Specifically, questions that referred to specific times and places in the respondent's life were much better at eliciting testimony grounded in personal experience rather than normative responses about the reasons why people emigrate (see appendix A for the list of questions used for interviews).

In recent years, an increasingly acrimonious debate has been waged between the Dominican government and international human rights organizations accusing it of enslaving Haitians on its sugarcane plantations. Both the accusers and the accused in this debate have mostly told the "truth," at least in the negative sense that neither has said much that could be proven false in a court of law. The testimony of Haitians in the Dominican Republic confirms that all the coercive practices denounced by advocates of Haitian workers' rights are real. To these well-known facts I add evidence of other little-remarked abuses. Yet most sociologists and ethnologists who have done research on the Dominican sugar estates agree that the condition of the Haitian *bracero* differs significantly from that of slaves on nineteenth-century Caribbean sugar plantations. For example, it is neither physical coercion nor the demands of social superiors but economic need which chiefly drives Haitian men to go to the Dominican Republic. And, in the sugarcane fields of the Dominican Republic, the primary means of maintaining labor discipline is not the threat of physical punishment or legal penalty but wage incentives.

My purpose here is not to pass judgment on where the truth may lie in the divergent opinions of activists and academicians. This book is not an analysis of the integration of Haitian labor into the Dominican sugar industry. Rather, it is primarily about the impact of labor circulation on the lives of the migrants and their kin. Even so, an indicator of the complexity of this case is that a judicious selection of the facts could produce two diametrically opposed representations of reality: slavery and free wage labor. My task as a social researcher is to draw together sometimes contradictory truths, to attempt to explain them as elements of a single system, and to admit to uncertainty where the facts do not fit together or where sufficient information is lacking. My great advantage is in being able to write at considerable length. Far more complexity can go into a scholarly monograph than will fit into an article for the *New York Times*. I am convinced that, among the relatively small audience this book will reach, more complexity will increase rather than diminish the conviction that this migratory labor system is unjust.

If at times I claim to shed light on little-remarked aspects of the experience of these migrants, it is with the realization that other perspectives may reveal hitherto unsuspected dimensions of the problem. In Haiti, there is a proverb: "Beyond mountains, lie more mountains" (*"Dèyè mòn, gê mòn"*). This is, of course, more than a commentary on Haiti's broken topography. Among other things, it calls attention to the hard fact that outward appearances may conceal as much as they reveal. In my mind, the proverb also contains a warning for all who wish to understand Haiti: The very act of situating one reality within a particular frame of reference necessarily conceals other equally important realities. Behind every truth lie others that may be equally enduring and persuasive. Even the most inclusive frame of interpretation excludes much of importance in rural life. It is therefore my hope that this study may serve not only as a point of reference to other scholars but as a stimulus to further study and reflection concerning this migration and others like it.

The organization of this book is simple. The introduction describes the migratory labor system that links rural Haiti and the Dominican sugar estates, situates this system within the global history of labor mobility since the mid-nineteenth century, and proposes that the Haitians who cross the border as cane workers have much in common with others who circulate between rural areas of the Third World. Chapters 1 and 2 are historical and trace the development of the migratory labor system from its origins to the present. Chapter 1 begins by placing Haiti and the Dominican Republic within the history of human geographical mobility in the postemancipation Caribbean. It then describes how a demand for immigrant labor first arose in the late nineteenth century among the sugar producers of the Dominican Republic, and seeks to shed light on why this demand has persisted up to the present. Demand for immigrant labor in the host area does not suffice to explain why people in migrant source areas might seek employment far from home. Accordingly, chapter 2 asks how it was that Haiti became a major supplier of plantation labor to neighboring countries. It focuses largely on how the structure of rural Haitian society was changing at the turn of the twentieth century, just as Haitian men first began to emigrate seasonally in large numbers.

Chapters 3 through 7 make up the ethnographic body of the work. Chapter 3 briefly sketches the company compounds and peasant villages in which I did my fieldwork in the Dominican Republic and Haiti. It also gives an approximation of the prevalence and spatial-temporal pattern of labor circulation, and it compares migration across the Dominican border to other streams of geographical mobility that originate in rural Haiti. Chapters 4 and 5 examine the role of labor circulation in the lives of the migrants and assess its impact on the migrants' home areas in Haiti. These chapters put forward the argument that labor circulation creates a difficult dilemma for the people of the major migrant source areas. On the one hand, Dominican money buttresses endangered peasant livelihoods in rural Haiti. On the other hand, people in rural southeastern Haiti have established a dangerous dependence on migrant earnings for the perpetuation of their peasant way of life. These earnings have recently proven vulnerable to cyclical downswings in the world sugar market, with painful consequences back home in Haiti.

Chapter 6 looks at the roles of women in the migratory system, as migrants and as wives left at home by emigrant husbands. Women migrants are not primarily employed in tasks that assure the daily reproduction of the labor power of the *braceros*. Women often as not have their own reasons for leaving home and seeking independent sources of livelihood on the sugar estates. Yet women gain little freedom socially or economically by emigrating, and they often seem driven to cross the border by desperate personal circumstances. The women who stay at home bear a burden of increased risk, deprivation, and drudgery fully comparable to that of the male *bracero*. Many absent men depend on their wives to assure the continuity of their households of origin, and women who stay at home often shape survival strategies around absent husbands' earnings. This degree of material dependence between spouses is unusual in rural Haiti. In these ways, the women who stay at home may participate, just as much as their husbands, in a system of capitalist production for export. Like more direct and enduring modes of capitalist incorporation, labor circulation may offer greater gains in freedom of economic maneuver to men than to women.

Chapter 7 attempts to shed light on why some emigrants stay indefinitely in the Dominican Republic, rather than returning shortly, as does the majority, to Haiti. Most nonreturning migrants experience great difficulty coping with poverty and economic insecurity. The risks involved in emigrating are made worse because the particular circumstances of this migration tend to isolate the *braceros* from their kin. This bears out Tilly and Brown's (1967) hypothesis that the poor who migrate outside the auspices of kinship are particularly vulnerable to the negative consequences of leaving home. By way of conclusion, chapter 8 attempts to draw out the implications of my study for U.S. policy, as well as for human rights advocacy and community development organizing.

Acknowledgments

If this book represents any kind of improvement in our understanding of the migratory system, it is largely because in preparing it I was armed with the observations and insights of earlier students of the Haitian peasantry and Dominican rural proletariat. The work of Franc Báez Evertsz, Martin Murphy, Gerald Murray, and Glenn Smucker perhaps helped me most to see patterns in the confusion of events and situations in the field.

At every step along the way from background research, through research proposal formulation, fieldwork, and writing, many people and institutions generously contributed knowledge and resources to this study. To conceal the identities of those informants who prefer to remain anonymous, it has been necessary in this study to use pseudonymous personal and place names. It is with regret that I am therefore unable to thank by name the peasants and plantation dwellers whose hospitality and cooperation made it possible for me to do fieldwork in Haiti and the Dominican Republic. On both sides of the border, the people among whom I did fieldwork showed tolerance and even enthusiasm for a project that must at times have seemed to them an unwelcome intrusion.

Friends and acquaintances in the Dominican Republic and Haiti made my research easier and more enjoyable by sharing their knowledge of the region, offering their hospitality, and assisting me in ways too numerous to list here. In the Dominican Republic, Carlos Dore Cabral, Franc Báez Evertsz, and José Ramírez more than once saved me from costly errors and delays in my research through their help and advice. Francis Charles, himself a former cane worker, provided invaluable assistance in the field.

Learning the Haitian Creole language under the tutelage of Juliette Salomon greatly facilitated my entry into the field. Shelagh O'Rourke first brought to my attention the high prevalence of Dominican-bound emigration in the Cayes-Jacmel area, where she had done her Haitian fieldwork, and she kindly introduced me to people there.

This book began as a doctoral dissertation at the Johns Hopkins University. The field research on which this book is based was carried out in the Dominican Republic and Haiti, between January 1985 and March 1987, under fellowships granted by the Doherty Fellowship Committee and the Social Science Research Council and the American Council of Learned Societies. In 1982, a grant from the Ford Foundation made possible two months of preliminary research in the Dominican Republic. The Museo del Hombre Dominicano and the Bureau National d'Ethnologie provided institutional backing in the Dominican Republic and Haiti, respectively. In 1987–88, the Johns Hopkins University Department of Anthropology provided twelve months of write-up support. In 1993–94, I completed the final draft of the manuscript during my residence as Rockefeller postdoctoral fellow at the Center for Afroamerican and African Studies of the University of Michigan.

At Johns Hopkins, the Interlibrary Loan Service of the Milton S. Eisenhower Library located many, often hard-to-find, articles and books. My fellow students at Johns Hopkins were a most supportive intellectual community. The assistance of departmental secretaries on too many occasions to mention eased the preparation of this study. Nearly every regular member of the Hopkins Anthropology faculty, past and present, at some point played a part in moving this work to completion. Preliminary drafts of one or more chapters were kindly read and commented on by Monica van Beusekom, Lanfranco Blanchetti, Bernadette Driscoll, Sidney Mintz, Martin Murphy, Richard Price, Karen Richman, Richard Shain, and Michel-Rolph Trouillot. As academic advisor, Sidney Mintz helped me through problem formulation, fieldwork, and writing. This book has benefited particularly from his comments and careful editing. As second reader, Michel-Rolph Trouillot, and my other thesis examiners, Joanne Brown, Alejandro Portes, and Erika Schoenberger, went beyond the call of duty in their insightful comments on this work. It was on the basis of their comments that I made my first revision of the thesis. Bonham Richardson prepared a kind, wise, and painstaking review of what was, in hindsight, an embarrassingly repetitive first revision. His comments, probably much more than he realizes, helped me move this study forward from dissertation to book. Later, he and Jane Collins also commented helpfully on the second revision. It has been a great pleasure to work with Meredith Morris-Babb, Kimberly Scarbrough, Stan Ivester, and Elaine Otto in bringing this book to completion. Of course, all findings, opinions, and other statements in this book, except where otherwise cited, are my own, and I am responsible for any remaining errors or distortions.

Finally, this study has demanded much patient support from my wife, Monica van Beusekom, and my parents. It is in recognition of their unstinting encouragement that I dedicate this book to them.

Glossary

âba fil (Haitian Creole)	Clandestine immigration
batey/es (Spanish)	Sugar company compound/s
bracero/s (Spanish)	Haitian seasonal immigrant cane worker/s
CEA (Spanish)	Consejo Estatal del Azúcar, the Dominican state sugar consortium
congó/ses (Spanish and HC)	Haitian seasonal immigrant cane worker/s
corte, the (Spanish)	Massacre of thousands of Haitian immigrants, carried out in 1937 by loyalists of Dominican dictator Rafael Trujillo
katye (HC)	"Neighborhood," small, informally defined urban or rural residential district
lòt bò lâmè (HC)	"Beyond the sea," countries outside the island of Hispaniola
nâ pâyòl (HC)	To or in the Dominican Republic
okazyô (HC)	Official recruitment voyage
plasaj (HC)	Consensual union
Sêdomêg (HC)	The Dominican Republic
viejo/s (Spanish and HC)	Haitian/s who maintain a permanent residence on a Dominican sugar estate

Introduction

The Dominican Republic is a poor, densely populated country that occupies the eastern two-thirds of the Caribbean island of Hispaniola. It meets the seasonal labor demand of its largest industry, sugar, by importing laborers from Haiti, its even poorer and more densely populated neighbor to the west. It has been remarked upon as a paradox that the Dominican Republic should import unskilled labor from Haiti, even as its own people slip into poverty and unemployment in growing numbers. The key to this paradox lies largely in the place the Dominican Republic has occupied in the world sugar trade and in the role sugar has played in Dominican history.

Even though recently surpassed by tourism as the country's largest foreign exchange earner, sugar exports are traditionally the backbone of the Dominican Republic's economy. Even so, historically, the Dominican Republic has not enjoyed preferential access to lucrative European and U.S. markets as consistently as most other world sugar producers have. Compared to other major sugar exporters, the Dominican Republic has had to sell a larger share of its sugar on the open world market. Throughout the twentieth century, with the exception of a few brief booms, the real value of sugar on the world market has dropped. The falling value of sugar has placed continuous pressure on Dominican sugar producers to minimize their unit costs of production. Only by keeping labor costs low have the Dominican Republic's sugar producers survived (Murphy 1991).

As early as the 1880s, Dominican labor began to prove too expensive to harvest the crop of the industry's rapidly expanding sugarcane plantations. By 1893, Dominican sugar companies were recruiting cheaper and more easily disciplined labor from other Caribbean islands (Hoetink 1988). Officially regulated recruitment of men in Haiti for labor on the Dominican Republic's sugar estates began in 1915. By the 1930s, Haiti had become the main source of cane cutters for the Dominican Republic's cane growers. It has retained that position despite episodes of political conflict between the two countries.

The migratory labor system has endured largely because powerful people and organizations profit from it. The sugar companies and the Dominican state have realized savings as a result of the lower wages, the substandard living and working conditions, the unpaid social security benefits, and the inferior labor unionization rights they have accorded immigrant workers. The continued availability of large quantities of cheap, nonunion labor from Haiti has also permitted company administrators to skimp on costly labor-saving technology in the cane harvest.

Haitian labor is attractive to the Dominican Republic's cane growers not just for its low cost and plentiful supply. The Dominican security forces and sugar company labor supervisors can also control the work schedules and mobility of Haitian seasonal migrants in ways that would be considered unacceptable if applied to Dominican nationals. Among the abuses routinely committed against the seasonal migrants are obligatory extra hours of labor, denial of a weekly day of rest, and compulsory relocation to the sugar estates from non-sugar-producing areas of the Dominican Republic.

The involvement of military and civilian authorities on both sides of the border has also favored perpetuation of the system. Labor migration, contractual and undocumented, has generated direct and indirect revenues for both governments and enriched the officials who have overseen it. Chief among the individual beneficiaries was Haitian president Jean-Claude Duvalier, who was paid over two million U.S. dollars in cash for each year's contract shipment of *braceros* (agricultural day laborers).

The terms and conditions of employment of Haitian *braceros* in the Dominican Republic are so inhumane as to be likened by human rights monitors to plantation slavery.[1] It is commonly assumed that if rural Haitians are willing to leave home for the inhuman conditions of the Dominican sugar estates, then the standards of living they leave behind in Haiti must be even worse. Yet the poverty and powerlessness of the Haitian *braceros* represent only one side of the story.

Another side is how these migrants cope (and, commonly, fail to cope) with brutal poverty and oppression, at home and in the Dominican Republic. In spite of all that is known about both the history of the migratory labor system and the *braceros'* conditions of work on the sugar estates, questions about the causes and consequences of emigration from the migrants' point of view remain unanswered. What motivates rural Haitian men (and, in smaller numbers, women) to risk going to the sugar estates, in spite of the low wages and subhuman conditions they find there? What role does emigration to the sugar estates play in the livelihoods and life courses of people in rural Haiti? In the political turmoil of post-Duvalier Haiti and in recent years of worsening economic hardship on both sides of the island, how has the migratory labor system changed, and how has it remained unchanged? In what follows, I seek to shed new light on these questions, drawing largely upon information that emerged from my fieldwork with Haitian migrants on one sugar estate in the Dominican Republic and with migrants' family members in one part of rural Haiti.

My main aim here is to develop a better understanding of the impact of labor circulation on the migrants and on the migrants' kinfolk at home in Haiti. I define the study this way largely to complement the several existing studies that have mostly looked at the migratory labor system from the Dominican side of the border.[2] Given its geographical limits, this study can reflect only a small part of the diversity of the places the migrants come from in Haiti and pass through in the Dominican Republic. Even so, having done village-level fieldwork on both sides of the border permits me in this book to span the border like no previous student of this migration.

One other aim of my study is to develop a clearer sense of where the Haitians who cross the border as cane workers fit among migrants worldwide. Just what sort of migrants are they? To what other migrants might they best be compared? Much of the evidence points to the particularity of the people who circulate between rural Haiti and the sugar estates of the Dominican Republic, when compared to other Third World migrants with whom social researchers are familiar. Yet, in spite of its peculiarities, the circulation of labor between rural Haiti and the sugar estates of the Dominican Republic is not an isolated phenomenon on the world scene. Rather, it exemplifies an important, if not often studied, dimension of international labor mobility. The Haitian *braceros* are among untold numbers of migrants across the Third World who neither move to the cities of the south nor emigrate to the countries of the north but circulate from one rural periphery to another. From what up-to-date information there is about these "peripheral migrants," it seems that many of them are among the poorest and least privileged of migrants internationally.

In this introductory chapter, I first sketch the main contours of the migratory labor system. I then compare this system to other cases of labor circulation in the world economic periphery. In particular, I aim to raise questions about the extent to which generalizations derived from the study of rural-urban and Third World–metropole migrations may apply to the "lower tier" of migrants who circulate within the rural periphery.

THE MIGRATORY LABOR SYSTEM

After Cuba, Hispaniola is the largest of the Antilles. It is one of only two islands in the Antilles to be divided between two sovereign states, the other being the small French/Dutch possession of St. Martin/St. Maarten. The land border between Haiti and the Dominican Republic is 275 kilometers long (Ireland 1941, 68).

Even though they share one island, the two nations are set apart by distinct histories of European colonization and divergent paths of economic

Map 1. The Caribbean region.

development. Several scholars have commented at length on the historical and sociocultural dualism of the island (e.g., Price-Mars 1953; Logan 1968; Palmer 1976). Language divides the two nations, Dominicans speaking Spanish and Haitians speaking a French Creole language. Haitians are predominantly of black African descent, and an African-American consciousness unites Haitians even as color distinctions divide them (Nicholls 1979). The people of the Dominican Republic, while mostly of mixed European and African ancestry, generally consider their national origins and culture to be at base Hispanic. Schools and communications media have encouraged Dominicans to consider themselves racially superior to Haitians (González Canalda and Silié 1985; WGBH 1993). Certain political and economic patterns also distinguish the two countries. Haiti is the preeminent "peasant" society of the region,[3] in the sense that its land lies mostly in the hands of smallholders, who grow subsistence foodstuffs and export staples for home consumption and the market (Mintz 1989, chap. 10). The Dominican Republic, like much of Latin America, has a bimodal land distribution pattern, in which large proprietors own the best land and smallholders get the rest (Greene and Roe 1989, 97). Whereas Haiti has long been one of the more densely populated territories of the Antilles, the Dominican Republic was for a long time among the most lightly populated (Castillo 1981a, 38). Equally important, as it concerns population movement between the two countries, Haiti lags behind the Dominican Republic in almost every basic indicator of national health and wealth (see table 1).

Table 1

Basic Indicators, Haiti and the Dominican Republic

Indicator	Haiti	Dominican Republic
Land area (square kilometers)	27,750	48,700
Total population (millions), 1990	6.5	7.2
Population density (persons per square kilometer), 1990	236	148
Population annual growth rate (%), 1960–90	1.8	2.7
Daily calorie supply (as % of requirements), 1988	84	104
Mortality rate before age 5 (per 1,000 live births), 1990	130	78
GNP per capita (U.S.$), 1990	370	830
Total adult literacy rate (%), 1990	53	83
% of population with access to safe water, 1988–90	41	63
% population urbanized, 1990	28	60

SOURCE: United Nations Development Programme 1992: 134–35, 146–47, and 170–71.

Both countries have experienced brutal family dictatorships: the Dominican Republic, under Trujillo, from 1930 to 1961, and Haiti, under the Duvaliers, father and son, from 1957 to 1986. The national constabularies established in each country by the U.S. Marines helped these dictators impose absolute control. After the dictators fell, both countries saw a freely elected government crushed by the military. In 1963, the Dominican Republic's Juan Bosch and, in 1991, Haiti's Jean-Bertrand Aristide each governed for only a few months before being forced into exile by military coups.

The two countries are on a par in at least one statistic. From each, some half-million nationals have emigrated to North America. This high incidence of emigration is all the more striking because neither country's citizens have been given preferential admission to an external metropole, as have the people of Puerto Rico, the British West Indies (until 1962), and the French Départements d'Outre-Mer. Since the 1960s, both countries have also seen greatly increased rates of rural-urban migration. Largely because of it, the capital city of each country—Santo Domingo in the Dominican Republic and Port-au-Prince in Haiti—contains more than 20 percent of the national population.

It is not known how many Haitian nationals there are in the Dominican Republic. The vast majority of them do not have proper immigration documents, and they seek to conceal their presence from state authorities. It is therefore perhaps not surprising that national census data has always drastically undercounted the country's Haitian population. Official Dominican estimates, on the other hand, have at times exaggerated the Haitian immigrant population, perhaps with the intent of arousing public indignation about the Haitian presence in the country. Unofficial estimates may more accurately reflect the true dimensions of Haitian immigration (see table 2). For lack of any more reliable figures, Báez Evertsz's (1992, 109) guess of 500,000 may be accepted as a credible estimate of the number of Haitian nationals now living in the Dominican Republic.

The sugar industry has long been the largest single employer of Haitian workers in the Dominican Republic. It seems safe to say that upwards of 100,000 Haitian nationals, including women and children, now live on the country's private and state-owned sugar estates. Today, 90 percent or more of the cane cutters in the Dominican Republic are Haitian nationals or second- and third-generation descendants of Haitian immigrants (Murphy 1986, 141). Of these workers, half are seasonal migrants, who enter the Dominican Republic before or during the cane harvest with the intention of returning to Haiti within a year (Báez Evertsz 1986, 158). More than one informed observer has concluded that, without immigrant labor, sugar production in the Dominican Republic would come to a virtual halt

Table 2

Estimates and Tallies of the Number of Haitians
in the Dominican Republic, 1920–92

Source	Year	Number of Haitians
Dominican census	1920	28,258
M. M. Knight	1925	100,000
Dominican census	1935	52,657
Balaguer	1935	400,000
Jimenes Grullón	1943	81,000
Dominican census	1950	18,772
Dominican census	1960	29,350
Border Commission	1968	200,000
Directory of Immigration	1970	42,142[a]
Lundahl	1979	300,000
ONAPLAN	1981	200,000
Balaguer	1989	over 2,000,000
Lawyers Committee	1991	over 1,000,000
Báez Evertsz	1992	500,000

SOURCES: Corten 1974, 67–68; Lundahl 1979, 626; ONAPLAN 1981b; Báez Evertsz 1986, 190, and 1992, 109; Lawyers Committee 1991a, 36; and Cedeño Caroit 1992, 104 n. 70.

[a]Registered, another 45,000 undocumented.

(ONAPLAN 1981a; Murphy 1986: 389–94). Hence, one can understand why Haitian cane workers in the Dominican Republic, in spite of their subordinate status, can say, "Haitians own the country" ("*se Ayisyê ki mèt peyi-a*").[4] It is upon their labor that sugar production, and hence the livelihood of tens of thousands of the country's citizens, depend.

The sugar estates are not the only destination in the Dominican Republic to which Haitian immigrants may go. Many thousands of Haitians reside in non-sugar-producing areas of the country. Just how many Haitian nationals live in non-sugar-producing areas is anyone's guess. The most careful estimate by economic sector of the country's Haitian population (ONAPLAN 1981b) is now out of date. A growing consensus has it that most Haitians in the Dominican Republic do not reside on the sugar estates (Caroit 1992, 73). Even so, no census or field survey has yet been made of the Haitians who do not reside on the sugar estates. Nor has any survey determined what proportion of that outside population passed through the estates on its way to its ultimate destination. These questions are of no small political importance. Dominican authorities have long maintained that those Haitians who reside off the sugar estates mostly entered the country as cane workers and subsequently abandoned their assigned places of work. This argument has justified a wide range of repressive measures against Haitian working people in the Dominican Republic.[5]

Dominican sugar companies have historically relied on two different channels of immigration from Haiti to recruit the harvest laborers they need. The first is voyages organized and paid for by agents of the sugar companies, with official approval on both sides of the border. These voyages, popularly called *"okazyô"* ("transport") or *"imigrasyô-â"* ("the immigration") by Haitians, were suspended in 1986 after the fall of Haiti's "President-for-Life," Jean-Claude Duvalier, and have not yet been reinstated by the military and civilian governments that have succeeded him in power. In its last years, contract migration brought over 20,000 seasonal workers annually to the Dominican Republic's cane harvest (Murphy 1986, 182).

A comparable number of seasonal migrants has entered by a second channel of immigration, clandestine passage by land. This route is called *"âba fil,"* meaning literally "under the wire," and is commonly traversed with the paid assistance of border guides, called *"pasè,"* similar to the *"coyotes"* who work the U.S.-Mexican border. With or without the assistance of a *pasè,* many of those who go *âba fil* cross the border undetected and pay their own passage, plus bribes to Dominican police officers along the way, to reach the destinations of their choice in the Dominican Republic. Even so, most *âba fil* entrants fall into the custody of Dominican military or police authorities soon after they cross the frontier. Often, the *pasè* turns the entrants over to the Dominican authorities at the border, for a fee of a few pesos for each Haitian man or woman he delivers. Other entrants turn themselves in at border garrisons, because they either lack enough money to travel further on their own or think it probable that they will eventually be detained by the authorities. Still others avoid immediate detention but are arrested at checkpoints further inside the country. From army garrisons, police stations, or nearby holding pens, army and police officers hand over the detainees for a fee of RD$15 to $30 (roughly U.S.$2 to $4, at 1990 exchange rates) per adult to agents of the state sugar consortium, Consejo Estatal del Azúcar (CEA), to be bused to estates that need harvest laborers. The buses travel under armed military escort, and make few stops on their way east, to diminish the chances of escape of their Haitian passengers. The detainees are not allowed to disembark until they arrive at the *batey* to which they have been assigned.[6]

Another, smaller avenue of undocumented immigration has been the recruitment of laborers in Haiti without official approval of the Haitian authorities. Both free-lancers and men who work for specific cane growers recruit unofficially in Haiti. Again, Dominican army officers commonly obtain a fee for holding these recruits at border garrisons until transshipment to a CEA estate is arranged. When a large number of men are recruited at the same time and place, migrants may also refer to unofficial recruitment voyages as "*okazyô.*"

Even in years when the influx of workers from Haiti has been heavy, the CEA has also made use of forced recruits, Haitian men whom the Dominican army rounds up in border towns, farms, and, more rarely, cities across the country. The military transfers these detainees to agents of the CEA, again for a fee, often together with *âba fil* entrants who are taken into official custody. During the harvest, the Dominican national police also routinely screen intercity buses and taxis for Haitian passengers, on highways Haitians are known to travel. The official rationale for both the round-ups and the surveillance of highways is to intercept any undocumented Haitians who circumvent border controls or who abandon the sugar estates to which they have been assigned by the CEA. In fact, during every cane harvest, many Haitian men and women who are in the Dominican Republic for reasons unrelated to work in the sugar industry are stopped by law enforcement officers. At the point of arrest, the Haitians are either made to pay a bribe for release or are detained as undocumented immigrants for shipment to *bateyes* of the CEA. In Yerba Buena and its surrounding *bateyes*, I met young men who had been detained and unwillingly relocated after having crossed the border just to buy a sack of sugar or other contraband trade goods. Other forced recruits included men who had entered the country with the idea of going to the city of Santo Domingo but were arrested by police on highways leading to the capital. Still others had homes and families in the Dominican Republic, but were taken from their places of work and sent to the sugar harvest, without even being given the chance to inform their people that they were being taken away. In years when the flow of workers from Haiti has faltered, the Dominican security forces have stepped up their persecution of Haitians in non-sugar-producing areas of the country.

Off the sugar estates during the harvest, Haitian-Dominican men may face many of the same official restrictions on their movements as Haitian nationals. (In this study, "Haitians" denotes only Haitian nationals, and "Haitian-Dominicans," Haitian immigrants of the second and third generations.) Each year, unknown numbers of Haitian-Dominican men are taken into custody and sent against their will to cut cane on CEA estates. It is also alleged that the most recent wave of deportations of Haitians from the Dominican Republic, from June to September 1991, swept up young Haitian-Dominicans as well as Haitian nationals. There is a certain controversy about whether the children born of Haitian nationals in the Dominican Republic are rightfully Dominican citizens. In the opinion of many, the Dominican Constitution is unequivocal on the matter. It states that any person born in the Dominican Republic has the right to Dominican citizenship. Yet the authorities do not necessarily respect the valid documents of Haitian-Dominicans. As Haitian-Dominican interviewees told one researcher, "When we show the *cédula* (identity card), the soldier tells us, as he rips it up, 'The *cédula* is Dominican, but you are Haitian'" (Dore Cabral 1987, 62, my trans.).

The Haitians whom CEA officials pick up from border garrisons and other holding points are generally given no choice about the estate to which they will be sent. Every busload of seasonal workers therefore contains some men and women who had plans to go somewhere other than the *batey* to which they have been sent. This other place may be a *batey* they know from a previous voyage, a *batey*, town, or urban neighborhood where family or fellow villagers reside, or a rural or urban area which they have simply heard is a "better place" to work. In the *batey* where I lived, I saw people sneak away literally the moment they got off the truck that had carried them there.

Not surprisingly, cane growers seek to curb the seasonal migrants' mobility. To prevent escape, local company bosses post armed guards at night outside the sleeping quarters of newly recruited workers. The guard is relaxed after one or two weeks, when each man among the new arrivals has cut enough cane to collect a paystub or two, and each woman has established a living arrangement with relatives, friends, or a single cane worker. At this point, it is assumed that inertia will keep many if not most of the recruits in place for the rest of the harvest. It seems that, given the ease and low cost of replacing workers who abandon the *bateyes*, cane growers find it uneconomical to implement strict surveillance for long. Maintaining a round-the-clock guard over the *braceros'* living quarters and workplaces for the entire harvest would cost several times more than recruiting a whole new batch of workers. It should not be forgotten that, porous though the system of labor control is, the threat of violence is what upholds it. Each year, unknown numbers of Haitians are killed, and many more are physically abused, robbed of their belongings, and denied basic liberties in acts of official oppression in the Dominican Republic. Yet company surveillance is not designed to prohibit all movement of Haitian immigrants. Its aim, rather, is to slow to a trickle the potential flood of labor from the estates.[7]

Poverty also acts to keep Haitian cane workers on the sugar estates. Few migrants leave home with more than the minimum amount of money they might need for travel expenses. By the time they arrive at the estates, most have spent their last dollar on food and transportation. Others have been robbed by *pasè* or by the authorities of what little money they had. Others still have been picked up from Dominican farms, orchards, and ranches and sent directly to a CEA estate in their work clothes, with hardly a penny in their pockets. Therefore, even without the surveillance of company security guards, many recruits would be obliged to stay on the sugar estates for at least a few weeks, until they saved enough money to move on to some other place in the Dominican Republic where they would rather be.

When Haitian men arrive in the company compounds where they are housed on the Dominican sugar estates, they find that the sugar companies offer them only one means of subsistence, cutting cane. From talking to veteran cane workers, the neophyte quickly learns the first rule of life for Haitian men in the *bateyes:* "cut cane or starve." Compared to Caribbean slave plantations of the nineteenth century, the modern Dominican sugar estates require very few supervisory personnel to keep the harvest going. Instead, the wage system quietly assures that the cane cutters will work their hardest even without close company supervision. In the piece-rate wage system under which they work as cane cutters, the migrants are paid according to the weight of the cane they cut. To get money for food, they must work, and work hard.

Outmoded, inefficient harvest technology restricts the cane cutters' productivity and hence their earnings to what is perhaps the lowest average in any modern sugar industry worldwide (ONAPLAN 1981a, 44; Corten 1985, 59–61; Báez Evertsz 1986, 232–49; Moya Pons et al. 1986, 291–99; Murphy 1991, 59–61). Haitian *braceros* must work days of 12 hours or longer just to earn barely enough to feed themselves (Murphy 1986, 284). A large part of their caloric intake comes from the cane juice that company foremen tacitly allow them to consume at work. Some nights, the *braceros* return to their quarters too tired even to undress, let alone to fetch water for bathing and cooking, and must return to the cane fields at dawn with the sweat and the hunger of the day before. Worse still are the days when the *braceros* go idle and hungry, because of a breakdown at the mill or while waiting for a foreman to give them a new work assignment or for a cart driver to come collect their cane from the fields. Illness and injury also commonly sideline individuals from work. The Dominican Republic's cane growers provide their cutters with none of the protective gear—boots, gloves, and goggles—that cane sugar producers in other countries consider essential. As a result, the cutters may suffer eye injuries from debris that flies off the cane plants as these are cut, and they risk deep wounds to their limbs, hands, and feet from errant strokes of the cutlass. Nutritional deprivation and the great physical strain of cutting cane also weaken *braceros'* resistance to illness. To pile injury on injury, a many-branched system of pay reductions and petty corruption deprives Haitian cane cutters, by my estimate, of at least one-third to one-half of their base income.

On top of these long hours of work, company bosses may require the *braceros* to work at night or on Sunday, so as to avoid shortages of cane at the mill, or to harvest accidentally burned cane before it goes dry. The *braceros* condemn the denial of proper rest on these occasions as being "like slavery" and a "shameless act" (*"vakabôday"*) on the part of the bosses. Breman's (1979, 186) analysis of the preference for migratory labor shown by sugar producers in South Gujarat, India, applies in its essentials to the Dominican sugar industry: "The seasonal migrants are available at all times (day and night), work (as little or as much) according to whatever is required and are immediately transferable (to any part of the harvest area) as is necessary. In all these respects, to employ local workers would be to diminish the degree of subordination and alienation—in principle, total—of labour in the production process."

At harvest's end, the Dominican authorities relax their restrictions on Haitians' movements. As a belated gesture of goodwill, CEA bosses may even provide free transportation back to the Haitian frontier to all who wish to go. All other Haitians are left free to stay or to go, as their individual means, needs, and preferences may dictate. It is only as the beginning of the next cane harvest approaches that the authorities once more tighten the net around Haitians in the Dominican Republic.

The year of my Dominican fieldwork, 1985–86, was unusual when compared to earlier years but perhaps typical of the years that have followed, in the heightened intensity of the repression that the Dominican authorities directed against Haitians. That year's cane harvest was the first to follow suspension of the official labor contract between the CEA and the Haitian government. In response to fears that the harvest might be lost through a shortage of cane cutters, Dominican authorities stepped up forced recruitment of Haitians residing off the sugar estates to a fever pitch (Plant 1987, 89–90). One sign of the unusual severity of official repression that year was the arrival, in the southern *batey* where I lived, of a large group of Haitian men, women, and children from the town of Esperanza in the center of the Dominican Republic. A few weeks into the harvest, they took the apparently very unusual step of volunteering as a group to go cut cane in the south. They did this out of fear that their men might be kidnapped for the sugar estates and even physically abused by the military. Recent reports from human rights monitor organizations (Americas Watch 1989, 1990; Lawyers Committee 1991a) suggest that CEA administrators are still turning to forced recruitment more frequently than in the years immediately before 1986.

In short, a combination of coercion and pressing economic need channels Haitian labor toward the sugar estates. Some *braceros* enter the Dominican Republic with the expectation of working on a sugar estate. Others only wish to spend a day buying trade goods in a Dominican border town, or they cross the border in search of work without realizing the risk they run of being arrested and shipped to a CEA estate. Others still live in non-sugar-producing areas of the Dominican Republic and are forcibly relocated to distant sugar estates. In spite of more than a decade of scrutiny of the industry's harvest labor recruitment practices by journalists, academicians, and human rights monitors, there is no broad-based survey data on how much each factor contributes to the harvest labor force.

Even so, my field observations sustain earlier evidence that most Haitian cane workers enter the Dominican Republic of their own volition and with the knowledge that they will probably be taken to work on a sugar estate. As late as 1985, each year's officially sponsored drive to recruit *braceros* for the Dominican cane harvest attracted men in numbers several times greater than the 20,000 or so who were hired. Many of the recruits were not only willing to tolerate the considerable inconvenience and danger of queuing up for recruitment under the batons and bullets of the Tontons Macoutes. They also *paid bribes* of up to U.S.$20 to obtain a place in the official *okazyô*. In 1986, at the height of that year's campaign of forced recruitment, the majority of the recent entrants whom I interviewed in one small group of *bateyes* (24 of 35 men, or 69 percent) had entered the country with the expectation of working on the sugar estates.[8] Unfortunately, this is to my knowledge the only quantitative data ever published on the relative prevalence of forced and fraudulent recruitment.

Nor is there convincing evidence that Haitians' interest in seasonal employment across the border is often a product of misinformation about the terms and conditions of employment on the sugar estates. On the contrary, in rural southeastern Haiti, I have found that details of abuses against Haitian workers in the Dominican Republic are known even to people who have never crossed the border. Returning kinfolk and neighbors have told them about the exploitation and mistreatment that Haitians experience on the sugar estates. Few young folk are likely to believe labor recruiters who tell them the streets across the border are paved with gold. (Even though not fooled, young men at times agree to go to the Dominican Republic with these recruiters.) Finally, misinformation cannot explain the high prevalence of repeat migration among Haitian cane workers in the Dominican Republic. If men went to the Dominican Republic as cane workers just because they thought they would find good pay and work conditions there, it is unlikely that many would return in subsequent harvests after they knew the bitter truth about working on the other side.

Few observers, however they might characterize the migratory labor system, would deny that the recruitment by force of even a minority of Haitian cane workers in the Dominican Republic is a crime that should be punished. Here, without intending to deny or minimize that injustice, I focus mainly on a lesser known and at times equally tragic story: that of the thousands of Haitians who have so few other economic alternatives at home that they cross the border of their own volition, knowing it likely that they will be taken to a sugar estate, where mistreatment and exploitation await them.

LABOR CIRCULATION IN THE WORLD ECONOMY

"If you want to get at the root of murder, look for the blacksmith who made the matchet": so advises a proverb from Chinua Achebe's fictional West African state of "Kangan." Even if this adage leaves something to be desired as a procedure of criminal investigation, it reflects a sound appreciation of the complex nature of causality in human relations. In the case of the migration of Caribbean islanders as cane cutters to the Dominican Republic, the matchets have—literally as well as figuratively—come from the highly industrialized, so-called core states of the world economy. Since the mid-nineteenth century, commerce between north and south has changed the scope and character of human geographical mobility across much of the tropical world. It is therefore appropriate to begin the search for the root causes of peripheral migration by briefly pondering these transformations.

In the last century-and-a-half, millions, north and south, have gone to places far from home for work producing commodities or building physical infrastructures for international trade. Long before this time, of course, extensive geographical mobility and extended absences from home were a part of people's lives in many human societies worldwide (Chapman 1982; Chapman and Prothero 1985). Yet, directly and indirectly, the explosive growth of international commerce of the last 150 years has led people around the world to move in greatly increased numbers. Just as importantly, this global economic revolution has changed the reasons why people move. Increasingly, people have left home as *labor migrants,* that is, as "individuals whose purpose in moving is to sell their work capacity in the receiving areas" (Portes and Walton 1981, 21).

Between 1845 and 1914, more than 50 million people left northern, eastern, and southern Europe for work in the Americas, southern Africa, the southern cone of South America, Australia, and New Zealand (Lewis 1978, 14). From this great wave of transoceanic migration came the west's most enduring popular images of the migrant experience. Little need be added to what has already been said about this massive displacement of people, except perhaps to point out that Europeans were not alone in this period of history in traveling far in search of work. At the same time in the tropics, little noticed in the north, there occurred a diaspora of perhaps even greater size and geographical spread.

In the late nineteenth and early twentieth centuries, probably many more than 50 million left tropical homelands temporarily or permanently for work in distant places. The largest of these migrations were those of Indians and Chinese, largely as indentured laborers. The Indians went in large numbers to Ceylon, Burma, and Malaya, to Fiji and islands of the Indian Ocean, to Natal and East Africa, and to the Guianas and the Antilles. The Chinese continued to go to established destinations in Southeast Asia and moved in large numbers to Australia, New Zealand, and various islands of the Pacific, to Mauritius in the Indian Ocean, to North and South America, and to the Caribbean (Look Lai 1993, 19–20). Across the tropics, dozens of smaller, less far-flung, but locally no less significant migrations brought people from rural homeplaces to mines, plantations, belts of smallholder export-crop cultivation, and large construction projects.

Migrants, north and south, largely followed where European and North American capital led. The global economic context of this rapid expansion of human mobility is perhaps nowhere better summarized than by Wolf (1982, 310): "During the latter part of the nineteenth century, production under capitalism took a great leap forward, escalating the demand for raw materials and foodstuffs and creating a vastly expanded market of world-wide scope. Whole regions became specialized in the production of some raw material, food crop, or stimulant. . . . Regional emphasis on a monocrop or single raw material product demanded, in turn, that other areas raise crops to feed the primary producers, or furnish labor power to the new plantations, farms, mines, processing plants, and transport systems."

Yet capital did not break down all institutional barriers to human migration. Remarkably, in spite of the enormous physical distances sometimes traveled, ordinary working people of the temperate and tropical worlds generally did not migrate as laborers into each other's latitudes. They remained, instead, within their respective tiers of the globe. By far the greater part of European emigrants of the time went to other temperate regions of the world. Tropical emigrants mostly traveled to other tropical regions, as laborers for export-oriented enterprises, large and small (Davis 1974, 96–99; Lewis 1978, 14; Mintz 1987, 47–49).

On occasion, interest in obtaining the cheapest and most easily disciplined labor led employers in the north to put aside their preference for Europeans and to opt instead for nonwhite workers from the tropics. Between 1863 and 1906, for example, the sugar estates of Queensland, Australia, imported at least 60,000 Melanesian islanders as harvest laborers (Docker 1970, 274, cited in Wolf 1982, 334). During roughly the same period, over 200,000 Chinese were recruited as temporary workers in agriculture, mining, and railroad construction in the western United States and Canada (Wolf 1982, 377). In these cases, as in other nonwhite labor recruitment schemes of the time, immigration laws and popular discrimination posed formidable obstacles to immigrant assimilation. Whereas European immigrants won uncounted niches in the economy from majority and minority group workers, nonwhite immigrants never succeeded in permanently displacing white labor from existing occupations. Nativism ultimately led all temperate countries except South Africa to curb further immigration of people of color.

It was not until the second half of the twentieth century that the by-then highly industrialized states of the First World would relax (but not lift altogether) their barriers to entry of immigrants of color. Beginning in the 1950s and 1960s, Western Europe and North America became targets for immigrants and guest workers from southerly neighbor states and imperial possessions on the road to decolonization (Davis 1974, 102–3). The rising tide of westward emigration from the former eastern bloc notwithstanding, international migration today consists mostly of people of the south trying to enter the countries of the north. Beginning also in the 1950s and 1960s, even greater numbers of people were swept into migration from rural to urban areas of the Third World. In these decades, many Third World states expanded government services and encouraged the growth of domestic manufacturing industries. Even people who could not get formal employment were quick to relocate to the city to sell goods and services to the full-time wage earners. Pioneer migrants helped later arrivals establish urban livelihoods that were relatively secure, if not often very satisfactory.

Today, three or four decades after the opening to immigration of the countries of the north and the cities of the south, it may seem paradoxical that migrations like the one I examine here might still exist. Diverse schools of social theory—including neoclassical economics, modernization theory, and social evolutionist strains of Marxism—coincide in predicting the imminent extinction of short-term labor circulation. They regard circulation as a transitional stage in mobility, halfway between largely sedentary, rural, "traditional" ways of life and very mobile, highly urbanized, "modern" lifestyles. Social evolutionist theories aside, one might reasonably wonder why anyone would still be willing or obliged to leave home for backbreaking labor and meager pay in Third World agricultural and extractive industries if they could obtain higher and more secure incomes, under better conditions, in a country of the north or a city of the south.

Yet, in every major region of the tropics, people continue to circulate as occasional laborers between impoverished homeplaces and agricultural estates, extractive industries, and infrastructural projects. Over the course of the twentieth century, many migrations like that of Haitians to the sugar estates of the Dominican Republic have died out. But new ones have arisen in response to fresh injections of capital into areas on the margins of global trade. Since 1930, even Latin America—the Third World region in which urban growth has been greatest (Skeldon 1985, 100)—has witnessed a significant expansion of predominantly short-term circulation, oriented toward agricultural regions of large seasonal labor demand. These migrations have arisen under various circumstances. Some have responded to growing inequalities in standards of living between certain countries of the region, as is perhaps exemplified most clearly by the migrations of Colombians to Venezuela (Gómez and Díaz 1983). Others have arisen with the introduction of a new cash crop to an agricultural frontier, as among the southern Peruvian highlanders who go as seasonal coffee farmers to the humid forests of the eastern Andes (Collins 1988). Still others have expanded with the growth of import-substituting domestic agroindustry, as did the migration of highland Bolivians as sugarcane workers to northwest Argentina (Whiteford 1981). At least one circular migration in Latin America has been set in motion out of the politically motivated desire to replace foreign workers with nationals, that of the Central Americans who displaced West Indians as harvest laborers on coastal banana plantations (Wolf 1982, 325). By looking further afield, to Africa, Asia, and the Pacific—where circular mobility is understood to predominate—many comparable migrations of recent origin could be added to this list.

Not only does rural-rural circulation persist, but much rural-urban mobility also now takes the form of short-term, circular displacements. Circular migrants of today, when compared to those of the past, work less often for large European/North American–owned firms and more often find employment in the urban informal economy. The "typical" circular migrant might now just as easily be an urban pedicart driver or a seasonal construction worker as an agricultural day laborer or a miner on short-term contract. By the same token, fewer circular migrants than in the past relocate under the auspices of labor recruiters or host area businesses, and more rely on their kin and fellow countryfolk to help them find lodgings and employment in their places of destination.

In short, even in the present global economic crisis, Third World migration shows few signs of becoming a single massive flow from the country to the city and from south to north. The emigration of Haitian men as cane workers to the Dominican Republic is unusual in having endured for almost a century. Yet the worldwide persistence of similar movements of labor raises doubts that this and other cases of labor circulation are simply vestiges of a bygone era of capitalism. Even the best-known modernization theorist in migration studies, Zelinsky (1979, 185, 187, in Chapman 1982, 96), has admitted that circulation in Third World countries may be "symptomatic of the problems of underdevelopment" and that it consequently "promises to endure, with further variations and complexities, as long as underdevelopment persists."

CIRCULATION AND MIGRATION THEORY

It is not just by having endured for generations that circulation poses a challenge to mainstream migration theory. There is also reason to suspect that the individual motivations of short-term circular migrants and the social consequences of their mobility may often differ from those of long-term migrants. "Our ideas about migration," van Amersfoort (1978, 18) remarks, "are strongly influenced by the forms of migration that were predominant in Europe and the U.S.A. in the 19th and 20th centuries: urbanization and colonization. These were processes in which, whatever the amount of local and individual variation, the net result was a lasting change of residence." Common sense, backed by neoclassical economic thought, holds that people move from one place to another because they think their quality of life will be better where they are going. This idea, made systematic, is "equilibrium theory," long the dominant perspective in migration studies. Equilibrium theory regards spatial imbalances in labor supply and demand, or differences in the quality of life between source and receiving areas, as a sufficient explanation for all voluntary, economically motivated population movements. In all its varieties, equilibrium theory reduces migration ultimately to individuals deciding in their thousands to move, based on a rational calculation of the personal costs of changing residence and the benefits of living elsewhere.

The concept of circulation focuses attention on an aspect of human geographical mobility that may be difficult to explain in terms of any simple variety of equilibrium theory: many Third World people go out as laborers not to establish lasting residence elsewhere but to return home shortly with enhanced means. Circulation confounds any simple interpretation of voluntary mobility as the outcome of invidious comparisons between home and host areas. If workers willingly alternate residence between two or more places over the course of the year, can one say without reservation that they consider one place "better" than the other? Leaving home in order to return challenges the assumption that successful emigrants from relatively "backward" areas will generally stay in their "adopted countries" and that only those who fail to adapt will return (Piore 1979, 50).

Even though it has long been considered marginal to mainstream migration theory, circulation in the periphery has not gone unnoticed by anthropologists, economists, and geographers. As early as the 1930s, social researchers asked why it was that people in noncapitalist or partially capitalist societies seemed often to prefer temporary or part-time wage labor or cash-crop cultivation over full-time employment in the market economy, even when the latter promised a higher real income. A series of pioneering studies, associated largely with the Rhodes-Livingstone Institute, viewed labor migration as a step taken only reluctantly by peoples of southern and central Africa, in response to the erosion of their customary sources of livelihood under colonial rule (Hunter 1936; A. I. Richards 1939; Wilson 1941–42). Yet few other early observers believed circulation to be a product of social and economic dislocation. Most held the opinion that peripheral people's temporary commitment to wage labor was a product of limited wants and conservative life-styles. As Greaves (1935, 114–15) summarized: "The continuity of a labour supply curve based on the need of money depends upon that need being constant, and people accustomed to a self-sufficing economy only feel this constancy of need if they have acquired a taste for necessities which must be regularly purchased from the outside. If their new tastes comprise only curiosities and occasional exceptions to their customary wants, . . . they will provide merely a discontinuous and short-term labour supply." The common wisdom of the time held that centers of wage opportunities in the periphery drew people from distant areas chiefly because they offered their workers a relatively quick way of attaining low and clearly defined income goals: e.g., money for head and hut taxes, with perhaps a little left over to purchase one or two consumer durables—a rifle, a bicycle, a steel ax, or machine-woven cloth.

Out of these ideas emerged the theory of the target worker and the backward-sloping labor supply function. Stated simply, this theory puts forward the possibility that in a dual economy—where a wage sector and a subsistence sector coexist—wage increases might paradoxically *decrease* labor supply. That is, a wage increase might boost the rate at which individual workers reached their savings goals and then left paid employment, but would not necessarily make paid employment attractive enough to people in the villages for new recruits to be mobilized in numbers greater than the early leavers. This is assuming that the potential migrant has both "a relatively low, clearly defined and rigid income goal" and "a strong preference to remain in the village" (Berg 1961, 474).

Even proponents of the theory of the target worker recognize that these assumptions might apply better to early migrations than to recent ones. Yet there is reason to doubt whether the target worker was ever an accurate representation of the motivations and behavior of nonwestern migrants. Recent historical research has tended to conclude that what brought people to emigrate from peripheral homelands was not the allure of industrial manufactures but the pressure of taxes, the displacement of small-scale producers from their customary land and water rights, the denial to them of markets for their products, and often physical punishment for noncompliance with outsiders' labor demands. As Portes and Walton (1981, 31) remark, "many 'backward' economies throughout history have not spontaneously exported labor and . . . , when labor has been needed, it has had to be coerced out of them." Often, in early tropical labor schemes, migrants were a captive work force in more than a figurative sense: many were recruited by force or deception, or under threat of imprisonment, or accepted contracts of indentureship or debt-peonage (Emmer 1986; Zegeye and Ishemo 1989; Breman 1990, chap. 4). In other societies, by contrast, such as the Pedi and Tsonga of southern Africa (Stichter 1985, 14–19) and in the Solomon Islands of Melanesia (Bathgate 1985; Connell 1985; Frazer 1985), people were quick to take up the offer of wages for labor in distant European-owned export enterprises, perhaps out of a desire to acquire useful and/or status-enhancing industrial manufactures unavailable at home.

All these migrations brought about a deeper integration of the migrants into circuits of global trade, and they often eventuated deep changes in the ways of life of the migrants' societies of origin. For many people from societies on the margins of global trade, migration was their first experience of being paid (or compelled by force) to "produce things of which they were not the principal consumers," and of "consum[ing mainly] things they had not produced, . . . in the process earn[ing] profit for others elsewhere" (Mintz 1985, xxiv). The advent of emigration on a large scale had similar meanings for the lives of the people who stayed at home in the migrants' places of origin. Emigration disrupted local production units, diminished agricultural output, encouraged dependence on migrant remittances, and necessitated increased imports of food, textiles, and other basic goods. Once integrated into external markets, few societies could retreat to an earlier, more self-reliant life-style. Thus, even in those places from which people went forth willingly as migratory laborers, emigration sooner or later became nearly obligatory, "as wants became necessities and taxes proved inescapable" (Connell 1985, 145).

At the level of individual and family decision making, recent research has also overturned the idea that circulation belongs to a stage at which rural folk have limited, customary wants. Social researchers have generally come to consider circulation to be not so much a product of a nonwestern mentality as a rational adaptation to poverty and economic uncertainty. One variant of this theme holds circulation to be a household or family strategy for optimizing utility from consumption. "A typical family that practises circular migration," according to Fan and Stretton (1985, 338), "has one or two members working in the city while the remaining members continue to live and work in the village. The migrant spends extended periods working and living in the city but makes frequent return visits to see his family." Sending out one or two highly productive workers may open access to higher urban incomes. Keeping the rest of the family in the village frees the domestic unit of the cost of supporting dependents and unemployed workers at higher urban costs of living.

Another variant of this perspective is that which holds circulation to be a way of mitigating risk. People who stand near the margin of subsistence may rationally give higher priority to increasing food security than to optimizing income. Keeping up small-scale farming and other customary sources of livelihood at home may be a form of insurance against unemployment or rapid wage-price fluctuation. "Peasants have greater opportunity to minimize risk, especially when they continue to produce a large part of their own food, and sustain an institutionalized system of reciprocity in full operation" (Brookfield 1970, 14–15, cited in Chapman and Prothero 1985, 19). According to Elkan (1959, 195), an African in paid employment who was "to withdraw permanently from the countryside, . . . would be giving up both a part of his income and also a form of insurance against unemployment or ill-health." Insecurity of employment in South Africa leads migrant workers from Lesotho to regard arable land at home "as a resource offering ultimate security" and to perceive "rural resources as being of greater significance than is promised by their potential, using present agricultural techniques" (Spiegel 1980, 115).

Both the family income optimization and the risk mitigation hypotheses hold circulation to be a means of optimizing individual or household utility in the face of severe economic constraints. In response to either, it may be pointed out that circulation is not always a pattern followed at the worker's initiative. At times, the migrant is sent home by employers seeking to undercut labor militancy or is expelled by host states wishing to rid themselves of redundant immigrants. This is perhaps nowhere more obvious than in the black homelands of South Africa. In many of these, agriculture has undergone such a marked decline that most people can no longer hope to sustain themselves through local production alone. Most people from these areas "are proletarianized workers who, were it not for their lack of legal access to urban areas, . . . would probably not be migrants at all, but full-time workers" (Stichter 1985, 90–91). Where a functioning subsistence economy survives in the migrants' home area, as is still the case for much of rural Haiti, it may not be easy to say for sure whether the pull of people and property at home or the push of obstacles to settlement in the host area is the stronger incentive to return.

HISTORICAL-STRUCTURAL PERSPECTIVES ON MIGRATION

These recent theories of circulation reflect a trend to view migration as a socially mediated and historically conditioned event. This approach owes much to a set of academic perspectives on migration termed "structural" (Portes 1981, 280) or "historical-structural" (Lomnitz 1977, 36; Kemper 1979; Wood 1982). Historical-structural perspectives explain migration not as a choice made by migrants and their kin but as a product of conditions beyond the control of ordinary people, conditions that make certain choices possible and others impossible. An enduring contribution of historical-structuralism is to have increased scholarly awareness of the role that distant, unseen actors and forces may play in promoting and guiding migration. As Portes (1981, 280) explains, "Obviously, individuals migrate for many reasons—to escape famine and political oppression, to attain wealth and status, to give better life chances to their children, and so forth. Nothing is easier than to compile a list of such motivations and present them as a theory of migration. This kind of analysis leaves unanswered the fundamental question of why, despite personal idiosyncrasies and varied motivations, population movements of known magnitude and duration occur with predictable regularity over extended periods of time." Or, as Sassen-Koob (1978, 515) suggests, "Migrants can be viewed as stepping or falling into a migratory flow, rather than initiating or constituting such a flow through their individual decisions and actions."

Perhaps the most serious potential pitfall of historical-structural analysis is to equate "structure" with the conditions that global capitalism imposes on subaltern populations. Recent historical-structural studies have recognized that it may be a mistake to attribute the conditions that encourage or discourage emigration from the periphery entirely to forces that emanate from the center of the capitalist world system (e.g., Massey et al. 1987; Trager 1988; Georges 1990; Grasmuck and Pessar 1991). Even before the advent of historical-structural perspectives, social researchers had argued that there might be much to learn by asking how migrant motivations and behavior related to levels of social organization between world and regional economic orders on the one hand and the individual migrant on the other (e.g., González 1969; Philpott 1973). Students of Third World migration have defined at least three levels at which economically motivated mobility may be studied as a social process.

The first of these levels is the household. Some social researchers, convinced of the shortcomings of methodological individualism but not wishing to attribute all determinacy to political and economic macrostructures, regard migration as part of household or family "strategies" of attainment. They point out that the decision whether or not to emigrate often reflects not individual utility but household needs and preferences. Some have gone so far as to posit that the household or family may mediate between the individual migrant and larger political and economic orders (Wood 1981; Pessar 1982; Trager 1988). Yet the conceptual point of departure of the household strategy model is still that migration is a form of utility-optimizing behavior. It simply transfers this voluntarist premise from the individual to the household or family. Valuable though its empirical insights may be, the household strategy concept may therefore represent a false start toward bridging the gap between studying migration locally and conceptualizing migration globally.

More promising in this regard is a second approach, which views migration as a process of network building. For the individual migrant, the assistance provided by kin and countryfolk in the host area may reduce the cost of relocating and help shield him or her from the worst effects of incorporation into the bottom of an alien social hierarchy. Friends and relatives help finance migrant voyages, put up new arrivals, find employment, transmit job skills, share information, and otherwise ease fellow immigrants' adaptation to the host area (Tilly and Brown 1967; Root 1987). In the aggregate, the migrant network may constitute "a significant undercurrent [of popular economic initiative], running counter to dominant structures of exploitation" (Portes and Walton 1981, 60). Ethnic enclaves in the cities of the First World may carry out similar functions (Portes and Bach 1985, chap. 6).

A third approach centers on the concept of "articulation of modes of production." The articulationist approach holds that dominant capitalist interests may benefit from, and even wish to promote, the survival of noncapitalist or partially capitalist subsistence economies in the periphery, even as those capitalist interests harness the labor of the periphery to the expanded reproduction of capital in the core. For example, the continuity of customary modes of livelihood and networks of reciprocity in the migrant's home area may help ensure that the worker's family can feed itself during his absence and later be able to support the worker in old age. This, in turn, may reduce the benefits and amenities host employers must provide in order to assure themselves a steady labor supply (Wolpe 1972; Castles and Kosack 1973, 374–75; Legassick 1974; Castells 1975; Meillassoux 1981, 117–19). Of course, externalizing the costs of labor renewal to an alternate economy or state does not by itself make immigrant labor cheap (Burawoy 1976, 1055–57). In southern Africa, for example, "until the monopsonistic organization of recruiting and wage determination came into full effect at the beginning of the twentieth century, migrant labor was in fact expensive in comparison to the wages prevailing in Europe at the time. It took some time for capitalism and capitalist coercion to penetrate and undermine rural economies enough to establish the low-wage tradition" (Stichter 1985, 8). The trick, it seems, is for agents of the dominant society to sap the subordinate population of its political and economic autonomy, but not to undermine that population's way of life so much that social chaos ensues.

Of these approaches, the articulationist perspective most closely resembles my own. Neither the household nor the migrant network emerge from my fieldwork observations as the main foci of migrant strategies of survival and economic attainment. Rather, I consider migrant behavior to be determined largely by the structural imperatives of the societies of origin and of destination. These social structures include not only the household and family but also land tenure, gender- and age-based divisions of labor, and the spatial and social distribution of wealth. Rural Haitian society, in turn, is not an autonomous entity but an open system, nested within a national and an international political economic order. In attempting to situate individual migrant behavior in structural and macrosocial contexts, my analytical approach intersects with the articulationist research agenda.

Even so, I hold certain reservations about the appropriateness of the articulationist model for this particular case. It may be particularly important to point out that postplantation Caribbean peasantries, unlike the African societies to which anthropologists have most often applied the articulationist model, cannot properly be called at root "noncapitalist." Well before emigration began on a large scale, rural Haitians were already participating as producers and consumers in internal and international markets, and they had felt the pinch of income-price fluctuations on their standard of living. Already in 1910, Aubin (1910, 126) evoked certain of the economic dilemmas of the cash-oriented peasantry of the village of Furcy, in the highlands southeast of Port-au-Prince: "From time to time, the women go down the mountain carrying to the nearest market the surplus of fruits, vegetables or coffee, gathered on the smallholdings. The money they earn will pay for the blue cotton cloth of their garments, the feminine adornments, *foulards* and earrings, and finally the foodstuffs, imported from the United States, to which the blacks have taken a liking—salt cod, red herring, lard and salt pork. Yet the exchange rate has gone so high that these are now luxury items, [a situation] to which the people of the mountain must pretty much resign themselves" (my trans.). These farmers' ability to acquire imported foodstuffs and urban manufactures hinged largely on the prices fetched in the market by their coffee and garden produce. Travelers' accounts testify to the existence as early as the 1820s of a cash-oriented domestic market system, probably quite similar to that which Aubin observed and which still thrives in Haiti today (G. F. Murray 1977, 82–88). In short, if rural Haiti may be said to possess a distinctive peasant mode of production, it is one that has long existed in intimate association with global capitalism. Surely, rural Haitians would ideally prefer that decisions about local production and consumption be kept as much as possible in local hands. Yet my firsthand observations and those of other Haitianist ethnographers suggest that Haitian peasants generally do *not* wish to escape the market economy and might even find that prospect difficult to imagine.

PERIPHERAL MIGRANTS

Probably, no single analytical approach could ever fit all cases of circulation worldwide. Circulation draws from source areas of widely differing levels of prosperity and selects individuals from various segments of the socioeconomic spectrum. Also, circular migrants do many kinds of work, and their motives for leaving home vary greatly. Like certain skilled building workers in Manila (Stretton 1985), circular migrants may be artisans who spend most of the year in the city and return to their villages only rarely, when urban demand for their labor is low. Others, like the ice cream vendors in Jakarta whom Jellinek (1977) describes, are young men and women who supplement their families' farm incomes with urban employment until they reach the age when they may inherit or purchase some land. Still others, like the "Pilamungas" of the Ecuadorian Andes (Lentz 1986), are farmers confined to a land base too small and impoverished for them ever to abandon seasonal employment in distant commercial enterprises. Or, as is commonly the case among dry-season emigrants from the African Sahel (Prothero 1957), circular migrants may be rural folk who go out mainly during periods of acute scarcity to reduce pressure on household food stocks at home. And this is just considering those who circulate as wage laborers. If one added to this list all those who leave home for relatively short periods of time—itinerant traders, pilgrims, nomadic pastoralists, and so forth—the concept of circulation would risk becoming so inclusive as to lose all specific content. If nothing else, these examples show that there is much room for generalizations to be formulated at levels below that of circulation in the periphery worldwide.

The Haitians who emigrate as cane workers to the Dominican Republic may have much in common with others who circulate between distant rural areas in the world's economic periphery—"peripheral migrants," for short. These migrants commonly belong to a "second tier" of lesser privileged migrants internationally, whose standards of living are inferior to those of most Third World migrants with whom social researchers are familiar. Unlike other migrants studied by social researchers worldwide (Graves and Graves 1974, 123; Simmons, Diaz-Briquets, and Laquian 1977, 28, 55–57, 89–91), peripheral migrants may most often come from backgrounds no richer than the rural average and have no higher than average levels of formal education and skills training (Rigg 1988, 75). One reason why I coin the term "peripheral migrants," rather than using the familiar concept of "rural-rural migration," is to distinguish peripheral migrants from those rural-rural migrants who travel as agricultural workers from poor countries to rich. Even the lowest paid, most insecure employment in the north may provide incomes superior to those available in the south. A case in point is the contrast between Mexican nationals who work on U.S. farms and those who occupy analogous seasonal positions in Mexican agroindustry. Access to U.S. wages may elevate even seasonal farm workers into the elite in their villages of origin (Mines 1981, chap. 5; Reichert 1981; Massey et al. 1987, chap. 8). Earnings from migratory labor in Mexico, by contrast, rarely enable migrants to emerge from the poorer strata of their communities of origin (Ángeles Crummett 1985). Road builders in India, farm workers in South Africa, and uncounted other rural migrant labor forces across the Third World may experience poverty of comparable severity. Of course, not all rural-rural migrants in the periphery stand below all rural-urban migrants. Many rural people whose economic prospects are also highly uncertain try their luck instead in the city. It is of interest, even so, why the people who circulate in the rural periphery appear to be on average less advantaged than those who move between the country and the city. What conditions and consequences of mobility go along with the unfortunate life circumstances of so many peripheral migrants?

The social and economic background of the migrant may be an important determinant of whether s/he takes a peripheral or urban/First World route. Following Connell et al. (1976, 197), it may be posited that migrants commonly emerge from either of two tiers of rural society, "the rather poor [or] the rather rich . . . , rather than, in general, the very poorest, the middle, or the very richest." The rather poor may be driven to accept relatively unattractive employment that presents few legal, educational, or economic barriers to entry. The rather rich more commonly move to the city to acquire or capitalize upon above-average formal education or urban occupational skills (Lipton 1980, 4).

Distinguishing richer and poorer migrants is an important corrective to sweeping generalizations about all Third World migrants. Yet it may often be incorrect to suppose that a migrant's economic standing seals his or her fate. A person's economic background often may not reliably predict the outcome of his or her migration. Migrants who emerge from the same stratum of society may end up going to very different types of destinations and experience differing conditions as they move. It is necessary to recognize that some rural folk can relocate in relative physical and economic security, while others who are not much poorer may do so only at considerable risk. For many of the rural poor, going out for work in distant places is a leap into the unknown and, at times, a gamble against desperate odds. Yet, for other comparably poor folk, emigration is a relatively reliable and risk-free economic resource.

It may therefore be useful to modify the Connell et al. scheme by dividing the "rather poor" migrants into two categories, according to their level of economic security in migrating. As Connell et al. propose, the most favorable emigration outcomes may be enjoyed most often by the relatively well-off and by those with above-average formal education. Even though not assured of success, they still hold important resources for gaining steady employment in the city. In the middle stand many villagers, who, in spite of their relative poverty and low levels of schooling, possess certain skills and social resources that permit them to emigrate at low economic risk. These migrants may generally have above-average occupational skills, move to known urban work, and relocate via ties with kin and countryfolk. The least economically secure may be those who possess only a greatly reduced subsistence base at home, who have no prized job skills, and who emigrate on their own or via labor recruiters (rather than under the auspices of kinship) as casual laborers or seasonal farm hands. To this group belong the Haitians who go as cane workers to the Dominican Republic.

Certain other shared characteristics may unite the Haitian *braceros* with other peripheral migrants worldwide. Commonly, peripheral migrants stand at the very bottom of regional and international divisions of labor. They go to the least desirable destinations and take the most arduous, worst paid, and least secure jobs available in the host area. Much the same, of course, may be said of many undocumented immigrants in the north. But poverty and economic insecurity may have different consequences for peripheral migrants. Peripheral migrants often begin from a position of dependence on wealthier people at home for access to the means of subsistence. The jobs they take as migrants do not often pay enough to permit them to diminish this dependence. Few can use their repatriated savings, like returnees from urban, industrialized societies, "to create a consumer environment and provide a fund capable of supporting their retirement" (Piore 1979, 117). Even in the best of cases, peripheral migration rarely enables people at home to abandon labor-intensive, small-scale agriculture. Commonly, low and insecure migratory incomes virtually guarantee that the least advantaged of peripheral migrants will remain near the bottom of the economic heap.

Communication links are generally not as good between rural areas in the periphery as they are between the country and the city and between the Third World and the First World. Bad communications may often make it hard for peripheral migrants to collaborate strategically with people from home in the host area. It may also place limits on their ability to participate meaningfully at a distance in the lives of people at home. It is not always easy even to send money home from certain peripheral migrant destinations. In this circumstance, the emigrant who wishes to maintain a place in security-enhancing production and consumption units and circuits of reciprocity may have to return; otherwise, the emigrant risks weakening these ties with people at home. It is therefore understandable that peripheral migrants might wish to return home more frequently than most urban or metropolitan migrants. For some, this may be their only way of renewing ties with kinfolk and fellow villagers. In spite of their poverty, the cost of relocating may generally be a lower obstacle to mobility for peripheral migrants than for other migrants. Home and host areas are often not far apart, and, where they are distant, host employers may subsidize transport costs. By the same token, peripheral migrants are often unusually vulnerable to being sent home against their will by employers. For these and other reasons, rates of circulation may generally be somewhat higher among peripheral migrants than among other migrants.

Peripheral migrants often come from remote and isolated rural areas and may be less well connected than other Third World migrants to people who can help them in the relocation process. At times, they have been passed up for migration to more attractive urban or First World destinations, in favor of better qualified relatives. Even though fewer peripheral migrants than in the past relocate via labor recruiters, many still depend on host area businesses and labor contractors for lodgings and employment in the receiving area (Breman 1978; Lwoga 1985; Spindel 1985; Radcliffe 1990). It may be predicted that those peripheral migrants who emigrate outside the protective umbrella of kinship will experience difficulty in adjusting to the host society more frequently than those who go under the auspices of kin and countryfolk (Tilly and Brown 1967).

Peripheral migrants generally have even less legal protection and more limited access to government services than is the norm among migrant workers internationally. They are often particularly vulnerable to arbitrary arrest and deportation. Many are victims of forced relocation and other flagrantly coercive labor control practices. The low visibility of peripheral migrants to urban-based journalists, human rights monitors, and social workers may give recruiters, employers, and security force officers a perfect cover to abuse these migrants with impunity. Community development professionals and human rights monitors are becoming increasingly aware of the plight of peripheral migrants. Yet frequent changes of residence and the fluid composition of the migrant population may make it difficult for these migrants to organize to receive outside support.

Peripheral migrants, like other migrant labor forces worldwide, permit employers and the state to exert greater control over labor, both in the firm and in society at large. There is little doubt that management can threaten, bully, and punish peripheral migrants more violently and regularly than would be tolerated with migrants who are more stable and likely to pursue legal recourse. Seasonal rotation and rapid rates of turnover help assure that peripheral migrants and local workers will not build ties of confidence but will remain mostly strangers to each other. Brief commitment to employment in the host area also tends to dissuade peripheral migrants from militating for long-term improvements in wages and conditions of work. Finally, the host populations of peripheral migration, even though they range from politically atomized peasants to the most highly unionized sectors of their societies, have generally been less capable than majority group workers in the north of resisting job competition by immigrants.

In short, there is reason to suspect that generalizations derived from the study of migration from the country to the city and from poor countries to rich might not always apply equally well to the rural-rural circulation of labor in the world's economic periphery. Both the persistence of peripheral migration and its often distinctive social circumstances and human consequences recommend that students of migration give it further attention. The need for more and better data on peripheral migrations worldwide is clear. In many world regions, our picture of labor circulation, particularly of the rural-rural variety, remains sketchy. Worse still, many of the best studies of peripheral migration are now badly out of date. The broadest significance of my study may therefore lie in what it adds, as a binational, community-based field study, to our understanding of the "lower tier" of labor circulation in the world's economic periphery.

1

The Origins of Demand

To a degree perhaps unsurpassed by any other world region, the societies of the Caribbean Sea are the products of immigration. After the aboriginal population was exterminated or genetically absorbed by its conquerors, "European colonizers were able to work out the problems of settlement, adjustment, and development to a very large degree *as if the Antilles were empty lands*" (Mintz 1966, 918). The Europeans brought enslaved Africans and other bonded laborers to the Antilles under duress, to repopulate and, with their labor, to give value to those lands. From the sixteenth to the nineteenth centuries, the region was settled in large part through bitter forced migrations, and much of its territory put into production by workers tied to the land through slavery or restrictive contracts.

Hence, it is not surprising that, after emancipation, geographical mobility was a primary means by which Afro-Caribbean people might assert their freedom. These postemancipation migrations were largely an effort on the part of freed people and their descendants to shake off the lingering bonds of the plantation system. To Afro-Caribbean people, migration did not signify quite what it had to migrants who had never before experienced the meaning of capitalist development for their labor. Laboring for wages in faraway places did not necessarily mean accepting a heavier yoke of capitalist exploitation than they or their ancestors had borne at home. On the contrary, as Richardson (1983, 6) remarks concerning the Commonwealth Caribbean, "Migrating away for wages, although the earliest destinations were often other plantation islands, was an assertion of independence. It was not a complete escape from the larger plantation sphere, but neither did it represent a docile willingness to accept local conditions dictated by former plantation masters." Across the Antilles, migrants' repatriated savings financed the purchase of agricultural, residential, and commercial properties. And, even where it did no more than subsidize consumption at home, migrant money helped Afro-Caribbean people distance themselves economically from direct plantation control.

The emigrants left islands where foreign capital, from an antecedent domination of the economy, was stagnating or being withdrawn, and moved toward places into which capital had been freshly injected. Following emancipation in the British West Indies (1838), thousands of laborers began to abandon the obsolescent sugar estates of the smaller islands of the British Antilles for better-paid temporary employment on the relatively thriving estates of Trinidad and British Guiana. Later, the abolition of slavery in the Caribbean possessions of France (1848), Denmark (1848), and the Netherlands (1863) and on the Spanish island of Puerto Rico (1876) added thousands more people to the ranks of those who were free to seek more remunerative employment on other islands. Beginning in the last quarter of the nineteenth century, steamship travel facilitated the circulation of labor around the Caribbean. This period saw the beginning of migrations from Jamaica to banana plantations in Costa Rica and to the French effort to build the Panama Canal, as well as from the Leeward Islands of the Antilles to sugar estates in the Dominican Republic. During the first quarter of the twentieth century, the number of important displacements of population in the region only grew. The outstanding migrant destinations of the time included Bermuda, for work in dock construction; Cuba, for work on sugar plantations; and Panama, for the construction of the canal. By the 1950s, when people from the Caribbean began to emigrate in large numbers to Europe and North America, a migration tradition had been established on many islands. Leaving home in order to return with enhanced means had become an accepted turn in the life course—and perhaps even an *expected* life experience—for millions of Caribbean people (Thomas-Hope 1978; D. I. Marshall 1982; Richardson 1983, chap. 1).

The character of postemancipation population movements varied from island to island, according to the political, economic, and geographic circumstances of each. At one extreme were those territories in which it was relatively easy for freed people to secure claims to land and other productive property. At the other extreme were islands where the politically managed scarcity of productive resources made it necessary for people hoping to expand their economic opportunities to travel to other territories (Mintz 1979).

On islands such as Barbados and Antigua, which were small, densely populated, and dominated by one crop, "those ex-slaves who wished to 'better' themselves away from the estates had to think of emigration" (W. K. Marshall 1968, 254). On many islands, even though the people were now free, the land remained firmly in the hands of a few leading families. What was worse, the wages of estate laborers were pitifully low. On many islands, standards of living deteriorated further as sugar production fell into protracted crisis.

In terms of land availability, Haiti stood at the opposite extreme from the small sugar islands. It differed crucially not just in size but in the historical circumstances of its independence. The French colony of Saint-Domingue (later to become Haiti) was founded in the late seventeenth century, after Spain ceded to France the western part of the island of Hispaniola. In the eighteenth century, through the brutal exploitation of the labor of hundreds of thousands of enslaved Africans, Saint-Domingue became the most profitable colony of its time for the production of export staples. The Haitian Revolution, from 1791 to 1804, dealt European fortunes across the island a complete reverse. Haiti was the first country in the world to have achieved its independence from European colonial rule through a revolution that sought freedom not just for the local propertied classes but for all its people, including the enslaved. After independence was won, Haiti's freed people had the advantage also of inhabiting an island with a rugged, sparsely populated interior. In Haiti, geographical mobility after independence consisted largely of freed people abandoning the plains, on which sugar and cotton production had been concentrated during the colonial era, to settle unused land in the interior.

It was only after the turn of the twentieth century that Haitian patterns of geographical mobility began to resemble those of the smaller islands. In the first quarter of the twentieth century, Haitians came to work side by side in the cane fields of the Dominican Republic with people from such classic plantation islands as St. Kitts, Montserrat, and Antigua. At the same time, Haitians and Jamaicans went in their tens of thousands to the sugar estates of Cuba (Pérez de la Riva 1979). In spite of Haiti's distinctive history and geography, it is not surprising that its streams of migrants eventually converged with those of other Caribbean islands. Each of these societies was a product of the same historical process, the sugar trade with Europe and North America.

From the sixteenth century onwards, island after island in the Antilles was swept into the forefront of world sugar production, only to be surpassed as the fertility of its land declined and other sugar producers grew more efficient (Williams 1944; Guerra y Sánchez 1964). The rise and fall of French Saint-Domingue was the bloodiest chapter in this history. But each of the other islands that sent workers to the Dominican Republic had seen its fortunes fluctuate with sugar. Haiti differed from these other islands, because after independence its land did not remain in the hands of a small elite. Yet it also resembled them, because its colonizers, too, had left a legacy of external economic dependence, from which postplantation Haiti never fully freed itself. Historians have correctly pointed to the decline of Haitian agricultural export production as an indication of the unwillingness of the freed people to remain tied to plantation labor. Yet, as Rotberg (1971, 38–40) cautions, even without a successful slave uprising Saint-Domingue/Haiti would have eventually lost its leadership of world sugar production and joined the list of labor-exporting islands.

The Dominican Republic also joined the "relay race" of sugar islands, but only as this succession reached its end. The history of Santo Domingo/Dominican Republic is a study in contrasts with Saint-Domingue/Haiti. Even though Hispaniola was the first place where sugarcane was planted in the Americas, Spanish efforts to produce sugar for export did not endure there beyond the sixteenth century (Ratekin 1954). Thereafter, the Spanish regarded the island chiefly as a way station between Europe and Middle America. In the eighteenth century, trade with French Saint-Domingue expanded, and the Spanish side of the island emerged from its doldrums. Yet, on the eve of the Haitian Revolution, Santo Domingo still lagged far behind its western neighbor in trade and population. In 1822, Haiti conquered and annexed Spanish Santo Domingo, but, in 1844, residents of the eastern territory seized the first opportunity to expel the Haitian occupiers and proclaim an independent Dominican Republic. Between 1845 and 1856, the Dominican Republic repulsed three Haitian attempts at reconquest.

The opposed destinies of the two nations took a new twist in the late nineteenth century. At that time, with the establishment of lasting peace, the Dominican Republic witnessed the creation of modern, mechanized sugar factories and extensive plantations of sugarcane. Between 1875 and 1930, under the pressure of international competition, the scale of sugar production in the Dominican Republic expanded at a dizzying pace. Yet, whereas global demand for tropical staples stimulated capital-intensive agriculture in the Dominican Republic, Haiti's century-old prohibition on the sale of land to foreign interests impeded foreign investment. This prohibition remained in place until 1915, when the United States invaded and took power in Haiti. In 1916, the United States also occupied the Dominican Republic. Before the American invasion, men from Haiti had already begun to emigrate as harvest laborers to the sugar estates of the Dominican Republic. Under U.S. rule, this migration expanded, and both countries took measures to regulate movement across their shared border.

Export production levels and patterns of labor circulation reflected the fact that the commercial center of gravity of the island had shifted from Haiti to the Dominican Republic.

The tardy arrival of the Dominican Republic on the international sugar scene distinguished it from all other Caribbean sugar producers. The Dominican Republic began its sugar experiment well after the emancipation of its slaves. It therefore did not go through a stage in which the production of sugar for export on a large scale depended on the labor of enslaved Africans.

Yet, in a closely related way, the growth of a modern sugar industry in the Dominican Republic conformed to a pattern as old and familiar to the Caribbean as sugar production itself. In its sparse population and in the ease with which its people could obtain land, the situation of the Dominican Republic in 1875 resembled an open frontier. The interior of the country still held enough open land to accommodate those rural people displaced by the expanding sugar estates. If left free, rural Dominicans could easily have earned a living as independent agricultural producers, without the necessity of selling their labor to large proprietors. As had happened so often before in the Caribbean, the new sugar industrialists of the Dominican Republic turned to external sources of labor. In this way, they sought to assemble a labor force whose access to the island's productive resources could be artificially restricted.[1]

Importing labor to produce sugar for export was a tactic with many precedents in the region and in the rest of the tropical world. "Sugar," Mintz (1959, 49) writes, "or rather the great commodity market which arose demanding it, has been one of the massive demographic forces in world history. Because of it, literally millions of enslaved Africans reached the New World, particularly the American South, the Caribbean and its littorals, the Guianas and Brazil. This migration was followed by those of East Indians, both Moslem and Hindu, Javanese, Chinese, Portuguese, and many other peoples in the nineteenth century. It was sugar that sent East Indians to Natal . . . , sugar that carried them to Mauritius and Fiji. Sugar brought a dozen different ethnic groups in staggering succession to Hawaii, and sugar still moves people about the Caribbean." Among immigrants from neighboring Caribbean islands, Dominican growers found a labor force whose freedom of economic maneuver would be severely constrained by poverty and social and cultural distance form the host population.

Yet the migratory labor systems that arose in the late nineteenth and early twentieth centuries in Cuba, Puerto Rico, and the Dominican Republic differed in at least one important way from earlier immigrations of labor in the region. This difference stemmed both from technical innovations in sugar production and from the need to adapt plantation agriculture to a nonslave labor force. The modern corporate sugar mill operated on a vastly larger scale than its semimechanized precursors. Yet, in spite of improvements in milling and refining technology, the work of cutting cane remained virtually the same as it had been for centuries. As a result, the new mills demanded much greater numbers of cane cutters than had the old. Also, the seasonality of that demand grew more pronounced. This was because mill owners found it profitable to concentrate production into that half of the year when the sucrose content of the juice of the cane plant was richest. "Thus," as Moreno Fraginals (1985, 6) writes, "there arose, in all its tragic dimensions, the problem of seasonal employment during four months of the year, which for the majority of workers meant seasonal unemployment for eight months of the year. This situation had not occurred previously because with . . . rudimentary manufacturing equipment, small daily millings, and long harvest seasons, there was almost always work for all hands. But the modern plantation required, for its optimal running, the existence of an army of unemployed workers, ideally located off *ingenio* (estate) grounds but subjected to economic pressure that forced them to sell their services cheaply and with a minimum of social benefits, as cane cutters." The problem faced by the new corporate sugar producers was less one of *holding* labor on the estates than of *recapturing* it every year, after it had been released from employment during the preceding "dead season." Old systems of legal constraint would prove cumbersome as a means of recruiting tens of thousands of workers on a yearly basis. Only where economic need drove workers back to the sugar estates each harvest season could an adequate supply of field labor be obtained, at sufficiently low cost, to feed the new mills with sugarcane. For this supply of labor, the Dominican Republic initially turned to islands of the Lesser Antilles and, not long after, to neighboring Haiti.

Labor supply was, of course, not the only obstacle to growth that Caribbean sugar producers had to surmount in the late nineteenth and early twentieth centuries. Few Caribbean sugar producers of the time competed successfully with subsidized European beet sugar producers. Even though Caribbean sugar production as a whole increased greatly from 1860 to 1914, this growth was concentrated in Cuba and Puerto Rico (see table 3). Even with a plentiful supply of cheap labor, it seems, early Dominican sugar industrialists were not assured of success. Yet low prices for sugar on international markets only heightened the pressure to find a cheap labor supply. It seems fair to say that without its immigrant labor the Dominican sugar industry might never have achieved the growth it did during this period.

Table 3

Sugar Production of Nine Caribbean Territories, 1860–1914 (in Thousands of Metric Tons)

Year	Barbados	Cuba	Dominican Republic	Guadeloupe	Guyana	Jamaica	Martinique	Puerto Rico	Trinidad
1860	35	428	—	33	55	26	31	53	29
1870	38	703	—	40	76	25	38	88	44
1884	60	626	9[a]	57	123	20	42	100	64
1894	59	1,111	36[b]	43	104	24	37	49	47
1904	56	1,078	48[c]	36	108	10	25	149	46
1914	30	2,622	101	41	109	21	41	318	56

SOURCES: Duarte 1980, 102; Schnakenbourg 1984, 93.

[a]1883 figure.

[b]1893 figure.

[c]1905 figure.

MEN, MILLS AND MONEY: THE FORMATION
OF THE MODERN DOMINICAN SUGAR INDUSTRY

In 1874, on the eve of its revolution in sugar production, the Dominican Republic had little experience of plantation agriculture and exported little to the outside world. Outbreaks of war with Haiti and fighting among political rivals within the Dominican Republic had discouraged capital investment. A poor infrastructure and scarce credit were perhaps equally important obstacles to commerce. And the few local entrepreneurs who surmounted these difficulties still had to adapt their investments to the prevailing labor scarcity. The country's population in 1875 numbered between 150,000 and 250,000 persons; the population density was between three and five persons per square kilometer (Hoetink 1982, 19).

Yet, once a measure of stability had been established, the ease with which good land could be acquired in the Dominican Republic sparked the interest of foreign investors. From 1875 to 1882, abundant land and liberal exemptions on taxes and duties for export agriculture attracted an influx of foreign entrepreneurs (Moya Pons 1978, 407–9; Castillo 1985, 216). Favorable world market prices for sugar led these men to attempt to duplicate the large sugar plantations and factories recently established in other Caribbean territories.

To satisfy the new mills' growing demand for cane, mill owners and independent cane growers steadily expanded the area of land they cultivated. Ancient forests were cleared for cultivation, and any small-scale agriculturalists who stood in the way were bought out, dispossessed through litigation, or simply driven off at gunpoint. Finding a legal pretext for taking over land was usually not difficult. The vast majority of cultivators and ranchers lacked formal title to their land (Hoetink 1982, 3, 10–11, 174).

In the 1880s, world sugar prices tumbled, putting the fledgling *ingenios* to a severe test. The producers who weathered the crisis were those who cut their cost of production per pound by improving their milling and refining capacity (Murphy 1991, 15–16). By 1892, fewer *ingenios* remained in business, but the country produced almost four times more sugar than it had a decade earlier (Báez Evertsz 1978, 26–27; Duarte 1980, 114).

During the industry's first two decades of operation, the harvest labor force was composed mainly of Dominican nationals. They were mostly seasonal proletarians, who took up wage labor during part of the year but were unwilling to relinquish a foothold on land of their own (Hoetink 1982, 171). As the century neared its end, price inflation made poor Dominicans increasingly reluctant to recur even seasonally to wage labor (Castillo 1981a, 43–44). Given the low prices at which sugar sold at the time, the sugar companies firmly refused to raise wages to compensate for inflation (Castillo 1978, 30). Also, by the 1890s, the *ingenios* had standardized their practice of issuing advances on monthly or semimonthly payments to workers via credit usable only at company stores. The exorbitant prices plantation workers had to pay at the company stores worsened the damage done them by rising prices and stagnating wages. Over time, the reduced buying power of the cane worker's wages made estate labor seem less and less attractive to rural Dominicans when compared to subsistence crop cultivation on their own smallholdings. As the pace of land expropriation quickened, displaced agriculturalists avoided the sugar estates and moved on to claim land elsewhere as their own (Calder 1981, 19).

In the 1880s and 1890s, estate owners increasingly perceived the labor supply for the growing sugar industry as inadequate. In 1884, a strike by field laborers foiled owners' attempts to cut back wages as a way of reducing costs (Bryan 1985, 236). Owners felt also that not enough labor could be gotten locally to bring in the harvest with the speed and regularity needed to run the mills with as few costly interruptions as possible. Dominican semiproletarians had a disconcerting tendency to leave the sugar estates after the first rains of spring, or as soon as they had saved a satisfying sum of money, whether the harvest had ended or not (Vidal 1926, 6–7). The importance of labor supply problems should not be exaggerated in comparison to the reduced revenues and increased indebtedness that sugar producers faced at the time. Yet the high cost and irregular supply of labor were among the factors that Sánchez (1976, 31) listed in 1893 as causes of the bankruptcy of so many of the industry's pioneers.

In the minds of many estate owners, all of the problems involved in recruiting harvest laborers from the local population had a single solution: to import cheaper labor from elsewhere. As early as 1884, workers from the Lesser Antilles had begun to find their way to the Dominican sugar-cane harvests (Bryan 1985, 241). In 1893, leading sugar producers formed an association for the recruitment of foreign *braceros*, the Immigration Society of Macorís. In October of that year an estate near San Pedro de Macorís received the Society's first shipment of workers. In the earliest years of recruitment, hundreds of Puerto Ricans also went to the Dominican Republic as contract workers, but soon migrants from the Lesser Antilles came to predominate (Castillo 1978, 32–34, 37).

Each year, between 1900 and 1930, thousands of West Indians migrated as cane workers to the Dominican Republic.[2] Some came from Jamaica, the Virgin Islands, and Barbados; most came from various Leeward Islands, including St. Kitts, Nevis, Anguilla, Antigua, Montserrat, and St. Martin. The West Indians who went to the Dominican Republic were mostly recruited by agents of particular plantations (Castillo 1978, 38, 41–42). After the harvest, most would return to their home islands, but others stayed on in Santo Domingo. Dominicans dubbed the West Indians "*cocolos*" or, more politely, "*ingleses*," whether they came from British, Danish, Dutch, or French possessions. As the latter nickname suggests, most of the migrants were recruited in islands of the British West Indies.

Certain Dominican elites viewed West Indian immigration with alarm, convinced that foreign labor and foreign capital were jointly turning sugar-producing areas of the country into a nation apart. Merchants were upset that the *cocolos* took home much of their savings rather than spending money in the Dominican Republic. As the second decade of West Indian labor recruitment (1903–13) neared its end, the Dominican press launched increasingly frequent attacks against the importation of *braceros*. Many interests based their opposition to West Indian immigration on frankly racist arguments and renewed the decades-old call for the Dominican government to promote a "desirable" (i.e., "white") immigration. The sugar companies and their Dominican allies, on the other hand, resolutely opposed any measure that might restrict their freedom to bring in laborers from wherever they wanted. In 1912, the Dominican Congress enacted tough restrictions on nonwhite immigration. Yet these tough regulations were ultimately ignored in the interest of protecting Dominican sugar producers (Castillo 1978, 44–47; Bryan 1985, 244–45). The government apparently considered the sugar industry too important to imperil by restricting its access to labor.

West Indian immigration enabled the sugar companies to keep a tight lid on wages. Whereas, in the 1890s, daily wages for harvest labor were 80 centavos to one peso, by 1907, the corresponding figures had dropped to 40 to 60 centavos (Castillo 1978, 30–31). These low wages drove away most of the remaining Dominican laborers. In 1912, a British colonial officer expressed the opinion that "if permission to enter the country is denied to [the West Indian] laborers the sugar industry will be brought almost to a standstill as native Dominicans can rarely be induced to work on the plantations" (quoted in Bryan 1985, 242).

In theory, many of the West Indians had consular representation as British subjects, but in reality there was probably little the British authorities could do to help an individual immigrant, once he entered sugar company property (Richardson 1983, 128). The "Wild West" atmosphere of the sugar estates in the 1920s is evoked in the life history of Alexander Charles, an immigrant from St. Lucia: "I make five years in Santo Domingo and I tell you I see dead people. I see dead, I see dead, I see dead. One kill another. In a dancing house, Easter Saturday night, you saw dead people like ants. No law for that at all" (Beck 1979, 22). Little more legal recourse existed for abuses suffered at the hands of employers.

Growers enjoyed a measure of control over West Indian labor denied them with Dominican semiproletarians. Unlike Dominicans, the *cocolos* were rarely immediately capable of retreating from the sugar estates into other forms of employment. And any threat of collective action the immigrants could muster was neutralized by the management's counterthreat of dismissal and deportation. The ease with which replacement workers could be recruited made employers' legal sanctions doubly effective. As a result, the *cocolos* had less power than Dominican seasonal proletarians to resist mistreatment and exploitation at work. Restraints on collective action may also have been self-imposed. As temporary workers, the *cocolos* were interested mainly in earning as much as they could within a short span of time and then returning home. They may have been reluctant to press for any long-term improvements, because they would probably not be around to benefit from these.

Yet, early on, *cocolos* captured at least two employment niches outside the cane fields. One was employment as dockers in the port of San Pedro de Macorís (Castillo 1978, 55). The other was in the sugar mills, where several found jobs on the basis of skills they had brought from their native islands (Castillo 1979, 33). Most of the *cocolos* could speak English with their North American bosses, and they used these contacts to find factory jobs for kinfolk, fellow islanders, and coreligionists. Today, very few *cocolos* of the second and third generations work as agricultural day laborers, and most have achieved upward mobility in the sugar companies or in commerce (Corten, Acosta, and Duarte 1976, 16, n. 8; Castillo and Murphy 1987, 58; Murphy 1991, 42–43).

In the late 1920s, decreasing numbers of West Indians went to the Dominican Republic. Many were discouraged from going there by falling real wage rates in the sugar industry. Others were diverted to more lucrative sources of income elsewhere in the Caribbean, including oil refineries in Curaçao and Aruba (Richardson 1983, 148–50). In much-reduced numbers, Leeward Islanders continued to circulate to and from the Dominican Republic. Many saw the Dominican Republic as a second home, where they had family members and friends on whom they could count for help in hard times. According to second-generation *cocolos*, as late as 1942, regular boat traffic still connected Dominican ports with St. Martin and St. Kitts.

For the Dominican Republic's sugar producers, a solution to the diminished supply of labor from the Leewards had already been found in immigration from Haiti. As early as 1920, official records suggest that nearly equal numbers of Haitians and *cocolos* lived on the sugar estates. In that year, of the 22,121 residence permits which the authorities granted to foreign *braceros* and their families, over 10,000 were for Haitians, compared to almost 8,000 for British West Indians, and another 4,000 or so for French, Dutch, Danish, and American (U.S. Virgin Islands) subjects combined (Castillo 1978, 53).

Official regulation of labor recruitment in Haiti began only in 1915. Because of the undocumented nature of the movement, the exact scale of emigration to the sugar estates before that time is not known. Apparently, Haitians did not begin to emigrate as cane workers in large numbers until 1900, when host country employers began to recruit laborers in Haiti (Dalencour 1923, 4; Laville 1933, 1; Dartigue 1938, 32; Thomas 1971, 431). At least one contemporary observer (Dalencour 1923, 4) sustained that it was only after the American invasion in 1915 that emigration to Cuba and the Dominican Republic attained "really frightening proportions" (my trans.). It is known that, after official recruitment procedures were established in 1915, large numbers of Haitian working people emigrated. Between 1915 and 1930, as many as 600,000 Haitian men emigrated to Cuba, mostly as harvest laborers in the cane fields of the eastern provinces of Oriente and Camagüey (Pérez de la Riva 1979, 34–35, 38–39). This figure might be inflated, because the average migrant may have traveled twice or more to Cuba and thus been counted on official immigration tallies more than once. In the opinion of Castor (1971, 84), Haitians emigrated in even larger numbers to the Dominican Republic. Southern Haiti alone was estimated to have "lost more than 80,000 men" to the cane fields across the border.

During and immediately after the First World War, sugar went through its greatest boom-and-bust cycle, a period named the "Dance of the Millions," in the Hispanic Caribbean. International speculation drove sugar prices from a little over 3 cents per pound in 1915 to 24.5 cents in 1920. Dominican sugar production expanded rapidly, and not even the sudden collapse of world sugar prices in 1920, to less than 2 cents a pound, brought this expansion to a halt (see table 4). As had been true during the crisis of the 1880s, it made economic sense to expand production after prices had dropped (Knight 1928, 135). Sugar, which had earlier been a rich man's game, came to be dominated almost totally by large U.S. corporations. By 1926, the sugar companies and other cane growers held over 16 percent of the total surface area of the country (Lozano 1976, 158). The Dominican Republic's export earnings came to depend to a dangerous degree on prices for sugar determined in Europe and North America (see figure 1).

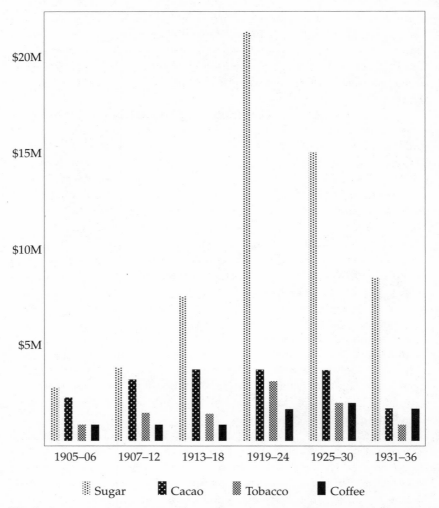

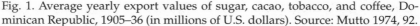

Fig. 1. Average yearly export values of sugar, cacao, tobacco, and coffee, Dominican Republic, 1905–36 (in millions of U.S. dollars). Source: Mutto 1974, 92.

Dominican governments between 1900 and 1915 proved more willing than ever to grant investors exemptions on taxes and duties related to export agriculture (Báez Evertsz 1978, 49–50). And, in 1911 and 1912, the Dominican Congress passed laws that gave the sugar companies improved legal grounds to contest the titles of customary landholders. These legislative tendencies gained further ground after the United States invaded and took power in the Dominican Republic in 1916.

Table 4

Dominican Sugar Exports, 1905–30

Year	Quantity (in Metric Tons)	Price per Metric Ton (in U.S.$)	Value (in Thousands U.S.$)
1905	48,169	68.34	3,292
1910	49,924	115.74	5,778
1915	102,801	72.55	7,458
1920	158,804	285.29	45,306
1925	301,106	51.33	15,447
1930	345,980	28.64	9,910

SOURCE: Duarte 1980, 102.

> A combination of naïve predispositions, of inexperience, and of strong influences from interested outside sources led to the creation of policies which were in many cases contrary to the occupiers' original intentions. In no other area was the contradiction between policy intentions and policy implementation so great as in land legislation. And in no other area did an economic policy have such a baneful effect on the future lives of ordinary Dominicans. New laws of the military government greatly improved the sugar companies' ability to procure land for their expanding domains and thus assured that the dominance of a one-crop economy, already possessed of a firm foothold in 1916, would be unshakable after 1924. (Calder 1984, 102)

As an unanticipated by-product of seizing power in both countries, the Americans also had an unprecedented opportunity to regulate labor practices across the entire island. (The impact of the U.S. military occupation on labor in Haiti is examined in chapter 2.) On the Dominican side of the border, the U.S. military government enacted decrees to bar the entry of foreign *braceros* not sponsored by Dominican employers and to regularize the residence status of authorized guest workers (Castillo 1978, 47–48). Yet perhaps more important than what the occupiers did was what they failed to do to regulate the sugar industry's labor practices. In spite of having introduced legislation that would restrict undocumented immigration, the occupiers made little effort to interdict clandestine entrants at the Haitian frontier or to inspect the sugar estates for undocumented workers. Nor did the Americans put forward any legislation aimed at improving the cane workers' conditions of life. Finally, they discouraged the formation of trade unions that, if able to organize freely, might have militated more effectively for wage increases, better working conditions, and stricter immigration controls.

CONTINUITY AND CHANGE IN THE MIGRATORY LABOR SYSTEM

The global business crisis of the 1930s triggered a wave of economic nationalism in the countries that had been willing if not enthusiastic hosts to Haitian labor during the previous three decades. The economic situation of Haitian workers in the Dominican Republic had already taken a sharp turn for the worse: in 1930, pay cuts had reduced cane workers' wages by half (Orbe 1981, 27). To make matters worse, anti-immigrant legislation soured the political climate for the Haitian *braceros*. In 1934, 1935, and 1938, the Dominican Congress passed laws requiring that all businesses in the country employ at least 70 percent Dominicans. The Dominican dictator, Trujillo Molina, and his puppet heads of state routinely granted exemptions to the sugar companies, but the Trujillo regime served warning that it wished to restrict the utilization of foreign labor to the agricultural sector of the sugar industry. In 1937, similar legislation in Cuba led to the deportations of thousands of Haitians and Jamaicans (Leyburn 1966, 271). In spite of these disincentives, rural Haitians continued to emigrate to the sugar estates, though apparently in smaller numbers than before.

During the 1930s, relations between Haiti and the Dominican Republic became increasingly conflictual. By this time, Dominican fears of Haitian military invasion had given way to apprehensions about a "peaceful invasion" ("*invasión pacífica*"). It was feared that Haiti might insidiously gain hegemony over all of Hispaniola through the infiltration of its numerically superior population onto Dominican territory. Spontaneous immigration from west to east was an old phenomenon on the island. It began even before independence when runaway slaves sought refuge in the Spanish colony, and it continued largely unchecked throughout the nineteenth century and into the twentieth. Neither government had much control over its frontier, and people on either side of the border circulated freely between the two countries. Over the decades, many thousands of Haitians settled as freeholders and farmhands in the sparsely populated region of the Dominican Republic adjoining the Haitian frontier.

This state of affairs was brought to an abrupt halt in 1937, when Trujillo unleashed the "*corte*" ("mowing-down") on Haitians living in the Dominican Republic's frontier region and northern Cibao Valley. This was one of the most horrid attacks on an unarmed civilian population in Latin American history. In a matter of days, as many as 25,000 Haitian men, women, and children were murdered, without warning or mercy, by members of the Dominican Republic's national constabulary and Trujillo loyalists. Thousands more who escaped the massacre fled into Haiti and never returned, even though many had been born in the Dominican Republic and had never known any other home. It is not clear what Trujillo intended this colossal atrocity to achieve politically. Yet it is significant that the killings occurred chiefly in areas neighboring the border with Haiti and spared Haitians who resided on the sugar estates (Crassweller 1966, 155–56). Regardless of the dictator's intentions, no more chilling way could be imagined of conveying to Haitian immigrants that the sugar *bateyes* would thereafter be their only secure place on Dominican soil. In response to the massacre, the Haitian government suspended permission for recruitment of *braceros*. Yet, within months, agents of the sugar companies may have resumed recruiting covertly in Haiti (Wingfield 1966, 97).

In 1941, Port-au-Prince reinstated officially regulated recruitment, but this ended just a year later when a diplomatic row broke out between the Haitian and Dominican governments (Price-Mars 1953, 230). On this occasion, the Haitian government headed by President Lescot not only suspended official recruitment but attempted to interdict clandestine emigration. Residents of the Cayes-Jacmel area remember that at this time government authorities destroyed all the small boats they could find, in an effort to impede maritime traffic with the town of Anse-à-Pitre, on the Dominican border. According to Price-Mars (1953, 230), after news of these measures crossed the border, "[t]he Dominican reaction was not slow in materializing against the Haitian workers resident in Santo Domingo. Their opportunities were limited by restricting their freedom to move from one place to another, and their salaries were reduced, condemning them virtually to servile peonage" (my trans.). The harvest of 1942–43 set a pattern to which the Dominican authorities would return every time the flow of migrant laborers was impeded. This was to send out troops to round up Haitian men living in non-sugar-producing areas of the Dominican Republic and to ship these detainees to the sugar estates, where hunger would force them to work as cane cutters. Therefore, if President Lescot achieved some success in thwarting emigration, he did so largely at the expense of Haitians living in the Dominican Republic. And Lescot's blockade on movement across the border did not last for long. Well before his term of office ended, *âba fil* emigration had apparently resumed on a large scale (Corten 1974, 80).

By the 1940s, crossing the border *âba fil* had changed in at least one important way. After the *corte*, the Dominican government built roads and expanded its military presence along the frontier. This made it possible for the Dominican military to intercept large numbers of undocumented entrants at the border and to transship these people to the sugar estates for a fee. This practice would thereafter greatly restrict undocumented immigrants' freedom to choose where they would work after entering the Dominican Republic.

Between 1950 and 1960, sugar production in the Dominican Republic doubled, with a near-proportionate increase in the number of men the country needed to cut cane. The renewed expansion of sugar production was largely caused by the entry of one powerful new player into the Dominican sugar industry, President Trujillo Molina. By this time Dominican authorities had involved themselves so deeply in channeling immigration that it was possible for Trujillo to succeed where Haiti's Lescot had failed, in interdicting the supply of Haitian labor as a means of exerting pressure on the sugar companies (Crassweller 1966, 245–55). Between 1952 and 1956, this and a variety of other methods of harassment forced the foreign owners of 10 estates to sell to Trujillo. At the death of the *generalísimo* in 1961, Trujillo-owned mills produced almost two-thirds of the country's sugar.

Trujillo's anti-Haitian stance and commitment to Dominicanize the sugar industry did not prevent him from reaching a new accord with Haiti in 1952 for the recruitment of *braceros*. Whereas previously the two governments regulated migration separately under their own laws, this accord placed it under an international treaty. Under its terms, employers still paid for recruitment, but the Haitian authorities took responsibility for organizing one or more centers each year for issuing contracts to *braceros* (Dorsinville 1953, 108–14). In 1959, Haiti and the Dominican Republic renewed their 1952 agreement.

Even so, friction between the two states would soon disrupt the flow of migrants, this time more drastically than ever. In 1963, Haiti's president François Duvalier came to fear that an armed invasion of anti-Duvalierists was poised to attack his regime from camps across the border. To meet this threat, he ordered that a strip of three or four miles be cleared of all human habitation across the entire length of the Dominican border. Duvalier declared this zone a no-man's land (Heinl and Heinl 1978, 638). Several migrants attempting to return home were put to death by hanging, and their bodies were displayed near the border as a warning to any others who would cross. It was rumored at the time that President Duvalier had said of Haitians in the Dominican Republic, "Let them plant coconut trees" ("*Yo mèt plâte kokoye*"). These words were enormously discouraging to Haitians on the Dominican side of the border because planting a coconut tree is a symbol of permanent residence. Duvalier's edict was taken to mean that he would never allow the emigrants to return. Many resigned themselves to staying in the Dominican Republic until Duvalier died or was thrown out of power, and they decided to use their harvest savings to make the best of their situation in the *bateyes*. One man, who eventually returned to Haiti, described his reaction as follows: "One day, I heard someone cry out, 'Duvalier says to Haitians in the Dominican Republic, "*Nu mèt plâte kokoye*"!' Well, I had some money [saved up], but when I heard that, instead of keeping the money, I went and wasted it all." After official contract migration resumed in 1966–67, many of those who had been stranded returned to Haiti. Others had put down roots in the Dominican Republic and chose to remain.

In 1966, in the wake of a second U.S. military intervention, the Dominican people elected a new president, Joaquín Balaguer, who had been Trujillo's last puppet head of state. In that same year, the Santo Domingo government created the CEA to manage the nationalized estates of the Trujillo family. An agreement was also reached with Haiti for the renewal of labor recruitment. The accord of 1966 differed from previous ones, in that it committed the Dominican government, rather than the private sugar companies, to pay Port-au-Prince a fee for organizing recruitment centers in Haiti. The sum which the Dominican government agreed to pay, around $1 million, was clearly in large part a bribe to ensure the goodwill of the Haitian authorities. Yet, between 1967 and 1969, fear of attack from Haitian insurgents again led President Duvalier to suspend the contract. In total, the Haitian government suspended official recruitment in 6 of the 10 years between 1960 and 1970. During these years, as in 1942–43, the response of the Dominican authorities was to redouble their persecution of Haitians already living in the Dominican Republic. President Balaguer crowed about having achieved the long sought-after "Dominicanization" of the cane harvest. In fact, the harvests of 1967–68 through 1969–70 were brought in mainly by *viejos, âba fil* entrants, and forced recruits. Official recruitment was renewed in 1970, less than a year before the death of President Duvalier and the accession of his son, Jean-Claude, to the presidency. The agreement of 1966 served as model for this contract and for those of all subsequent years.

In 1977, disagreement over the "sale price" that Duvalier asked for the *braceros* led to the suspension of that year's contract. The following year, the contract was renewed, apparently with the increase in payment Duvalier had demanded. The number of *braceros* that the CEA recruited each year also increased in 1978 from 12,000 to 15,000. Also that year, for the first time since 1962, a new government had taken office in Santo Domingo through fair and open elections. It is rumored that Duvalier wished to mark the occasion by sending the Dominicans "a higher class" of people than the peasants who normally turned out for Dominican recruitment. In the fall of 1978, Haitian state radio announced that the Dominican Republic immediately sought workers of all kinds, to be paid as high as U.S.$15 per day. Urban Haitians, normally indifferent to calls for employment in the Dominican Republic, swamped the CEA recruitment center in Croix-des-Bouquets. The urbanites got preference, if only because they generally had fewer problems raising the bribe necessary to be escorted to the front of the line, out of reach of the Tontons Macoutes. Many of the men who went to the Dominican Republic that year abandoned relatively well-paid jobs as cab drivers, shopkeepers, and craftsmen in Port-au-Prince and its environs. One of that year's recruits, who ultimately stayed in the Dominican Republic, told me that before he left Haiti, friends and neighbors in his crowded Port-au-Prince neighborhood came round to wish him luck and brought plates of food to strengthen him for the journey. These he refused in jest, saying he was going to a country where he would earn enough to buy all the food he might want. In his words, "I was haaappy! I thought I was going abroad, I would eat well, [and] handle plenty of cash."

The chagrin of the urbanites upon arriving in the *bateyes* was indescribable. Who, they wondered, could possibly believe that they would accept being housed four to eight men per room, in rooms no more than 12 square meters large; tolerate being called a *"congó"* all the time (an epithet reserved in Haiti for "hillbillies"); and, to top it all, be willing to *cut cane* for barely over one U.S. dollar per *ton*? As Lemoine (1985, 75–98) recounts vividly, thousands of recruits that year refused to work or abandoned the estates—on foot, if necessary—to demand decent employment or repatriation to Haiti. CEA officials had no recourse but to repatriate most of the urban recruits, whom they regarded as incorrigible. Afterward, the CEA made do as it had in many recent harvests with undocumented entrants, *viejos*, and Haitians forcibly recruited in other parts of the country.

The following year, tardy renewal of the contract delayed the opening of the harvest on a number of CEA estates (Castillo 1981b, 101). Also in 1979, the Anti-Slavery Society for the Protection of Human Rights denounced the labor contract between the two governments and other aspects of the Dominican Republic's treatment of Haitian *braceros* as a form of slavery. The recently inaugurated government of President Guzmán flatly denied the charge of enslaving Haitian cane workers and claimed that it had already improved many of the bad conditions the Society described in its report (Plant 1987, 1). In 1981, Lemoine's fictionalized account of life in the sugar *bateyes, Sucre Amer,* added further intensity to the controversy surrounding the issue. Some improvements resulted from the international attention focused on the plight of the *braceros*.[3] But the *braceros'* situation in fact deteriorated during the 1980s, as inflation ate steadily into their wages (see chapter 5).

During the years of booming sugar prices of the 1970s, the CEA floated a few pilot projects aimed at reducing the industry's dependence on Haitian labor. Little came of these other than the construction of some new, improved barracks for the Brazilian or El Salvadoran men or Dominican families who, it was hoped, might replace the Haitians. Enterprising *batey* residents promptly stripped these buildings of their shower facilities, washbasins, and electrical fixtures.

The CEA failed to make good use of its windfall profits during the sugar boom, and it was unprepared for the slump in world sugar prices that set in after 1981 (Rodríguez and Huntington 1982, 24–25). The root of the market crisis lay in U.S. and European Community price supports for cane and beet sugar production in their own countries. For example, in 1985, while world sugar prices hovered around 3 cents a pound, sugar producers in the U.S. and EC were enjoying prices between 19 and 22 cents a pound (Coote 1992, 39). Even a low-cost sugar producer could not break even at a price much below 12 cents a pound. As if to make matters worse, American protectionist measures increased Dominican sugar producers' exposure to the depressed world market. In 1984, the United States lowered the price of sugar on its preferential market from U.S.$0.22 to $0.17 per pound. In 1986, it cut the Dominican Republic's quota in this market from 535,000 to 362,000 metric tons (Greene and Roe 1989, 166). Since 1987, the CEA has been forced to close 3 of its 12 plantations, and sugar's percentage of Dominican total exports has plummeted. It is uncertain whether these developments signal a lasting turn away from sugar exports. In recent years, undetermined quantities of sugar produced for domestic consumption have in fact been smuggled to Haiti (Caroit 1992).

In 1985–86, the growing financial crisis of the CEA, combined with civil unrest in Haiti, led to the suspension of official recruitment. To make matters worse for Dominican cane growers, Haitians were reluctant to cross the border as undocumented migrants during that time of trouble. By February 1986, two months after the cane harvest should have begun, most of the Dominican Republic's sugar mills were idle, awaiting the arrival of the *braceros*. The crisis came to a head when, on 7 February, President Duvalier fled Haiti to exile in France. Local company bosses did not sit idly waiting for a solution to the labor shortage to come from Santo Domingo, but dispatched Haitian employees to recruit men in Haiti. These recruiters met with fierce opposition from civilians in Haiti, some barely escaping with their lives. Yet, as early as May 1986, CEA recruiters could again work openly in some parts of southeastern Haiti, as the people's anti-Duvalierist ardor cooled.

The harvest of 1986 dramatized the Dominican sugar industry's dependence on Haitian labor. After Duvalier fled Haiti, Dominican president Jorge Blanco declared the harvest a national emergency. In a well-publicized move, the government formed brigades of civil servants to cut cane on weekends. The CEA also launched advertisements that exhorted Dominicans to join the cane harvest. These promised free medical care, cheap food, and good pay. To my knowledge, no Dominican rural or urban people arrived in Yerba Buena to take up the offer. In addition to these largely symbolic measures, the government assigned Air Force troops as cane cutters to CEA *bateyes* around the country. The soldiers did not prove adept at the task. By my calculation, based on local company weigh station records, the soldiers were only one-fortieth to one-eighth as productive per capita as the Haitian cane cutters. Given the extra housing, food, and transport costs they incurred, it is possible that the soldiers cost more than they earned the CEA. In an election year, Jorge Blanco may have wished to keep the soldiers in the cane fields as a visible sign of government action on the crisis. The soldiers moved out of Yerba Buena soon after the May elections, leaving room to house a new shipment of undocumented workers from Haiti.

Since 1989, international human rights organizations—most notably, Americas Watch and the Lawyers Committee for Human Rights—have brought increased pressure to bear on the Dominican Republic to put an end to the forced recruitment of Haitian immigrants as cane cutters on government estates. In 1990, human rights organizations petitioned the U.S. Trade Representative to suspend benefits to the Dominican Republic under the U.S. Generalized System of Preferences and Caribbean Basin Initiative, until such time as the Dominican Republic improved its treatment of Haitian workers. President Balaguer responded with a decree intended to show his government's commitment to protecting the rights of Haitian workers. The decree proposed procedures to regularize the residence and employment status of Haitians who cut cane, and it forbade those under the age of 14 to work in the cane harvest. Unfortunately, abuses continued in the recruitment and employment of Haitian *braceros* (Lawyers Committee 1991a, iii–iv). The Dominican government, it seems, was more interested in avoiding U.S. trade sanctions than in improving the situation of its Haitian workers. The following year, human rights organizations renewed their pressure. On 30 May 1991, the ABC television network broadcast a report on child labor on the Dominican sugar estates. On 11 June that year, a U.S. Congressional committee heard testimony from human rights activists recommending trade sanctions against the Dominican Republic. Two days later came the first substantive action on the issue by the Balaguer government: for the first time since Trujillo's *corte* in 1937, Haitians would be expelled from the Dominican Republic en masse. President Balaguer had decreed the expulsion of all Haitian nationals under 15 and over 60.

The Dominican security forces quickly overstepped the presidential decree by apprehending many young adults. The deportations followed no legal proceedings. The military and police authorities simply picked up men and women they thought were Haitian, sent them to improvised holding centers, and packed them off in buses to Haiti. Many deportees bore legal papers that identified them as Dominican citizens; these the authorities simply ignored, assuming that all those determined at the point of arrest to be "Haitian" were in fact Haitian nationals. Between June and September, 6,000 "Haitians" were deported. Many more fled the country in fear of losing all they possessed. In his speech of 25 September 1991 before the United Nations General Assembly, Haitian president Aristide spoke of 50,000 returnees. Other sources estimate the number to have been 30,000 (Corten 1992).

Hard on the heels of the deportation campaign, on 30 September 1991, a military coup toppled the Haitian president. After Aristide's ouster, the Dominican Republic suspended further deportations. Haitian sources in the Dominican Republic indicate that many of those who fled between June and September soon found their way back into the country. The decree of 13 June broke with the decades-old practice of turning a blind eye to the presence of Haitians on Dominican territory during the sugar industry's dead season. In earlier years, apart from the yearly end-of-harvest repatriation of contract *braceros,* the Dominican security forces had carried out only sporadic, localized round-ups of Haitians for deportation. It remains to be seen whether or not large-scale deportations will be repeated. If they are, it may mark a new turn for the worse in the Dominican Republic's treatment of Haitian immigrants.

In summary, the migratory labor system set up by Dominican sugar planters in the last quarter of the nineteenth century was a new version of an old Caribbean theme. The new sugar industrialists imported workers whose access to livelihood opportunities could be restricted to create a cheap and easily disciplined work force for their plantations. Like the sugar planters of the era of slavery, managers of the new corporate sugar mills sought in effect to eliminate the field worker's alternatives to estate labor.

Observers of the Dominican sugar industry have often remarked that Dominican nationals have historically rejected cane work as labor unworthy of decent folk. It would be more accurate to say that the sugar companies *drove out* ethnic Dominicans by importing cheaper and more easily controlled labor from neighboring territories. In the industry's first two decades, a mostly Dominican labor force brought in the cane harvests. Dominicans withdrew from cane work only when consumer price inflation and downward pressure on wages made further employment in the cane harvests unattractive, when compared to the cultivation of subsistence crops on their own smallholdings. Global overproduction of sugar and the resulting instability of international sugar markets pushed estate owners to look for the cheapest sources of labor possible. The Dominican ruling elite accepted the denationalization of the harvest labor force as the price of ensuring the survival of the country's sugar producers.

At the risk of repeating the obvious, it can be observed that the development of sugar production on an industrial scale in the Dominican Republic was not just a consequence of favorable market conditions and natural endowments. It was also aided at nearly every step by a compliant host state. Similarly, even though spontaneous immigration preceded recruitment, it took the active intervention of the sugar companies to set immigration in motion on a large scale. As the twentieth century wore on, the Haitian and Dominican governments would play an ever more visible role in assuring that Haitian labor would continue to flow in large quantities toward the sugar estates.

Since 1986, the Haitian government has abandoned any official role in organizing labor recruitment. Yet the Dominican security forces remain active in channeling Haitian entrants toward the sugar estates. It may be predicted that, as long as the cane growers depend on seasonal migrants, and as long as cutting cane pays lower wages than any other work in the Dominican economy, the CEA will need to continue its coercive recruitment and labor control practices.

2

Mobilizing Labor

Until the turn of the twentieth century, few signs suggested that Haiti might become a large supplier of plantation labor to neighboring countries. Haitians showed little inclination to work for wages on large agricultural estates at home, much less to emigrate as agricultural wage laborers to distant lands. The history of labor in nineteenth-century Haiti was largely one of failed elite attempts to channel rural people's efforts toward production of exportable commodities. Even before independence was definitively won, Haiti's rebel leader, François-Dominique Toussaint L'Ouverture, sought to restore production of export crops—chiefly, sugar, coffee, and cotton—to its prerevolutionary levels, in order to place the new state on a secure fiscal footing (Moral 1961, 12–30; G. F. Murray 1977, 57–64; Dupuy 1989, chap. 3). To do this, it would have been necessary to make large numbers of freed people return to estates like those where they had worked as slaves. That was something the freed people were reluctant to do, except perhaps under the most liberal conditions as sharecroppers (Moral 1961, 36–37). As Gerald F. Murray (1977, 54) phrases it, "The desires for freedom which must have been felt by the majority of the slaves were not desires for freedom in the abstract, but for freedom to dedicate all of their labor to their own economic pursuits."

Jean-Jacques Dessalines, the first head of state of independent Haiti, 1804–6, kept up export production, as Toussaint L'Ouverture had, by compelling large numbers of former slaves to work on large agricultural estates. After Dessalines, between 1807 and 1820, two rival states divided Haiti's territory: a northern kingdom led by Christophe, formerly the most senior officer in the army, and a southern republic, under the presidents Pétion (1807–18) and Boyer (1818–43). Pétion made an important innovation in land policy. While still attempting to maintain harsh discipline on the large estates, Pétion moved to secure the loyalty of his soldiers by giving them land (Moral 1961, 30–33; Dupuy 1989, 85–93). After the overthrow and suicide of Christophe in 1820, the republic and its policy of land distribution were extended to the north. Several historians credit (or blame) Pétion's land distribution policy with having created Haiti's free peasantry (G. F. Murray 1977, 77). Yet Pétion and Boyer probably never intended to endow all, or even most, of the freed people with land (Lepkowski 1968, 122). The republican leadership envisioned Haiti not as a nation of free peasants but as a three-tiered society of large proprietors, yeomen, and landless laborers. Controlling the labor of the large mass of freed people was to make or break this vision of Haiti's future. Without plenty of cheap labor, neither large proprietors nor the yeoman middle class could put their land into production.

In the struggle for control of their own labor, the freed people had at least one decisive advantage: the availability of large tracts of unused land in the interior of the country. Immediately after the Revolution, there was enough land for all who wanted it to claim a parcel of their own. Having the option of working their own smallholdings, few Haitians were content to work the land of others for wages or willing to pay rent or grow cash crops on demand for absentee landlords. Landowners who were loath to work the land with their own hands could find no one to work for them as day laborers or tenants. Many beneficiaries of state land grants may have made the best of their bad situation by selling out to people who had no legal title to land (G. F. Murray 1977, 102). Thus, small property replaced large as the country's leading form of landholding, and subsistence farming supplanted export production as its dominant economic orientation. Of the major colonial exports, only coffee proved well enough adapted to independent cultivation on a small scale for large quantities to be exported.

The continuing importance of coffee shows that after independence the freed people did not seal themselves away in the fastnesses of the country's rugged interior. On the contrary, "it seems that the link between production in the *mornes* (highlands) and commerce based in the coastal towns was never broken. Rather, coffee provided the peasants a source of limited, but even so significant, revenue" (Girault 1981, 56, my trans.). A cash economy was one enduring legacy of slavery. The colonial economy was oriented heavily toward cultivation of a few export staples, and such items of everyday necessity as cloth, soap, and smoked or salted meat and fish were imported. After the Europeans were overthrown, a need or preference for some of these items endured. Also, on plantation provision grounds, the enslaved had grown their own food and thereby gotten a taste of what it would be like to dispose of their own labor as they saw fit. In local markets, slaves had even sold the surplus of these gardens to the free people of the colony (Mintz 1989, chaps. 5 and 7).

After independence, effective control of the land and possession of skills needed to put that land to profitable use should have afforded ordinary Haitians a long period of prosperity. Yet Haitian leaders were not about to let the freed people prosper and the state go to ruin. In taxes, Haitian rulers found a foolproof tool for getting revenue out of even the most remote rural areas. Lacking the will to tax wealth, the Haitian state had little way of raising revenues except by taxing ordinary consumer goods and placing duties on basic imports and exports, particularly exports of coffee. Merchants reduced the price they paid peasants for raw coffee to compensate for the large fraction of the final selling price that export duties would claim (Tanzi 1976; Girault 1981, chap. 9). Marketplace taxes and import duties on such basic consumer goods as cloth, fish, and flour also bore down disproportionally on poorer Haitians. As Trouillot (1985, 13) remarks, "It is not too much to suggest that the peasantry, almost alone, was subsidizing the Haitian state."

The hostility and greed of the world's great powers also helped push Haiti into poverty. To guard against European reconquest and reimposition of slavery, Haiti's early rulers kept the country continually on a war footing. The demands of national defense grew lighter after 1825, when France granted Haiti tentative diplomatic recognition. Yet the price of increased security was enormous: Haiti's president, Jean-Pierre Boyer, agreed to pay France an indemnity of 150 million francs (Rotberg 1971, 66–67). The indemnity was later reduced to 60 million francs, but it took over a century for Haiti to repay the loans taken to finance its payment. Haiti, like many other primary commodity exporters of the south, has suffered also from the unfair trading practices of the north. For instance, escalating tariffs, which increase with each stage of processing, have discouraged Haiti from roasting and further processing its own coffee before export. Tariff barriers like these persist even today. For example, the European Community tariff on raw coffee beans is 9 percent, while soluble, or instant, coffee carries a tariff double that amount (Coote 1992, 94–95).[1]

In short, the poverty that was a necessary condition for rural Haitians to emigrate in large numbers was largely a product of regressive taxation and other forms of exploitation imposed by Haitian rulers, the great powers, and international commodities traders. Even so, for many years, the emigration of the rural masses was probably one of the last things Haitian leaders would have wished to encourage. They may have hoped that rural folk would eventually become so poor as to offer their labor willingly to large landowners in Haiti. But, time and again, even well into the twentieth century (e.g., Dalencour 1923), elite observers bemoaned the *scarcity* of farmhands in Haiti as an obstacle to the renaissance of export agriculture. It is doubtful that Haitian elites would have wished to encourage the emigration of what they considered scarce labor.

Also, as late as the last quarter of the nineteenth century, the few agricultural estates established around semimechanized sugarcane mills in Haiti's Cul de Sac Valley encountered resistance to plantation-style work discipline. In 1873, Hazard visited the only steam-powered sugarcane mill then operating in Haiti. This estate was probably the same one that Rigaud (1930, 105) mentions as having been held jointly by a Haitian, Félix Duthiers, and an American, Captain Cutts, which was to go out of business in 1877. Concerning it, Hazard (1873, 457–58) observed,

> He [the white proprietor] has under cultivation a thousand acres of cane, which is growing all the year round, . . . no attention being paid to the weeding, hoeing, or care of the cane, as is done in Cuba.
>
> His labourers are all blacks, all living on the place or in the vicinity, . . . the average wages per hand being about twelve cents per day, and this he esteems expensive labour for the quality furnished.
>
> He has little or no strong control over this labour, being compelled to humour the hands in great degree in their holidays, fandangos, and church celebrations. . . .
>
> Contrary to every other sugar-producing country, the mills stop every day; and when I ask if this is as profitable as running the mills night and day during the regular season, the reply is, "If I attempted such a thing my plantation would be burned by the people."
>
> Although some $50,000 have been invested in the place, it yields, owing to the poor labour and the irregular system of agriculture, a rather slim return, and this is only in rum and tafia, little or no sugar being produced.

Some sense of the attitudes behind Haitians' resistance to plantation-style work discipline may perhaps be drawn from the following anecdote, which St. John (1971, 366) recounted in 1884: "The prejudice against sugar-making is still strong. . . . A friend of mine tried to persuade one of his cultivators to aid him in a sugar-making project, but the man answered sulkily, 'Moué pas esclave' ('I'm not a slave'), and walked away. The negroes do not like a bell to be used to ring them to work, as it reminds them of colonial days, but some bold innovators have introduced and continued the practice, without producing any other effect than occasional grumbling."

Around the turn of the twentieth century, a sudden change seems to have come over rural Haitians in their attitudes toward estate labor. Haitian men in their tens of thousands came to consider the offer of meager wages for backbreaking work attractive enough to risk injury or death by emigrating as cane workers to Cuba and the Dominican Republic. After 1900, why did so many rural Haitians drop their aversion to a proletarian life-style, at least for a few months each year?

THE SOURCES OF EMIGRATION

Even though emigration to Cuba and the Dominican Republic seems to have accelerated after 1915, there is little evidence that the Americans who ruled Haiti at that time purposely promoted emigration (but, for an opposing opinion, see Castor 1971, 85). Labor recruitment at that time was a private affair. Each employer hired agents in Haiti to do its recruiting and paid for its contract workers to be transported in steamboats to the ports nearest its properties. The American military authorities in Haiti did not at first attempt to control emigration but simply levied a modest tax on it. Even after it was increased in 1923, this tax was no more than a minor disincentive to emigration (Moral 1961, 69–70). Also, after 1924, the Haitian-American "joint dictatorship" (Haitian only in name) required that each recruiter carry an official license, for which they charged a fee of U.S.$100 for Haitians and U.S.$500 for non-Haitians (Pérez de la Riva 1979, 43). By the late 1920s, the official attitude toward emigration had cooled. In 1928, the government went so far as to prohibit contract emigration altogether, but apparently took no steps to enforce this regulation (Moral 1961, 70).

Even so, certain American initiatives may have unintentionally provoked emigration. Some contemporary observers, such as the Union Nationaliste (1930, 15) and Renaud (1934, 172–74), considered that the major reason Haitians emigrated to Cuba and the Dominican Republic was the dispossession of thousands of Haitian smallholders of their land under the U.S. occupation. Some later authors (Bastien 1951, 155; Romain 1959, 33, 107; Castor 1971, 82–83; Millet 1978, 58, 108–9) have accepted this conclusion, citing the Union Nationaliste as their authority. Yet the claim that the U.S. military occupation triggered large-scale emigration is not at all certain and merits skeptical reconsideration.

It is clear that the American occupiers changed Haitian land laws to permit foreign entrepreneurs to obtain secure claims to land in Haiti. Before the American invasion, if there was one point on which Haiti's leaders and its rural masses agreed, it was that white foreigners should be prohibited from acquiring Haitian land, even if this meant slowing economic growth. After 1915, the American occupiers excluded opponents of foreign investment from the puppet regimes through which they governed Haiti, and, in 1918, they lifted the prohibition on foreign land ownership altogether. By Castor's (1974, 55) count, 33 legislative measures were enacted between 1915 and 1930 to attract foreign capital to Haiti. These made it possible for foreigners to buy or lease land in Haiti on secure terms (Castor 1971, 76–77). Beginning in 1915, foreign investors amassed large properties for export agriculture on the Plaine du Nord, in the Cul de Sac Valley, and on the plains of Léogâne and Les Cayes (see table 5). Each estate probably dispossessed thousands of smallholders.

The dislocations caused by American rule were not limited to land expropriations. Untold thousands also fled their homes to avoid the *corvée* (forced labor in road construction). And, between 1918 and 1920, thousands more fled the war against the Cacos, peasant guerrilla armies who resisted American rule.

Unfortunately, it is not known where most of the displaced people went or how they earned a living after they lost or abandoned their land. In the end, all there is to the alleged link between expropriation and emigration is the coincidence that, just as thousands of Haitian peasants were uprooted from their land, thousands also emigrated to neighboring countries. On close examination, this coincidence seems not so exact as it may have appeared to the Union Nationaliste authors at the time.

First, blaming the occupiers for emigration runs aground on the historical chronology of emigration. Before the U.S. invaders had displaced a

Table 5

Major Land Acquisitions by U.S. Owned Companies, Haiti, 1915–34

Date of Acquisition	Company Name	Acres of Land Acquired
1915	Haytian American Sugar Company	24,000
1915	Haytian Products Company	10,000
1918	United West Indies Corporation	16,000
1918	Société Commerciale d'Haïti	3,000
1922	North Haytian Sugar Company	400
1923	Haytian Pine–apple Company	600
1926	Haytian American Development Corporation	14,000
1927	Haytian Agricultural Corporation	2,200
Total		70,200

SOURCE: Moral 1961, 63.

single person, Haitians were already emigrating in large numbers to Cuba (beginning in 1900) and to the Dominican Republic (ca. 1915). This suggests that conditions for large-scale emigration were in place at least a decade before the first U.S. Marine disembarked in Port-au-Prince.

Second, it seems unlikely that the total number of displaced people came anywhere close to the hundreds of thousands who went to Cuba and to the Dominican Republic at the time, not to mention the hundreds of thousands of immediate family members whom the emigrants—mostly men—left behind in Haiti. For the U.S. occupation to have been the main cause of emigration, it would have had to have uprooted upwards of 500,000 men, women, and children, or at least one-fifth of the entire population of Haiti at that time. In reality, North American investors only took about 1 percent of Haiti's total land area, and could not conceivably have been responsible for emigration on the scale at which it occurred.[2] The American program of legislation came too late, it seems, for export agriculture in Haiti to have benefited from post–world war highs in prices for sugar and other tropical exports. By the time the new land laws were in place, world prices for these products had tumbled. Therefore, in spite of the unprecedented ease with which land could be acquired in Haiti, the prevailing global overproduction of tropical staples discouraged much foreign investment. At the end of the American occupation in 1934, the hemp plantation, Dauphin, and the Haitian American Sugar Company (HASCO) were the only large agricultural estates that survived. It is perhaps significant that HASCO was founded in 1915 and began grinding at close to full capacity in 1918, whereas the sugar estates that came into production in Haiti after the 1920 crash of world sugar prices all failed.[3]

Third, the displacements of people caused by the American occupation cannot explain the geography of emigration. The largest number of emigrants to the Dominican Republic did not originate in areas where much land was expropriated, such as the Plaine du Nord and the Cul de Sac Valley. Instead, they came from the southeast, an area untouched by expropriation on a large scale. Both the war against the Cacos and, after 1918, the *corvée* were largely restricted to the Plateau Central (Schmidt 1971, 101–2; Millet 1978, 77–81), a secondary source of emigration to the Dominican Republic. The main source areas of emigration to Cuba, the northwest and southwest, were not spared from expropriation but were far from being the most heavily expropriated parts of the country. In short, the upheavals of American rule probably added thousands of displaced people to the ranks of the emigrants. Yet the U.S. occupation was not the main engine of emigration.

It seems more likely that, in the decades *before* the United States took power, increasing foreign involvement in Haiti might somehow have played a role in setting emigration in motion. The period between 1880 and 1915 saw a gradual but politically significant growth in European and United States interference in Haitian politics, commerce, and finance (Caprio 1985; Nicholls 1985, chap. 5; Plummer 1988, chap. 2). Foreign merchants set up business in increased numbers in Haitian port towns and meddled brashly in Haitian politics. Unfavorable international market conditions may also have placed increased pressure on peasant livelihoods. From 1891 to 1910, the annual export values of Haiti's key crop, coffee, fell steadily (Rotberg 1971, 394). It is suggestive that the three heartlands of emigration to Cuba and the Dominican Republic—the Southwest Peninsula, the southeast, and the northeast—were also Haiti's major coffee-producing regions. Yet, again, it is not clear precisely how all these factors—growing political instability, worsening terms of foreign trade, and increasing foreign business involvement in Haiti's coastal cities—might have led to the development of conditions conducive to emigration in the countryside. Increased foreign financial and commercial domination may well have signaled a turn for the worse for small farmers when compared to earlier exploitation by Haitian elites, but concrete evidence of this is as yet lacking.

POPULATION PRESSURE AND EMIGRATION: SEARCHING FOR A LINK

While the land tenure of the vast majority of Haitians remained unchallenged during the U.S. occupation, rising population pressure raised the specter of dispossession for undetermined numbers of Haitians. At least two conditions were necessary for overpopulation to have become a problem: first, that rural people would remain largely tied to the land and, second, that the productivity of farm labor would improve little over the years. These conditions are not explained by population growth but are part of a larger syndrome of poverty. Any approach that takes the immobility of the rural population and the stagnation of agricultural technology as givens will deceptively isolate population growth from other causes of rural poverty. This may convey the mistaken impression that the negative consequences of population growth were natural and inevitable outcomes of the redistribution of land to the freed people during Haiti's first decades of independence.

That said, it cannot be denied that increased population pressure may have played a substantial role in setting the stage for emigration. According to Gerald F. Murray (1977, 410), "Though one cannot fix exact dates, by the last quarter of the nineteenth century probably few tracts of arable soil were not either under cultivation or at least under the claim of one or another owner." Palmer (1976, 62) estimates that it took only 50 years after independence for all of Haiti's habitable land areas to be occupied. Either way, by the time emigration began on a large scale, Haiti's population had already expanded to cover all its usable land, except perhaps in the country's most isolated regions.

At least one author, Lundahl, draws a very direct link between population pressure and the origins of emigration from Haiti. He posits that "most of the emigrants . . . were landless peasants," uprooted by rising population pressure (Lundahl 1983, 97–98). Lundahl finds support for his position from two other authors, Moral and Wingfield, who lay emphasis on the extreme poverty of the migrants. Neither source bases his opinion on systematic observation. Moral (1961, 70) only notes in passing that "emigration brought . . . only destitute peasants to Cuba" (my trans.). Wingfield (1966, 94) comes to the same conclusion but cites only Moral as his authority.

Contrary to this opinion, there is evidence that the landless may have been no more prone than other rural Haitians to emigrate to Cuba and the Dominican Republic. This evidence is found in Dartigue's survey of 884 families, carried out in the mid-1930s in villages throughout rural Haiti. The purpose of this survey was to gather basic information on living conditions in several regions of the country. In the course of this survey, Dartigue's enumerators came across 115 individuals who had worked in Cuba or in the Dominican Republic. Of these, 96 (about 83 percent) reported that they owned land. Surprisingly, this was *higher* than the percentage of landowners in the sample population at large (75 percent) (Dartigue 1938, 30, 38). The absence of data on absentees means that Dartigue's data cannot be regarded as a representative sample of the entire migrant population. Perhaps more importantly, Dartigue did not indicate whether the returnees had owned land before emigrating or had only acquired it afterwards, perhaps out of money repatriated from abroad. It is therefore impossible to say conclusively whether land ownership predisposed men to emigrate, was itself a product of emigration, or bore no significant relationship to it at all. Yet, in searching for clues concerning the status background of most migrants, it seems reasonable to place greater confidence in Dartigue's numbers than in one author's unsubstantiated impressions, even when that author is someone as trustworthy as Moral. The conclusion one must draw from Dartigue is that most of the men who emigrated as cane workers at this time probably had at least a realistic hope of acquiring land in their rural home places in Haiti, if they did not already own land before emigrating.

Yet what overpopulation alone can least explain about emigration to the sugar estates is that this was basically a *circular* movement of people. Most migrants, it seems, returned every year and ultimately settled into nonmigratory occupations at home. At the height of the first wave of emigration, in the 1920s, immigration records documented that at least two-thirds of the Haitian men who went to Cuba ultimately returned home (Millspaugh 1931, 143, n. 37; Balch 1927, 77). Pérez de la Riva (1979) estimates an 80 percent rate of return, but it is not clear whether by this he means annual circulation or permanent return. I leave it until the next chapter to examine the reasons why this migration has had such an important return component. For now, suffice it to observe that population pressure doubtless worsened resource scarcity for many Haitians, but it did not make life so difficult as to preclude the return to Haiti of most emigrants.

In short, the role of demographic pressure in setting emigration in motion was perhaps less direct than one might expect, given Haiti's historically high levels of population density. Little evidence sustains the notion that emigration to Cuba and the Dominican Republic in the early twentieth century was a product of desperation, brought on by landlessness. It would clearly be an oversimplification to suppose that high population density pushed rural Haitians, as if by hydraulic pressure, to emigrate to neighboring lands in search of work. The early links between population growth, rural poverty, and emigration remain poorly understood and demand further study.

CHANGES IN THE PEASANT LIFE CYCLE AS A STIMULUS TO EMIGRATION

The structure of rural Haitian society places as strong an imprint on migrants' motivations and behavior as the income gap, the difference in population densities, or any other invidious distinction between Haiti and the Dominican Republic. This social structure is not timeless but has evolved over Haitian history. What relationship there might have been between social change and the origins of mass emigration is clouded in uncertainty. The available documents from nineteenth-century Haiti give only tantalizing glimpses of rural society. Yet it is suggestive that, at roughly the same time as emigration was taking off, a transformation seems to have been under way in the character of relations between young and old in rural Haiti. I refer here to Gerald F. Murray's (1977) thesis concerning the "arrival of stress" in Haiti's agrarian system. Murray holds that, before actual crowding of the land became a problem, population pressure may have brought about lasting changes in the social mechanisms whereby Haitian smallholders recruited the labor of their dependent offspring. This growing break with former custom may have been one reason why Haiti so *rapidly* became a leading supplier of immigrant labor after 1900.

As early as Herskovits's fieldwork in the Mirebalais Valley in 1934, students of rural Haiti have observed that young men engage in local agricultural wage labor and sharecropping as a normal phase in the life cycle. Young men do this largely to accumulate the resources they need to establish their first conjugal union (Herskovits 1937, 109, 133; A. Métraux 1951, 86; G. F. Murray 1977, 469–72; Smucker 1982, 317–18, 356). This is an old pattern. Yet Murray's synthesis of Haitian agrarian history suggests that in the nineteenth century it may have been an exceptional strategy, followed only by the very poor and by youths who had renounced or been denied access to their inheritance. In former times, most young men in rural Haiti took a different path toward acquiring the material resources that they needed to enter adulthood.

Murray (1977, 409) writes, "After the expulsion of the Europeans, and for many decades thereafter, there were too few people to cultivate all of the land." Nearly all of the material resources that young people might need to take their first steps toward establishing households of their own— wood and thatch to build a house and land, seed, and livestock for agriculture—were commonly found in relative abundance in the possession of their adult guardians. Labor, on the other hand, was scarce. It was therefore possible up to a certain point for young people to dictate the conditions under which they would remain loyal to the parental estate. Out of countless implicit negotiations between parents and offspring, it became customary for parents to give their sons of marriageable age one or more parcels of land as a preinheritance grant, on condition that those sons continue to provide regular unremunerated labor on the parental estate.

Over time, the countryside grew more densely populated, and each generation of elders found itself more constrained than the last in the amount of land it could cede provisionally to the young. As the implicit price of labor declined relative to that of land, elders also felt progressively less need to give up land in order to ensure the availability of filial labor. Murray (1977, 418–19) posits that the relative value of filial labor eventually dropped so much that land grants gave way to sharecropping as the most common way for elders to recruit the labor of the younger generation. He documents a trend away from preinheritance grants and toward intergenerational sharecropping over a span of three generations among the living informants in one village in the Cul de Sac Valley. Increased demographic pressure may therefore have made itself felt first not as a declining standard of living but as a change in the ways the old transmitted wealth to, and recruited the labor of, the young.

In the short term, the young might have found the shrinkage of their preinheritance grants more damaging than the increasing overall scarcity of land. This was because the withdrawal of preinheritance grants cut into the resources that young adults received from their parents to help them get started in life. Following this change in custom, during the late nineteenth and early twentieth centuries, increased numbers of young Haitians may have been left largely to their own devices to acquire the customary necessities of life. Many young men may have emigrated in the hope of accumulating assets more rapidly than would be possible by staying at home.

It is also possible that emigration itself contributed to the decline of the obligations that formerly tied the young to their parents' land. Some young men may have emigrated as a way to escape from increasingly unrewarding filial labor obligations. Mintz (1964, 258) speculates that the advent of new wage labor opportunities after 1910 may have hastened the obsolescence of the extended family residential compound (*laku*) as an agricultural production unit. So little is known for sure about how the *laku* functioned at that time that it is difficult to say how heavily parental authority in it may have weighed on the young or how easily the young could have escaped that authority by pursuing outside incomes. Even so, it seems likely that the opening of new sources of income in the early twentieth century only accelerated the diminution of obligations between parents and offspring in agricultural production. Rising population pressure and increased international labor circulation went hand in hand with major changes in rural Haitian household organization, the male life cycle, and smallholder land tenure and agricultural labor relations.

That said, the economic impact of emigration in early twentieth-century Haiti should not be overstated. In Haiti, as in most other parts of the circum-Caribbean region, emigration was probably far less destructive of indigenous economic institutions than it was in areas of the world that had previously been little integrated into global trade. Because the market already dominated so many other aspects of the rural Haitian economy, the impact of migrant money was probably limited largely to furthering an existing trend toward monetarizing agricultural labor relations.

Where emigration may have had its most far-reaching effects on rural Haitian society was in the growing dependence of the peasantry on external labor markets for the generational reproduction of their livelihoods. After the advent of labor circulation on a large scale, people in rural southeastern Haiti would continue farming the land and taking their garden produce to market much as they had before. Yet the young would thereafter look increasingly to temporary employment on distant commercial farms in attempting to reproduce customary standards of living at home.

One thread connects the macrosocial history reviewed in this chapter with the microsocial strategies of attainment that will be described in what follows. This link is the remarkable perseverance of a peasant way of life in rural Haiti. When people cling to this way of life as tenaciously as rural

Haitians have, it is not just conservatism or a lack of viable alternatives that impels them to do so. Rather, within the terrible constraints under which they live, rural Haitians consider their modes of livelihood to have retained some advantages relative to other possible life-styles.

Against this background of continuity, the incomes of the migrant cane workers and the profits of Haitian coffee growers have fluctuated significantly with the ups and downs of international commodities markets. The personal histories on which the ethnographic body of this study is largely based reflect the experience of migration during both "good" times and "bad." Therefore, in what follows, I do not so much turn away from history as turn toward a different window on the past, one that looks out on how rural Haitians have experienced changes and continuities in the migratory system.

3

The Setting

Strikingly different forms of commerce, architecture, landscape, agricultural technology, and labor relations distinguish the Dominican Republic's Ingenio Santa Ana and the Cayes-Jacmel/Cap Rouge area of Haiti. This is hardly surprising. Not only are the two separated by the cultural and political boundary between Haiti and the Dominican Republic, but one is a modern corporate plantation, and the other, a dispersed settlement of free peasants. The two places also occupy different niches in the imaginary landscapes of their inhabitants. No sugar estate resident, Dominican or Haitian, even those born and raised in the *batey*, speaks of Yerba Buena as anything more than a stopping point on the way to where he or she would rather be. No matter how long one lives there, the *batey* will always be a place one wishes someday to leave behind for good. It is a place for sojourners, not settlers, and only the unfortunate (many though they may be) remain there indefinitely. By contrast, Cayes-Jacmel and Cap Rouge are and always will be "home" to the people who come from those areas of Haiti, even if they spend an entire lifetime abroad. It may be significant that people in southeastern Haiti speak of circulating between Haiti and the Dominican Republic as "going *up* to Spanishland" ("*môte nâ pâyòl*") and "coming *down* to Haiti" ("*desân ân Ayiti*"): s/he who goes up to the Dominican Republic should eventually come down to Haiti. Circulation, not permanent emigration, is the normal, expected pattern of mobility. This chapter briefly sketches these two places to give the reader a clearer sense of what sort of human environment the migrants are leaving behind in Haiti and going to in the Dominican Republic.

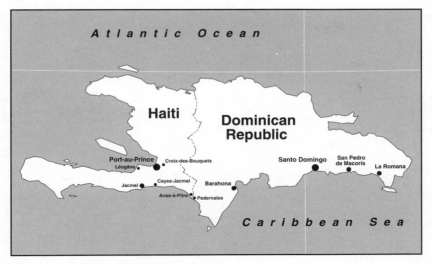

Map 2. Haiti and the Dominican Republic.

YERBA BUENA: A COMPANY TOWN

The Ingenio Santa Ana is one of 12 estates that belong to the CEA. It lies in the middle of the primary region of sugar production in the Dominican Republic, the rolling plain that stretches along the southeastern coast of the island, from the city of Santo Domingo to the Mona Passage. It was here, in the southeast, that sugar production expanded most vigorously during the industry's formative period, 1875 to 1925, favored by good harbors, a relatively flat topography, and enough precipitation to grow sugarcane without irrigation. The estate is a massive field-and-factory combine. It controls about 20,000 hectares of land under sugarcane and owns thousands more hectares of pastures and woodland. Cane is transported from distant fields to the central mill by rail and truck. The mill and refinery complex produce over 50,000 tons of raw sugar in a full grinding season.

As is common among Caribbean sugar industries, the yearly cycle of sugarcane cultivation comprises two periods, *zafra* (harvest) and *tiempo muerto* ("dead season"). The harvest runs four to six months, from December through June, and is the peak period of employment. The dead season lasts six to eight months. As its name implies, the dead season is a time of reduced employment and, for many *batey* people, real hunger. The dead season population of Yerba Buena is a little over 800 persons. Among 420 full-time adult residents of Yerba Buena in 1986, 172 (41 percent) were ethnic Dominicans, 88 (21 percent) were Haitians, and 135 (32 percent) were

Haitian-Dominicans and people of mixed Haitian and Dominican ancestry (see table 6). During the harvest, the population is augmented by about
300 people. The seasonal residents are mostly men who come from Haiti
as seasonal *braceros* (popularly termed *"congoses"* in Spanish), but also include the wives and children of a few of the *congoses*, a few single Haitian
women, and Dominicans and Haitians who keep a dwelling in the *batey*
but reside elsewhere in the Dominican Republic during the dead season.
(In this book, the seasonal migrants are called *"bracero/s"* rather than
"congó/ses" because the latter term is pejorative both in Haitian Creole and
Dominican Spanish.) Much of the seasonal population is highly transient,
and it is hard to say how many Haitians spend only a few days in the *batey*
before moving elsewhere.

The *bateyes* of the CEA vary considerably in size. A handful resemble
small cities with populations numbering in the thousands. Others consist
of nothing more than two or three barracks lost in the cane fields, capable
of housing no more than 200 people. The vast majority fall somewhere between the two extremes. Yerba Buena is a relatively large *batey*, of the type
called *"principal."* It is distinguished from the handful of smaller *"bateyes
satélites"* that lie in its vicinity by the presence in it of certain administrative and maintenance personnel and facilities (Moya Pons et al. 1986, 90–
93). My fieldwork included Yerba Buena and three of its four *bateyes
satélites*. I do not have a census of the population of these *bateyes satélites*,
but it seems that, compared to Yerba Buena, a larger proportion of their
inhabitants are ethnic Haitians.

Yerba Buena occupies a narrow strip of land, situated at a node in the
company transport network. To the south and east, settlement is bounded
by company rail lines. To the north and west, company barracks hug the
main north-south road and a branch road that connects Yerba Buena to
bateyes to the northwest. Sugarcane is planted to the very edge of the *batey*.

Table 6

Ethnic Composition of Yerba Buena's Year–Round Adult Population, 1986

Ethnic Group	Men	Women	Both Sexes
Dominican	97	75	172
Haitian	64	24	88
Haitian–Dominicans and mixed ancestry	59	76	135
West Indian	15	7	22
Unknown	1	2	3
Total	236	184	420

SOURCE: Based on survey in Dominican Republic, March 1986.

As you walk the dirt roads and cane alleys around Yerba Buena, you often lose sight of the *batey*'s low buildings behind the tall cane. From a distance, the *batey*'s location is recognizable only because tall trees mark the spot amid the rolling fields. All the land in Yerba Buena and its immediate surroundings and nearly all the buildings in the *batey* are property of the Ingenio Santa Ana.

The purpose of the *batey* is to house the personnel and equipment needed to plant, cultivate, and harvest the company's sugarcane. True to this purpose, the company has designed the *batey* to be a settlement of men and oxen, the former to cut the cane and the latter to haul it, once cut, on heavy carts in the first leg of its journey from field to mill. The *batey* makes no specific provision for families and provides little space for alternative subsistence activities. Yet, of Yerba Buena's permanent residents, nearly half are children under the age of 15, and of 420 adults who maintain permanent residence, 184 (about 44 percent) are women. Only a handful of these women work in the cane fields, at most occasionally and in the company of their husbands or grown sons. Other employment for women is in short supply and is grossly underpaid.

Batey housing is ceded to company workers free of rent but is woefully inadequate in quantity and quality. The typical family inhabits one or two rooms in barracks (*barracones*) built for groups of single men to live in. The *barracones* are long, boxy, unadorned, single-story wood or concrete structures. Depending on their size, they may contain from 4 to 24 small rooms. The rooms of a typical *barracón* are arranged in either a single row or a double row. Each room has one door and, in some cases, a window that face out. In a single-row *barracón,* the doors and windows all face out on one side, and the other side is entirely closed. A double-row *barracón* is like two single-row *barracones* placed back to back. Most *barracones* in Yerba Buena stand on concrete foundations. Yet, in most *barracones,* wind, rain, and pests can penetrate through rust holes in the sheet metal roofs and gaps in the walls. The *barracones* have not been laid out according to plan but have been added haphazardly in any available space as needed. Usually, this has occurred because "*viejos*" ("old hands," i.e., Haitians who take up permanent residence on the estates) and Dominican nationals have gradually occupied the existing structures, creating a need for new dwellings to house the *braceros.*[1]

Permanent residents attempt to adapt their surroundings to their personal needs and preferences. In and around the *batey,* tiny, rain-fed subsistence gardens cover nearly every bit of land not taken by roads, footpaths, buildings, and sugarcane. As you wander the paths that snake around the *barracones,* yard fowl scatter underfoot, and you inevitably tangle with one of the clotheslines (often made of barbed wire!) that *batey* women string all about at shoulder level. Most permanent residents fence off a bit of space adjacent to their rooms as a private yard, and some plant these with ornamental and medicinal shrubs and forbs. To add a kitchen, an extra bedroom, or a family shop, many residents build small annexes onto their rooms, with cast-off scraps of wood, cardboard, and sheet metal. A household with some space and money to spare will furnish one room in front as a living room and reserve it for hospitality and leisure. By contrast, a large household with only two rooms at its disposal can scarcely avoid the intrusion of bedding, clothing, and charred and dented cooking utensils into all parts of the dwelling.

The company lodges *braceros* and permanent residents in separate barracks to facilitate surveillance of the *braceros* by company security personnel. But, because the *braceros'* barracks stand right next to those of the *batey's* permanent residents, the two groups cannot be said to be residentially segregated. One *congó* barracks, which housed about 60 during the *zafra*, stood directly in front of the *barracón* in which I had taken residence. The harsh shouts and clanging machetes of predawn wake-up calls, the sickly sweet evening smell of dried cane burning as a crude cooking fuel, and, at night, the *braceros'* voices raised in conversation and often in song became inescapable features of my daily experience. Two other *barracones*, identical to it, stood within a stone's throw and housed the rest of the *braceros* assigned to live in Yerba Buena.

The *braceros'* barracks are as crowded as those of the permanent residents. Company bosses generally put four to eight men together in each room, only 9 to 12 square meters large. In Yerba Buena, the CEA equips each room in the *braceros'* barracks with two or three steel-frame bunk beds. Generally, the *braceros'* rooms are otherwise almost bare. A few tattered sheets, one or two plastic jugs for carrying water to the fields, perhaps a small stack of wood in one corner, and large tins blackened by use as cooking vessels make up the range of household items typically visible in the *braceros'* barracks. The *bracero* travels light because, for him, picking up his belongings and moving to another *batey* may at times mean the difference between meeting and failing to meet his harvest savings goal. Poverty and the danger of theft also tend to discourage acquisition of consumer goods until the harvest is over and the migrants prepare to return to Haiti.

The *braceros'* barracks are grimy and battered, but, having been built relatively recently of concrete, they are not as badly deteriorated as the *barracones* of most permanent residents. For the *braceros*, a more serious problem is getting water for bathing and cooking in the evening after work. When the *batey's* well pump breaks down, as was more often than not the case during my stay in Yerba Buena, water is available only at distances of over 1.5 kilometers.

To most Haitian cane workers, the channels of communication through which Haitians in North America may remain active participants in the lives of people in Haiti—telephone, audio cassette, and Haitian transfer houses—are in effect as far out of reach as the moon. Even postal facilities are available only in the mill town of Santa Ana and are little used by Haitians in Yerba Buena. The only way most migrants have of sending a message or money to people at home is to entrust these to someone from their village to carry home when that person returns to Haiti. Because relatively few migrants return before the harvest ends, a suitable messenger is commonly not found until then.

Viejos stand higher than *braceros* in the *batey* social hierarchy, and they share residential space with Dominicans. In Yerba Buena, as in most other *bateyes*, towns, and urban slums where large numbers of Haitians reside in the Dominican Republic, Haitians and Dominicans mingle constantly in their daily affairs. Ties of reciprocity between households, cooperation between people at work and leisure, and mixture of the two ethnicities through intermarriage dull the animosity against everything Haitian expressed by Dominicans in non-sugar-producing areas of the country.

Even so, the yearly sojourn of the *braceros* helps preserve the boundary between "*dominicano*" and "*haitiano*." Local reckonings of status reflect the occupational structure of the sugar company, which in turn largely follows ethnic and national lines (Báez Evertsz 1986, 199–207; Moya Pons et al. 1986, 36–55; Murphy 1986, chap. 13 and 431–35). Generally speaking, the workers who physically touch the industry's raw material, sugarcane, stand at the bottom of the company job ladder. The further one gets from the cane, the higher one's income goes and the better one's conditions, hours, security, and benefits of employment become. Haitian immigrants, seasonal and permanent, occupy the lowest-paid, most physically punishing, and least secure jobs as agricultural piece workers and day laborers. Cutting cane is the province of Haitian men, but many second- and third-generation Haitians and ethnic Dominicans—particularly young men and boys—take it up occasionally during the harvest. Cart driver and wagon loader—jobs that also involve handling cane but that pay slightly better and demand less effort than cutting—employ Haitian men alongside Haitian-Dominicans and ethnic Dominicans. Few Haitian men are promoted to positions as company "*empleados*," which pay a fixed daily wage. Moving further up the ladder to achieve management status is almost unheard of for a Haitian national and is exceptional even for a Haitian-Dominican.

When I left Yerba Buena in August 1986, a newly elected national government was about to take charge in Santo Domingo under President Joaquín Balaguer. Yerba Buenans feared that the new government might introduce drastic economic reforms, including perhaps the closure of the Ingenio Santa Ana. To date, these fears have not materialized. Correspondence with *batey* residents and brief visits in 1987 and 1992 have brought to my attention only a few important changes: a few mechanical harvesters have been introduced, a community dispensary has been established, and a reliable hand-pump well has been installed near the *braceros'* barracks.

ROCHETEAU AND CABROUETTE: TWO NEIGHBORHOODS IN RURAL SOUTHEASTERN HAITI

At first sight, the town of Cayes-Jacmel may appear to be little more than a jumble of small, mismatched buildings, clinging to a stretch of dusty coastal road. A few emigrants to North America, prosperous merchants, and government officials have built one- or two-story concrete structures there. Most of the dwellings in town are low, rectangular, wattle-and-daub houses of one to four rooms. These dwellings are distinguished from the houses that dot the local countryside only by being squeezed closely together, rather than being separated by subsistence plots and tree-shaded yards. Yet, in spite of its modest appearance, the town acts as a gateway to the surrounding countryside. Whether one approaches the area by sea or by land, one generally passes through the town of Cayes-Jacmel. For example, the Haitian capital, Port-au-Prince, lies almost dead north of the *commune* of Cayes-Jacmel. Yet to travel there, the inhabitant of the plain or the surrounding highlands usually walks *south* to town and boards a vehicle that first takes him or her *west* to the city of Jacmel. Only after reaching Jacmel does the vehicle bear north on the paved road that snakes through the mountains. This circuitous route is often traveled by local women as itinerant traders. A number of brightly painted, privately owned minivans and light trucks converted into buses carry goods and passengers along it daily. From Cayes-Jacmel wooden boats equipped with outboard motors carry on a lively maritime trade with the Dominican Republic. (Towns on Haiti's southern coast are not well connected to the international frontier by road.) The same boats carry migrants to the Haitian border town of Anse-à-Pitre, from which point they cross into the Dominican Republic by foot. In town, rural people also attend the twice-weekly market, go to school, obtain official documents, attend Catholic or Evangelical services, or just visit friends. Employment in government administration, trade, transport, and fishing has attracted many to settle there. In town also reside a few merchants, coffee brokers, government bureaucrats, military officers, and other "notables," placed above the peasant masses by wealth, literacy in French, and connections to people in power.

The Cayes-Jacmel area is far from the poorest in Haiti. One of the first things remarked upon by visitors familiar with other parts of rural Haiti is the unusually large number of houses in the area with sheet metal roofs and concrete floors. Older people remember a time when nearly all local houses had thatch roofs and when a concrete floor was a sign of unusual prosperity. In recent decades, many local men have bought sheet metal roofing and cement with money earned in the Dominican Republic. Also, for a brief time, families with young children received these materials as a gift or on easy credit from an American charity, Foster Parents Plan.

The local landscape is perhaps also not quite what one would expect of "tragically deforested Haiti." Breadfruit, mango, star-apple, avocado, and other fruit trees, as well as a handful of palm varieties, stud subsistence gardens and form dark groves in the residential yards of the plain. It is only by marching up to the Cap Rouge Plateau that one may see that the vegetation, even though abundant, is in the wrong place. The plain below is carpeted with trees. Yet, seen from elevated points on the plateau, the mountains to the northeast appear frighteningly bare. Uncontrolled tree-felling has stripped the mountains of southeastern Haiti of the vegetation essential to their role as precipitation-condensers and water towers for the surrounding agricultural lands. In spite of this, soil degradation in the Cayes-Jacmel and Cap Rouge areas has not reached the shocking extremes seen in other parts of Haiti. Deforestation poses a clear ecological menace, but the area remains a major producer of coffee and subsistence crops. Soil-laden runoff is also a potential threat to hydraulic resources, which are of importance even beyond the local area. A hydroelectric plant, located in a small concrete building at the foot of the slope that leads up to Cap Rouge, provides electricity for the city of Jacmel and several nearby towns. The availability of electric power has yet to attract any processing or manufacturing industries to Cayes-Jacmel itself.

The two *katye* in which I did my fieldwork reflect the geographical diversity of the area. The lowland *katye,* Cabrouette, straddles an all-weather road that connects the hydroelectric plant with the town of Cayes-Jacmel. Many of Cabrouette's houses cluster along this road. Yet nowhere in the plain is there a gap in settlement or cultivation, and the whole area is fairly densely inhabited. Cabrouette is a *katye* of small farmers, but households there supplement farm-related incomes through work as fisherfolk, crafts producers, wayside vendors, local market intermediaries, itinerant traders, owners of family shops, transport workers, school teachers, voodoo priests, and ritual healers. The soil there is generally not as fertile as on Cap Rouge, and precipitation is far less reliable. Even so, lowland farms produce much the same wide range of annual tilled crops as highland farms. The fruit and palm trees that blanket the plain are a drought-resistant alternative source of cash and calories.

Rocheteau stands at the edge of cliffs that rise steeply from the plain to a height of 600 to 800 meters. Its air of tranquility differs considerably from the bustle of townward-bound pedestrian and vehicular traffic passing through Cabrouette on busy mornings. Rocheteau is only accessible from the plain via a steep two-hour climb by footpath. On many a highland path, hemmed in on one side by dense, wild-looking coffee shrubs and on the other by multiple-cropped subsistence gardens, it is easy to think oneself far from human habitation. Yet that is an illusion: Cap Rouge is one of the most densely populated rural areas of the country, and nowhere on the plateau is one ever far from a peasant homestead. The fertile soil and plentiful precipitation of the plateau make it one of the best places in Haiti for labor-intensive smallholder agriculture. The "prodigiously dense planting of small gardens of banana-trees, coffee, and food crops," of which Moral (1961, 155, my trans.) wrote in 1961, still blankets the red earth of the plateau.

Distinct as the lowland and highland habitats are, it would be a mistake to draw a neat boundary between the ways of life of lowlanders and highlanders. The livelihood space of the areas' residents in fact overlaps considerably. Many residents farm land both in the plain and on the plateau, and trade goes on constantly between the two areas. Thus, in the production and consumption activities and strategies of survival of local smallholders, the plateau and the plain are not so much distinct productive zones as linked components of a single, complex agricultural subregion.

In spite of the relative prosperity of the Cayes-Jacmel area, local farmers encounter many of the same constraints that confront farmers in most of Haiti. Rudimentary technology severely limits agricultural productivity. Only simple steel hand tools—hoes, machetes, and picks—are used to clear and cultivate the fields. The positive side of low technology is that wealthier farmers must hire laborers to cultivate their fields, which helps poorer farmers survive the hungry season between planting and harvest. An equally important economic constraint, with particularly visible effects on the lowland plain, is the steady toll on productivity taken by soil degradation. As in other parts of Haiti, apart from the ash produced by burning underbrush before planting, the "only source of soil replenishment . . . is the rotting of the post-harvest stubble purposefully left on the fields after a cropping cycle, or the droppings of cattle and horses which are frequently sent to graze on fields not currently under cultivation. Such techniques are simply unable to restore fertility to overworked land" (G. F. Murray 1977, 202–3).

Another important dimension of the Haitian syndrome of poverty is the scarcity of credit and of income opportunities locally for the young and the land-poor. The 1987 wage for a six- to eight-hour "day" of agricultural labor was four or five gourdes (U.S.$0.80–$1.00). A peasant cannot find wage employment every day, even if he or she wants it, because only a minority of local farmers have the wealth to rely largely on hired labor. Nor do government credit institutions generally reach rural smallholders. Local lenders advance sums over U.S.$10 only to farmers who expect substantial returns from irrigated parcels or coffee harvests. Only seasonal migration to the Dominican Republic and itinerant trade in Haiti offer local lenders sufficient guarantee of return to justify loans over U.S.$20, and then only at rates of interest (e.g., 100 percent after the six to nine months of a typical Dominican sojourn), which take a large chunk out of the earnings of would-be entrepreneurs.

Bearing in mind Haiti's formidable material obstacles to human development, it may seem superfluous to bring into consideration certain "cultural" motivations for emigrating. To understand these motivations, it helps to know that, in spite of Haiti's general poverty and scarcity of land, the rural population is stratified by wealth. The stigma attached to soliciting work from wealthier neighbors may well motivate some men to go far from home in search of work. Patterns of land distribution in rural Haiti generally approximate a finely gradated continuum rather than a bimodal distribution (Zuvekas 1979; Mintz 1989, 273; but Casimir 1964, 41–46; Pierre-Charles 1967, 64–78; Girault 1981, 92–95 have opposing opinions). This continuum ranges from those who own no land and depend entirely on wage labor and sharecropping for a living, to those few who own too much land to manage on their own (Smucker 1982, 248–68). Land tenure data for rural Haiti are sparse and uncertain, but ethnographic evidence indicates that in most rural areas only a handful of people owns more than 5 *carreaux* (7.25 hectares) of land (RONCO 1987, 162–67).

Smucker, in his monograph on the village-level politics of a development project in northern Haiti, finds that many men prefer to walk several kilometers to neighboring villages in search of paid work, rather than asking for work in their own villages (also G. F. Murray 1977, 300). Smucker (1982, 318) argues that the stigma has its roots in the rural Haitian man's "dual role as peasant farmer and wage laborer": "The wage laborer often has his own separate house, family and gardens like any other peasant farmer. Consequently, the peasant-worker prefers to work in other nearby communities rather than for his neighbors: '*M pito glé louin pou yo pa konn mizè-a-ou*' [I prefer to go far away where they don't know your poverty]." It should perhaps be stressed that the stigma attaches neither to working for a neighbor, nor to soliciting work per se, but to the combination of the two. That is, it is shameful to solicit work from a neighbor, rather than being invited to work by that neighbor. By soliciting work, one would admit to standing lower on the social ladder than the neighbor does (Murray 1977, 293–94).

Significantly, on more than one occasion, local people told me they would prefer to work locally for a business entrepreneur rather than emigrate to the Dominican Republic. According to them, if, say, a processing plant were to open near by, it would have no problem recruiting labor locally, even at low wages. This suggests that the men who emigrate as cane workers to the Dominican Republic are *not* turning down stigmatized labor at home just to take very similar work abroad. Most rural Haitians would regard soliciting employment from an outsider who might set up shop locally as something very different—and less shameful—than going hat in hand to ask a neighbor for work. Clearly, the stigma does not come just from being seen by one's neighbors handling a machete or a hoe in the sun under another person's orders. Rather, it may depend entirely on what is the social identity of the proprietor and how the laborer was recruited and is being put to work.

An enduring myth about rural-rural migrations is that the migrants generally leave home only during slack periods in the agricultural calendar. The seasonal migration of Haitians as cane workers to the Dominican Republic, and I suspect many comparable migrations worldwide (e.g., Collins 1988), do not fit this pattern. Rather, emigration conflicts with the agricultural calendar of the source area and may deprive people at home of needed labor during seasons of peak activity. In the Cayes-Jacmel and Cap Rouge areas, as in most of Haiti, there are two main planting seasons (see figure 2). These coincide with the rainiest months of the year, March through May and August through November. If the rain begins when expected, most farmers sow crops on all of their parcels in both seasons. Some farmers also plant a "November garden" during the dry season (November through March) on any land they might have adjacent to stream beds, in ravine bottoms, or on low-lying parcels that retain moisture or can be irrigated from streams via shallow ditches. The months of peak labor demand are those when fields are cleared for planting: February-March and July-August. Emigrating to the Dominican Republic for the entire sugarcane harvest (December through June) prohibits the migrant from preparing fields for planting in the spring. In short, it is the alternation of dead season and harvest on the sugar estates, rather than the agricultural calendar of the migrant source areas, which sets the schedule for labor circulation.

Before moving on to the next chapter's discussion of the role of labor circulation in the reproduction of peasant livelihoods in rural southeastern Haiti, it remains only to give an approximation of the prevalence and spatial-temporal pattern of this migration and to situate it among certain other streams of geographical mobility that originate in the area.

Month		Cultivation	Planting	Harvest
Jan.	*early*	Prepare fields for planting spring gardens		pigeon peas and sorghum
	late			
Feb.	*early*			beans from November gardens
	late			
Mar.	*early*			
	late		After first heavy rains, maize, beans, pigeon peas, sorghum, yams, manioc, sweet potatoes, and bananas	
Apr.	*early*	weeding		
	late	Build yam mounds		
May	*early*			beans
	late			
June	*early*			maize
	late			
July	*early*	Prepare fields for summer gardens		
	late			
Aug.	*early*		maize, beans, manioc, and sweet potatoes	
	late			
Sept.	*early*	weeding		coffee (at lower elevations)
	late			
Oct.	*early*			beans
	late	Prepare fields for November gardens		
Nov.	*early*		beans, manioc, sweet potatoes, and sorghum	maize coffee (at higher evelations)
	late			pigeon peas and sorghum (sown in spring)
Dec.	*early*			
	late			

Fig. 2. Synopsis of the agricultural calendar, southeastern Haiti. Based on author's fieldwork in southeastern Haiti, 1986–87.

In the Cayes-Jacmel and Cap Rouge areas, nearly all adults are aware of the option of crossing the border for work or for trade. Information provided by returnees constantly updates local knowledge of the terms and conditions of employment in the Dominican Republic. When asked how they first learned of the opportunity of emigrating as cane workers to the Dominican Republic, most men either say that a friend or kinsman one day invited them to come along on a trip there, or they reply that they cannot even remember a time when they did not know about the Dominican Republic. From early childhood, local people hear older folk talk about "Sêdomêg" (the Dominican Republic, pronounced as in the French, "Saint-Domingue") and are aware of its involvement in the goings and comings of their older kinsmen. Sêdomêg looms large in local stories of violence, magic, madness, and intrigue. These stories perpetuate popular negative stereotypes of Dominican men—as dishonest, greedy, and willing to perpetrate any abuse to separate a Haitian from his or her hard-earned possessions— and of Dominican women—as being mostly whores. Spanish words pepper the language of many veteran migrants. A few Hispanicisms, or perhaps more precisely, "batey-isms," have even entered the speech of local people who have never set foot in the Dominican Republic. Not surprisingly, the most common of these are the terms by which the migrants denote the sugarcane harvest and dead season in the Dominican Republic: "lasaf" (from the Spanish, "la zafra") and "tchêpomwèt" or "kêpomwèt" (from "tiempo muerto").

Region of origin channels the rural Haitians who go to the Dominican Republic into different streams of geographical mobility. Residents of the Plaine du Nord and Plateau Central, which lie far to the north of Cayes-Jacmel, tend to go first to the closest agricultural zones across the border, the Cibao and San Juan Valleys, respectively. Historical tradition and proximity to the southwestern border of the Dominican Republic predispose men from southeastern Haiti to emigrate to the sugar estates of southern Dominican Republic (Corten 1976, 97, 99; 1985, 73; 1986, 255–56; Murphy 1991, 103–4, 106). As many as half of all Haitian braceros in the Dominican Republic claim the southeast as their region of origin, many more than any of the eight other administrative regions (départements) of Haiti (Báez Evertsz 1986, 64).

From the time of the U.S. military occupation of Haiti, 1915 to 1934, to the late 1960s, the sugar companies transported workers by ship from Haiti to southern ports in the Dominican Republic. Jacmel was the primary port of embarkation because of its relative proximity to points of destination in southern Dominican Republic. Recruitment later shifted to Léogâne and Croix-des-Bouquets in western Haiti, but by this time emigration had become entrenched in the southeastern way of life. Today, geographical proximity still favors people from this region who try to cross the border by clandestine means. Two ports near Cayes-Jacmel are entrepôts for the debarkation of contraband goods bought in the Dominican Republic and the embarkation of *âba fil* migrants.

Emigration to urban Haiti and to countries *"lòt bò lâmè"* ("beyond the sea," i.e., beyond the island of Hispaniola) is less common in Rocheteau and Cabrouette than emigration to the Dominican Republic.[2] Yet the Dominican Republic is not the only important destination for migrants from Cayes-Jacmel and Cap Rouge. A number of forms of short-term circular mobility link the area with other parts of Haiti and the rest of the world. Men, women, and children commute daily from home to gardens, marketplaces, and local schools. Female market intermediaries take days-long trading journeys to the city and to distant rural markets. Older children may circulate weekly or for longer periods to Jacmel or Port-au-Prince for schooling. And men may emigrate seasonally as day laborers to other rural areas of Haiti. Among the other destinations that figure prominently in local people's migration histories, the most notable are the cities of Jacmel and Port-au-Prince in Haiti and New York, Miami, and Boston. In the recent past, a few local people have also emigrated to Venezuela, to French Guiana, and to other islands of the Antilles.

Emigrants to all these destinations tend to be young and to travel as individuals rather than in family groups. Even so, emigrants to the Dominican Republic, on the one hand, and emigrants to countries *lòt bò lâmè*, on the other, seem to draw largely upon distinct groups of people. It is rare for the households of overseas emigrants also to have members who have emigrated to the Dominican Republic. This may be largely because remittances from North America free many of the close relatives of these migrants from the need to emigrate to the Dominican Republic. Conversely, emigration to the Dominican Republic rarely serves as a springboard for emigration to a more desirable urban or overseas destination. Dominican savings are generally too small relative to the immediate needs of the migrants for money to be set aside from it to finance further emigration.[3]

Emigrants to urban Haiti and North America tend to have higher levels of formal education than the rural average, and they generally come from households that are wealthier than average (Dejean 1978, 24; Ahlers 1979, 58; D. I. Marshall 1979, 25–30; Stepick and Portes 1986, 332). The Dominican Republic seems by contrast to attract mainly those rural people who are too poor to emigrate elsewhere. Field research in the Dominican Republic indicates that Haitian cane workers there have levels of formal education and job skills no higher than average for rural Haiti (Hernández 1973, 67; Veras 1983, 118–19; Murphy 1991, 100, 105).

Retrospective migration history data from Rocheteau and Cabrouette makes it possible to estimate the number of people from this area who emigrate to and return from the Dominican Republic.[4] Among men 35 years and older, including both residents and absentees, about 66 percent (91 of the 138 cases reported) have made at least one trip to the Dominican Republic. Emigration is more prevalent in Rocheteau than in Cabrouette (79 versus 56 percent), which may reflect the highlanders' more restricted alternatives to farming, when compared to the roadside villagers (see table 7). The mean age of first voyage for men is about 23 years old.

Another striking difference between this migration and Haiti's other major migrant streams is that many more men than women go to the Dominican Republic. Among women over 35 in Cabrouette and Rocheteau, only about 9 percent (14 of 157 women) have been to the Dominican Republic. By contrast, in urban- and North American–bound migration, with the possible exception of boat emigrants to the Bahamas and South Florida (D. I. Marshall 1979; Buchanan 1981; Allman and Richman 1985), women are more likely than men to emigrate (Bertrand 1973, 51; Ahlers 1979; Buchanan 1979, 20; Labelle, Larose, and Piché 1983, 85–86; Locher 1984, 330; Stepick and Portes 1986, 332).

Because few whole families emigrate to the Dominican Republic, genealogies in the migrants' home areas in Haiti reveal many absentees. I estimate that, including these absentees, about 16 percent of men over 35 from Rocheteau and Cabrouette (22 of 138) have spent most of their working lives (ages 15 to 60) in the Dominican Republic. Even under the most pessimistic assumption, that all absentees for whom precise information

Table 7

Number of Nonmigrants, Returnees, and Nonreturning Emigrants among Men over 35 from Rocheteau and Cabrouette, 1987

Category	Rocheteau	Cabrouette
Nonmigrants	12	35
Returnees	37	32
Nonreturning emigrants[a]	9	13
No information	10	7
Total	68	87

SOURCE: Based on migration history census, gathered in rural neighborhoods in the Cayes–Jacmel and Cap Rouge areas of southeastern Haiti, January and February 1987.

[a]Men who had emigrated to the Dominican Republic and subsequently disappeared were counted as nonreturning emigrants, as were those who had spent most of their adult lives in the Dominican Republic, regardless of how many times, or how recently, they might have returned to Haiti.

was lacking have emigrated permanently to the Dominican Republic, 64 percent of male emigrants (69 of 108) ultimately return and settle into nonmigratory livelihoods at home in Haiti. It seems also that the great majority of those who return do not scatter to urban and suburban locations in Haiti but go back to their rural places of origin.

Labor circulation between southeastern Haiti and the Dominican Republic is also mostly short-term and repetitive. Men's sojourns in the Dominican Republic typically last only three to nine months.[5] Each year, on average, between 1955 and 1986, about 14 percent of men aged 15 to 60 have gone to the Dominican Republic. About 88 percent of each year's migrant cohort have returned within a year, and about 91 percent have returned within two years. Repeat migration is common. The median number of trips per male migrant over 35 not "lost" to migration is four. The norm is to cease migrating after having made between two and five seasonal trips. Yet it is not rare for a man to make 10 or more seasonal visits to the Dominican Republic in a lifetime.

In summary, any account of the emigration of people from this region to the sugar estates of the Dominican Republic must ask why most of the migrants are young, poor men and why they return home shortly, rather than staying away indefinitely. Yet it must also ask why a large minority of the migrants—on the order of one in five to one in three—consists of men who return home irregularly, if ever. Similarly, even though nine of every ten migrants are men, attention must be given to the impact of labor circulation on the lives of women both as migrants and as wives and family members left behind in Haiti.

4

Poverty, Labor Circulation, and the Reproduction of Rural Livelihoods

In recent harvests, Haitian cane workers in the Dominican Republic have recognized the futility of trying to save money from their daily wages, given the inflated prices of everyday necessities there. Their only hope of obtaining enough money to return to Haiti lies in the "incentive" payments the sugar companies promise at the end of each year's harvest. The CEA bases this payment on the RD$0.60 per ton of cane that it withholds from each cutter's wages throughout the harvest, as an incentive to stay on the plantation until his labor is no longer needed. Summarizing his experiences in the Dominican cane harvests, one seasonal migrant remarked, "You break your body, but you have hope of having some money at the end."

Even with the incentive payment, the typical migrant brings home only between U.S.$25 and $75. At times, this is scarcely enough to repay any debt he may have incurred to finance his voyage to the Dominican Republic. Some succeed in scraping together greater savings through lottery winnings or occasional labor off the sugar estates. But, just as often, theft, bad luck in the lottery, or a prolonged illness or injury sinks the migrant's savings beneath the amount he needs to return to Haiti. This may force him to stay in the Dominican Republic for another year, in the hope of saving enough money to return after the next harvest. For some, this yearlong delay begins a chain of misfortunes that prevents them from ever going home again.

Why do so many Haitians still seek employment in the Dominican Republic if they are so cruelly exploited there? Many observers answer this question by evoking Haiti's well-known image as a "Caribbean Calcutta."

One Haitian scholar writes that "the failure of the agricultural system of Haiti to produce enough food is the cause . . . [of] migration to the Dominican sugar mills" (Latortue 1985, 56, my trans.). A Dominican sociologist and advocate for Haitian rights concludes that, inspired by hunger and oppression, "a kind of mass psychosis . . . propels the Haitian to flee" his or her homeland (Madruga 1986, 71, my trans.). Outsiders are, if anything, more prone to hyperbole, as is exemplified by the following statement of the Puerto Rico-based Ecumenical Center for Human Rights: "[The Haitian people] are leaving their country by any route which will take them out, however painful the voyage, in search of another way of life, . . . like a new tribe of nomads which has decided to start again from scratch now they have lost their tribal garden" (quoted in Plant 1987, 59–60).

Other recent authors seek to balance their assessments by attributing emigration equally to conditions of abject poverty in the Haitian countryside *and* the relative improvement in standards of living it is assumed the migrants find in the Dominican Republic (ILO 1983, 54–55; Moya Pons et al. 1986, 31). Glaessel-Brown (1979, 236) suggests, "The economic disparity between the two countries makes the low-paying, insecure jobs shunned by Dominican labor acceptable to the Haitian worker who does slightly better than he would at home while earning a cash income." Grasmuck (1982, 365) observes, "Large numbers of Dominicans leave their country every year . . . to suffer in unattractive jobs in New York because they do not like the nature of suffering in their own country. Haitians, in turn, leave their country every year . . . to suffer in the sugarcane fields of the Dominican Republic because they consider suffering on the Dominican side of the island more attractive than suffering on the Haitian side." Grasmuck's paper has the merit of pointing out that "there are a number of things to be learned from the 'desire' of so many Haitians to work in the worst jobs in the Dominican Republic beyond the fact that there are, apparently, degrees in hell" (ibid., 365–66). Other authors go little beyond this point. Lundahl (1979, 628), for instance, concludes: "Given the conditions which the temporary or permanent emigrants are likely to meet abroad, . . . it is difficult not to interpret emigration very much as a result of the conditions in the countryside. The absolute unattractiveness of some of the countries of destination is turned into relative attractiveness when it is compared to the situation within rural Haiti itself."

Does the poverty of Haiti—absolute or relative—really tell all that need be known about the conditions that lead rural Haitian men to cross the border as cane workers? I think not. These migrants respond not just to invidious comparisons between home and host areas. They leave home not to find a better life elsewhere but to return shortly with enhanced means. Specifically, the need to improve long-term food security may have much to do with why these migrants mostly follow a circular pattern of mobility. I work largely from the premise that migrant behavior assumes specifiable patterns, in response to forces of which the individual migrant may be only imperfectly aware. In keeping with this premise, I seek to bring migrants' stated motivations into interpretive tension with the record of behavior taken from their personal histories. Admittedly, there is the danger that, in seeking to elucidate the migrants' motivations and behavior, I may succeed too well in making sense of a situation that to the migrants might often seem very uncertain. It therefore bears repeating that going to the Dominican Republic is perhaps for most men more a conscious gamble than a source of predictable monetary returns.

ABSOLUTE POVERTY AND RELATIVE POVERTY AS DETERMINANTS OF MIGRATION

Students of Haiti agree that much of the blame for recent increases in rates of emigration from Haiti rests with the deterioration in the quality of life that took place there under the dictatorship of the Duvaliers (Holly, Labelle, and Larose 1979; Buchanan 1981; Stepick 1982a; Nicholls 1985; DeWind and Kinley 1988). Structural poverty is an incentive to emigration, even in situations, like the Haitian one, where individual poverty may be an obstacle to departure (Locher 1984, 332). The scholars who see emigration to the Dominican Republic as a flight from poverty are probably correct in implying that the decision to leave is not often an outcome of free choice. Many, perhaps most, rural emigrants find no other viable sources of income besides emigration to choose from. It might even be apt to characterize certain population displacements from Haiti, such as the emigration of boat people to South Florida, as a flight from intolerable conditions of life at home and a search for a better life elsewhere (Stepick 1982b).

Yet this would not be an entirely accurate description of emigration to the Dominican sugar estates. "Flight" implies that the migrant has split with his or her place of origin, abandoning claims to property and contacts with people at home for an indefinite period of time, without clear hope of soon renewing those ties. It is stretching the meaning of the word very far to suggest that "flight" is compatible with a pattern of seasonal return to the sending area, such as I have found among Haitian men who emigrate as cane workers to the Dominican Republic (chapter 3).

Also, people who are incapable of surviving in the countryside, because of property loss and disruption of ties of neighborhood assistance, tend strongly *not* to emigrate to the Dominican Republic. The cost of the trip, even though exceptionally low, is generally beyond the reach of the poorest Haitians. Going *âba fil* may cost between U.S. $10 and $40, because the migrant has to pay many of the expenses of his or her voyage: transportation, food, a fee to be guided surreptitiously across the border, and sometimes bribes for Dominican police officers along the route. Migrants commonly borrow money or sell livestock to cover these expenses, an option scarcely available to the destitute. Instead of emigrating to the Dominican Republic, rural people who lose their homes and sources of livelihood tend to go to towns and cities within Haiti, where they subsist on begging and casual employment (Smucker 1982, 105).

Interviews with migrants also indicate that direct persecution by agents of the state has not been a major cause of emigration to the Dominican sugar estates. Many Haitians went to the Dominican Republic to escape Duvalierist oppression. (The presence of several hundred Haitian political refugees in the Dominican Republic was undeniable proof of this.) Yet few of these refugees, it seems, settled on the sugar estates. In Yerba Buena, only one permanent resident was reputed to be a political refugee, and only two of the dozens of seasonal migrants whom I met claimed to have entered the Dominican Republic to escape persecution by agents of the Duvalier regime. Nearly all Haitians in the Dominican *bateyes* insisted that they would return to Haiti tomorrow if given the money to do so, and this certainly does not suggest that they feared persecution at home.[1]

If the evidence does not sustain a picture of emigration to the sugar estates of the Dominican Republic as a flight from poverty and oppression, how well does it fit the alternative "equilibrium theory," which considers migration to be a response to marginally better conditions of life elsewhere? A disparity in expected incomes between geographical areas is always necessary for voluntary labor migration to occur. The availability of more jobs, at higher wage levels, on the Dominican side of the border is surely a strong incentive for Haitians to go to the Dominican Republic. As Lundahl (1983, 111) observes, "Haiti is the poorest country in Latin America with a gross national product per capita . . . [of] U.S.$260 in 1978 whereas the corresponding figure for the Dominican Republic was 3.5 times as high, or U.S.$910. . . . This income gap has led to a steady stream of temporary and permanent migrants from Haiti to the Dominican Republic for a full century."

What I question about the equilibrium approach is its assumption that rural Haitians are attracted to the Dominican Republic by the better quality of life they can reasonably expect to achieve there (ibid., 137–42). If this is so, why, then, are Haitian *braceros* generally so committed to returning home at the end of the cane harvest? No simple variety of equilibrium theory can explain why short-term circulation, and not long-term emigration, best describes the migration histories of most *braceros*. To understand the migrants' return orientation, one must take into account other factors besides the income gap between the two countries.

The Reasons for Return

During their time on Dominican soil, most migrants live literally at the margin of subsistence. Báez Evertsz (1986, 303) reports that the average Haitian *bracero* experiences a daily nutritional deficit "of 29.4 percent in calories and 41.5 percent in protein" (my trans.)—that is, 880 calories and 37 grams of protein less than the 3,000 calories and 90 grams of protein which a Brazilian study of the 1940s estimated to be the average daily needs of a cane cutter.[2] Báez's survey also reveals "marked deficiencies . . . in consumption of vitamin A, niacin, calcium and thiamine." In 1983, food expenditures took 80 percent of *braceros'* earnings (ibid., 286). Given that the fraction of their income spent on food could hardly get much higher, it can be assumed that double-digit consumer price inflation since 1983 has only worsened the *braceros'* nutritional status.[3] Haitians exaggerate little, therefore, when they say, "You lay waste to your body" working in the cane fields of the Dominican Republic. The sugar companies' piece-rate wages are in effect geared slowly to squeeze the life out of the workers who must subsist on those wages.[4]

Yet, ultimately, as an outsider looking in at the migrants' plight, it is impossible for me to say with certainty whether, materially and socially, life in rural Haiti is better or worse than in the Dominican *bateyes*. It must suffice to reiterate an observation that several recent students of the problem have confirmed (Corten 1976, 1981, and 1986; Veras 1983; Lemoine 1985; Báez Evertsz 1986; Moya Pons et al. 1986; Murphy 1991): working as a cane cutter not only pays pitifully low wages; it is also a highly *insecure* means of earning a living.

It is likely that people as poor as the Haitian *braceros* would rationally place as high a priority on income security as on the marginal rate of return on their remunerative employment. Concerned with income levels though they are, Haitian migrants may understandably be loath to remain indefinitely on the sugar estates, where their standards of living lie wholly at the mercy of wage-price fluctuations and where an incapacitating injury or illness can leave them without any means of putting food on the table.

For several reasons, the Haitian smallholder may attain more secure access to food than a similarly impoverished wage earner on the sugar estates. One advantage of smallholder agriculture in southeastern Haiti is its great diversity (Kermel-Torrès and Roca 1991). This diversity has at least two dimensions. The first is that the Haitian smallholder typically pursues a number of occupations besides the cultivation of annual tilled crops. Working the land may be the Haitian farmer's main tangible guarantee of survival, but he or she rarely does without other sources of livelihood. I have already noted that men may do occasional wage labor on neighbors' farms. Other sources of income for men include carpentry, masonry, husbandry of neighbors' animals or of their own smallstock (mainly goats and poultry), weaving fiber mats, hats, nets, and baskets, cutting wood for fuel or building material, making charcoal, and making lime for whitewashing houses. Women may take a lead in any of these activities, except carpentry and the building trades, and may also supplement their incomes through a variety of petty trading activities.

The second dimension of diversity relates to how agriculture is practiced, that is, whether the farmer grows one crop variety or several on each parcel of land, and whether the landholding is homogeneous or heterogeneous in soil type and microclimate. By planting a variety of crops that differ in their capacity to withstand drought, flooding, and attack by pests, farmers in southeastern Haiti diminish their risk of crop loss. Heterogeneous cropping also reduces their exposure to fluctuations in farm commodity prices. If one of the crops the farmer wishes to sell—say, coffee—drops suddenly in price or is wiped out by pests, the prices of the other crops he or she sells—e.g., pulses, vegetables, fruit, wood, and smallstock—may hold firm. Or, if a particular dietary staple—say, maize—should rise in price, the farmer may turn to sorghum, breadfruit, or root crops standing in his or her gardens as an alternative source of complex carbohydrates. In short, the more diverse a farmer's agriculture is, the better able he or she should be to withstand the shocks of a variable climate, ecology, and marketplace.

Farmers of the Cayes-Jacmel and Cap Rouge area also mitigate risk by planting gardens on parcels of differing soil types, microclimates, and levels of natural moisture. The broken topography of the Cayes-Jacmel and Cap Rouge area provides local farmers with a variety of agricultural habitats. Renting and sharecropping neighbors' land may permit even a man or woman who owns little or no land to gain access to a number of small plots. A farmer of modest means may cultivate 10 or more widely scattered small parcels of varying elevation, soil type, and water-retention characteristics. A Haitian farmer often prefers half a stake in two pieces of land over a full stake in one plot, if it seems that this may reduce his or her exposure to the risk of crop failure (G. F. Murray 1977, 488–94). Thus, as farmers purchase land over the course of their lives, some prefer to keep their old sharecropped parcels and give out their newly acquired parcels to tenants.

Sharecropping in Haiti is often a way of sharing risk among kin and neighbors. Often, a man is landlord on one parcel of land and tenant on another. Perhaps equally surprising, to those used to thinking of sharecropping as a system of inequality, is that the Haitian sharecropper's tenure may be fairly secure. In most of Haiti, unlike in many other agrarian societies, landlord and tenant generally do not belong to different classes or castes but are fellow villagers and often status equals. Often, landlord and tenant are kin: sister and brother or uncle and nephew. It is therefore not surprising that norms of reciprocity at times effectively bar the owner of the land from evicting certain tenants. In the Cayes-Jacmel and Cap Rouge areas, it is common to find farmers in their middle years who have worked the same one or two plots in sharecrop for over 20 years. Custom and practice also seem to accord the larger share of the crop most often to the sharecropper, rather than to the landlord (A. Métraux 1951, 19; G. F. Murray 1977, 385–86; Woodson 1990, 514). This favors those (mostly poor) farmers who take in more land in sharecrop than they give out to neighbors.

It is significant that Haitian cane workers speak of the money they spend on their own needs in the Dominican Republic as "wasted," and they commonly refer to the Dominican Republic itself as a "blood-sucking country" or "hooker's country." The meaning of the last metaphor may relate in part to Haitians' distinctive attitudes toward prostitution. Haitians look down on the prostitute not just for being immoral. They condemn her also for exchanging use of her "natural" assets for ephemeral gain rather than trading these for a commitment of lasting support (Lowenthal 1984, 33, n. 15). In like manner, the Haitian *bracero* knows that, no matter how hard he works, he will gain little or nothing in long-term income security by remaining on the sugar estates. Only by returning home to Haiti can he convert his Dominican money into assets of his own, with which to meet future family health, ceremonial, and educational needs. In short, rural Haiti's poverty is severe, but the diversity of its sources of livelihood makes it a more secure place in the long term than the Dominican sugar estates for the poor to earn a living.

Also, the Dominican Republic may be the only place in the world where Haitians are accorded fewer civil rights than in their own country (Anti-Slavery Society 1979; Veras 1983; Lemoine 1985; Plant 1987; Americas Watch 1989 and 1990; Lawyers Committee 1991a). Even those few Haitians who achieve some upward mobility in the Dominican Republic rarely feel at ease in their good fortune. Dozens of cases of official and unofficial intimidation, physical abuse, and seizure of property against Haitians were brought to my attention during my fieldwork. If, to these abuses, one adds the Dominican government's well-documented record of denying Haitian immigrants basic freedoms of the work place, of movement, and of association, it becomes clear why fear for the safety of their persons and property in the Dominican Republic may be a strong incentive for Haitian workers to return home.

Another incentive to return to Haiti is to resume participation in kin-based and neighborhood networks of reciprocity. Ties with people at home may take on particular importance for these migrants, because the migrant network works for them only in relatively limited ways, when compared to other Third World migrants (see chapter 7's examination of the migrant network). Given the isolation the migrants experience on the sugar estates, returning home may be their only reliable means of renewing ties with people in Haiti.

In returning to Haiti, *Sêdomêg* migrants may not only seek to improve their personal security. They may also wish to fulfill obligations toward parents, siblings, and other relatives at home. For example, it is the solemn duty of a son or daughter to assure the subsistence in old age of their mother and father. After their parents die, the surviving offspring bear the responsibility for carrying out a series of elaborate mortuary ceremonies (G. F. Murray 1977, 528–32). Fulfillment of these ritual obligations "is required for the successful passage of the spirit from this world to the next, and for the eternal repose of the spirit which death *should* portend; and as the final, public demonstration of the individual worth and personal prestige of the deceased" (Lowenthal 1987, 232). Extraordinary expenses of catastrophic illness and of mortuary ceremonials may force peasants to sell land and valuable livestock (Herskovits 1937, 132; Bastien 1951, 104; A. Métraux 1951, 193–94; G. F. Murray 1977, 534–40). Men commonly go to the Dominican Republic to try to recoup these losses, or they use their Dominican savings to pay back debts incurred by family members during family crises.

Worries about the fate of their own souls after death also may encourage Haitian cane workers to return home. The moderately well-to-do in rural Haiti unabashedly make advance preparations to depart from the material world in proper style. Rural Haitians consider it proper for a living adult to build a tomb, ready a coffin, and set aside a good suit of clothing for his or her own funeral. Their preparations for death are complete only when they have purchased livestock and a plot of land and have designated these to be sold to pay for the mortuary ceremonies (Lowenthal 1987, 233). For many, the fear that their souls may suffer torment after death, if they have no family members to carry out the proper mortuary ceremonials for them, may give added urgency to the longing to return to Haiti voiced by nearly all nonreturning migrants.

Even if a migrant loses all contact with people at home, he or she cannot escape the influence for good or bad of his family's ancestral spirits, or *lwa* (Richman 1990). The isolation of the nonreturning emigrant sometimes translates into an unfulfilled spiritual need. For example, it is said of a handful of *viejos* with lingering ailments in Yerba Buena that they might only be cured if they return to the place of their "family *lwa*" in Haiti or arrange for relatives to conduct a ceremony there on their behalf. It is held to be extremely unfortunate that these people are either unable to get in touch with their kinfolk in Haiti or lack the money to pay a spiritual healer at home for diagnosis and treatment.

Besides these incentives to return, there are also sanctions in Haiti against prolonged absence. Haitian land tenure and property relations do not easily accommodate years of continuous absence. In principle, local land should be available to local people and not sit idle just because its owner is absent (Smucker 1982, 282; G. F. Murray 1977, 320–22). Migrants must periodically renew claims over land and other productive property at home or else risk losing these. Emigrants to North America ensure their claims to property in Haiti by periodically sending money home. For Haitians on the sugar estates, by contrast, remitting is often difficult. A man who spends a lifetime in the Dominican Republic may come home only to find that his kinfolk have divided up or sold his property as their own, or that all the relatives he once knew have died or moved away.

This was the fate of one old man, whom I met in 1985 in the Port-au-Prince slum district of Cité Simone (now Cité Soleil). His case is highly exceptional, but even so may serve to dramatize the dangers to which I refer. In 1980, after an unbroken absence from Haiti of 52 years, he left his home in Oriente, Cuba, and sailed to Miami in the Mariel boatlift. Sympathetic South Floridians, informed by the local press about his desire to return to his birthplace, helped pay his passage to Haiti. When he arrived in his hometown of Corail, near Jérémie, on Haiti's Southwest Peninsula, he found no one who remembered him. The distant relatives he located disclaimed all responsibility for caring for him and sent him back to Port-au-Prince. There, he wandered the streets, penniless, for weeks. If Catholic sisters in Cité Simone had not found him and given him shelter in a home for destitute older men, there is no telling how long he could have survived. He had apparent difficulties adjusting emotionally to return. He was unable to speak Creole without interjecting Spanish words, and he had frequent arguments with neighborhood children and fellow residents of the shelter. If stories like his are rare, it may be because few Haitians who have spent most of their lives on the sugar estates of the Dominican Republic would attempt what he did. In recent years in Rocheteau and Cabrouette, only one individual over the age of 60 has returned from the Dominican Republic after an absence of many years. Significantly, this man was sought out in the Dominican Republic by his sister's son with the intention of bringing him home.

In this context, it is not surprising that the migrants' personal histories and subjective evaluations of experience reveal a set of motivations for emigrating quite different from that which equilibrium theories of migration would lead one to expect. For most migrants, the point of going to the Dominican Republic may be not to seek an improvement in their standard of living while abroad but to bring money back to Haiti. One frequent seasonal migrant from Cabrouette summarized: "It is not nakedness, not hunger that would make you leave, because . . . the hunger cannot be avoided (*fòk u gêyê-ni*), neither here nor there. When we eat, we eat. When we go hungry, we go hungry. It is the money situation, the money you need, that makes you go. . . . He who can, resigns himself, really resigns himself and goes. He goes through hardships (*pase mizè*); he goes after the bucks. Because after you go in it, really, you can earn some bucks. When you return, you meet your obligations for the moment. It is all because the money situation is very, very hard here."[5]

This observation calls for an examination of the "obligations" Haitian men seek to meet with migrant money. Most migrants make their first voyage to the Dominican Republic as young adults, when they are still dependent members of their parental households. Many told me their first migrant voyage was the first time in their lives they had experienced severe hunger and deprivation, having depended previously on adult guardians for food, shelter, and clothing. "I left school, I had nothing to do," said a former seasonal migrant in Rocheteau:

> So, I got up and went to *Sêdomêg*. But, when I got to *Sêdomêg*, . . .
> I fell upon harder times. When I was here [in Haiti], I was under the care
> of Father and Mother. I was eating, I was drinking, everything. I had no
> problems.
>
> When I arrived over there [in the Dominican Republic], it was in the
> time of Trujillo. They treated Haitians badly. When you arrived, they threw
> a sack at you for you to sleep on, with an old unsharpened machete. That
> was what most broke my heart. . . . And, at the time, you worked for nothing. You could not even make enough money to eat. During seven months,
> you could not even buy a pair of pants. It was a very hard time. They paid
> 45 cents per ton of cane. It was not every day you could earn a dollar.
> Sometimes, you had to go to sleep without eating. . . .
>
> So I returned just as I had left, without money. But when I arrived at
> my house, the people were very happy to see me. It was not deprivation
> which made me go, because I was under their [his parents'] care. They
> were able to give me food; they gave me drink. Even though they could
> not set me up at ease, they at least sent me to school.[6]

The predicament of impoverished young men striving to attain the customary means of entering manhood is the first issue I will examine, to attempt to advance understanding of migrant motivations and behavior beyond explanations that dwell solely on the absolute or relative poverty of rural Haiti.

In what follows, it may be remarked that the migrants appear to pursue largely individualized strategies of economic attainment. This should not be confused with *methodological* individualism, a scholarly perspective which supposes that migration may be adequately described as if it involved no one but the individual migrant him/herself. Contrary to that perspective, I found numerous examples in Cayes-Jacmel and Cap Rouge of how the emigration of a particular individual might affect others: siblings who alternate their absences from home in relay fashion so that there may always be one on hand to farm for single mothers or look after elderly parents; emigrants to North America whose remittances free relatives of the need to emigrate to less desirable destinations, such as the Dominican Republic; women who are hampered in their own trading activities by the responsibility they assume for managing farms in their husbands' absence. At issue here, rather, is the difference between making a living *on* one's own and making a living *of* one's own. Very few rural Haitians ever make a living *on* their own, that is, without more or less constantly turning for help and giving assistance to kinfolk and neighbors. In fact, attempting to make a living on your own might be seen by rural Haitians as a very peculiar, even insane, pattern of behavior. An individual's best assurance of survival in adversity is through the support of kinfolk and neighbors. Yet *Sêdomêg* money may help young men begin making a living *of* their own, insofar as it enables them to begin accumulating the means to build a house, to marry, and to cultivate gardens under their own management, perhaps years before they could if they stayed at home. In short, even though few rural Haitians are individualists, I think no analysis of this migration would be complete without recognizing the migrants' individuality. What these migrants strive for is perhaps not so much personal economic autonomy as a personal economic identity.

MIGRATION AND THE LIFE CYCLE

Young men in rural Haiti generally start their adult lives with few productive assets of their own. Most hire out their labor locally as agricultural wage laborers and sharecroppers in an effort to accumulate the resources they need to establish a conjugal union and to embark on careers as small-scale agricultural and petty commodity producers.[7]

Consensual union (*plasaj*) is much more common in rural Haiti than legal marriage. Establishing a *plasaj* presents somewhat fewer material impediments than legal marriage. Even so, to many a young man, meeting his obligations to his prospective spouse poses a formidable challenge. A woman, if she has been active in trade for some years, may bring a substantial amount of productive property into a newly formed union. Yet unequal distribution of land between the sexes and Haitian gender ideology generally hold the man responsible for providing the initial material basis for their joint household (G. F. Murray 1977, 326–42; Smucker 1982, 236–37). According to Lowenthal (1984, 29), rural Haitians speak of the conjugal relationship as a straightforward exchange of men's labor for women's sexuality: "An honest union requires of the man that he (1) *okipe fanm-nan jan li kapab* (take care of the woman in the manner that he can), (2) *rete ak fanm-nan* (stay with the woman), in the sense of establishing some regular pattern of coresidence with her, even if only partial, and (3) *mete l nan yon kay* (put her in a house). Of the woman, an honest union makes a unique demand: sexual fidelity (*ke li pa tronpe msye li*; literally, that she not fool her husband)." Not every union conforms to ideal expectations of what a husband should do for a wife. Yet young men strive to attain these standards often enough that the effort to accumulate material assets for establishing conjugal union may be said without exaggeration to mark a normal phase in the male life cycle.

Rural Haitians think it proper for a recently wedded man to provide his wife a house. Failing to make his union "honest" in this way invites ridicule, even if the man's wife is willing to go on sharing a relative's house or procures their shared abode herself. In building and furnishing a peasant wattle-and-daub house, even one without a cement floor and sheet metal roof, such building materials and household necessities as hinges, nails, and cooking pots must be purchased from nonlocal sources. Certain local products—wooden posts and planks, lime (for whitewash), kitchen utensils, and chairs, stools, tables, and cabinets—are generally also bought with cash.

As of 1987, migrant savings had provided seed money for about half of the houses standing in highland Rocheteau and for about one-third of those in lowland Cabrouette. These fractions may underestimate the real importance of *Sêdomêg* money for local housing, because many people had already torn down houses built with migrant savings and replaced these with second or third houses built with locally earned capital and material salvaged from their first homes. When asked to recall what first motivated them to go to the Dominican Republic, 19 of 31 men questioned in Rocheteau and Cabrouette (about 61 percent) said that their primary goal was to earn money to build a house. (By comparison, the second most common response—to repair storm damage to houses and replenish lost seed and livestock—was mentioned by only three men [about 10 percent].) A Rocheteau man, who made his first voyage to the Dominican Republic in 1960, recalled, "At that time, all the young people like me were struggling to buy those [wooden] posts, to raise the frame of the house. Me, I had no cow, I had no trade, I was not getting a wage. I got up and left, too." The response of a much younger man, from Cabrouette, who emigrated for the first time in 1981, also typified the majority: "I went to work [in the Dominican Republic] to find money so that I could build a house and buy a piece [of land], a place to give the woman [his wife] to live. So that, when I die tomorrow, God willing, these children here would . . . find a place to eat a mango . . . and drink a coconut."

The dilemmas of young men seeking to establish their personal economic identities also lie behind the other immediate reasons, besides building a house, that lead men to make their first voyage across the border. Dependent young men in households of humble means cannot rely on their guardians to provide them with anything more than basic food, clothing, and shelter. They have to fend for themselves, for instance, to acquire the one pair of dress shoes and good change of clothing deemed appropriate for important trips to town and other serious occasions, or to buy a piece of jewelry, a wristwatch, or some other prestige item to hold as a symbol of adulthood and urbanity. "My mother did not have the means to dress me," said one man of Rocheteau, whose single mother owned almost no land. "I went to *Sêdomêg* after a pair of pants. I saw everyone my age wearing their pants. Well, I did not have any to wear, so I went looking for a way to buy a pair of shoes, a shirt, my underwear, a hat to wear." Quite often, the inexperienced migrant returns home with little more than a new outfit and a few dollars to distribute as gifts to relatives. If he wishes to acquire more through outside labor, he may attempt one or more subsequent journeys across the border.

Many also see their first voyage in retrospect as a passage into adulthood. These men experienced a severe test of self-reliance as first-time *braceros*. "It is your wrist [*pôyèt-u*, i.e., your own strength] which is your mother and father *nâ pâyòl* [in the Dominican Republic]," said one young man, holding his hand clenched, palm upward, before his chest as if to grasp a machete. An older man, who first went to the Dominican Republic in his late teens, said, "I had made gardens for my mother already [i.e., before his first voyage]. It was when I returned from *Sêdomêg* that I came of age. I became an adult. [In the Dominican Republic,] I had built my [cooking] fire, I had done all my own laundry, I had taken care of myself for six months. I worked on my own account. I saw I was an adult. After that, I began to make gardens for myself."

In spite of the role that *Sêdomêg* money has played in helping the young get a start in life, parents generally take no interest in assisting the departure of their sons to the Dominican Republic. This is in part because they and other family members rarely expect the returned migrant to give them much of his savings or to contribute money for the education or emigration of other relatives. (The savings with which the migrants return from *Sêdomêg* are simply too small to permit such generosity.) Also, parents worry with good reason that their children will be terribly mistreated in the Dominican Republic or might even fail to return and be lost to them forever.[8]

In all but a handful of the personal histories I recorded in the Dominican Republic and Haiti, the migrant's first voyage to the Dominican Republic resulted not from the orders or advice of his guardians but from the migrant's own initiative. A few men say they made their first voyage on a "vagabond" whim, without informing their guardians of their intent to go. These men are unusual in admitting to flouting their guardians' will. Yet, when asked if their relatives had approved or disapproved of their decision to emigrate, most men say their people had no choice but to accept it, that "they had to agree." The Rocheteau man whom I quoted above, about his difficult first voyage to Trujillo's Dominican Republic, responded as follows:

> Author: "Were your relatives in favor of your going *nâ pâyòl*, or not in favor of it?"
>
> Abner, the returned migrant: "They were not in favor. It was not they who sent me, it was I who wanted to go."
>
> Jean-Robert, a neighbor: "Was it your idea?"
>
> Abner: "It was my idea. They were not happy I went. I did not steal out on them, no. But, in the end, when I had decided to go, they had to let me go."
>
> Jean-Robert: "Did they advise you not to go?"
>
> Abner: "They said I better not go, because the country [i.e., the Dominican Republic] was a terrible place."

Parents can offer their sons of marriageable age little to dissuade them from emigrating. Most peasant households can only raise sums of money over U.S.$50 by liquidating assets, such as large livestock, trees (for wood and charcoal), and land. Besides being productive resources, these things may be the only form of savings owned by peasants living near the margin of subsistence, their only means of paying for emergency expenses of ceremonial/health crisis management, and their only guarantee of survival in time of drought. Most rural parents are thus unable to offer much material support for their dependent offspring when these seek to take their first steps toward establishing households of their own. Finally, it should be recalled that the cost of going to the Dominican Republic is nowhere near as great an obstacle to departure as the cost of relocating to an urban area or of traveling to North America. Therefore, a man who contemplates crossing the border as a cane worker generally finds little use in mobilizing the financial support of relatives at home. On the contrary, he may wish to avoid taking debts he may later find difficult to repay.

It is not that a young man renounces his claims on his kinfolk when he emigrates to the Dominican Republic. The support that relatives give is largely passive and falls far short of the active sponsorship that rural Haitians commonly provide for emigration to relatively desirable destinations, lòt bò lâmè. Even so, parental support is often vital to the success of a young migrant's strategy of petty accumulation. In the dead season between cane harvests, the young migrant generally returns to his parents' household and resumes his former place there. If he did not do so, he would at best have a highly insecure basis for investing his savings, and at worst he would be left unemployed, homeless, and hungry, with no other resources to fall back on but his hard-earned Sêdomêg money.

Nor does the returnee turn his back on needy friends and relatives. The returnee almost always distributes part of his savings in small cash gifts to a wide group of people. Returnees recognize certain social obligations, as one frequent migrant described: "When you return with a little money, you know already that all the family is needy. You have people to whom you must give five gourdes (U.S.$1), a sister of your mother, a family member. Like me, I have seven brothers and sisters. You must give each brother some money. Here, a certain 'dear one,' 10 bucks ($2). There, a certain 'little sister,' 10 bucks. The money shrinks in your hand. The country is a poor country, Haiti. Everyone is always needy. If you did not have need, you would never have left. . . . So, when you return, he, who was not able to go, he, too, must find a little something in your hand." Migrants' estimates of past gift giving and personal expenditures commonly fall in the range of U.S.$25 to $50. This is a substantial sum when compared to the $50 to $250 that migrants of the mid-1960s to mid-1970s typically repatriated from the cane harvests. Today, the much smaller savings that migrants bring back from the Dominican Republic scarcely allow returnees to share their Sêdomêg savings at all and certainly not as generously as past migrants saw fit.

Returnees give to their relatives out of self-interest as well as out of moral compunction. As one veteran migrant put it, "You must give the family life [i.e., help ensure their subsistence] for them to be able to give you help one day." In case of serious illness or other misfortune in the near family, the migrant may be called upon to share the bulk of his Sêdomêg money with relatives. Returnees claim not to resent such demands for assistance. Some say, in fact, that they regret not being able to give more to their kinfolk. Even so, *Sêdomêg* migrants do not face the intense pressure to become the economic leaders of the family that emigrants to North America encounter. People in rural southeastern Haiti understand that a man rarely brings home much money from the Dominican Republic. Relatives and neighbors sooner view *Sêdomêg* migrants as people in need of assistance than as individuals who are in a position to disburse aid to others. Skinner's (1960, 383) observations concerning returnees to Mossi country in former Upper Volta apply also to the returning *braceros:* "Migration itself brings little lasting prestige. It is not seen as a *rite de passage* or even an unusual feat. The men who go away are not considered brave but poor."

"PUTTING THE *Sêdomêg* MONEY TO WORK . . ."

A Haitian man who goes to the Dominican Republic as a cane worker usually cannot save enough money in one harvest to build a house. The wages he earns abroad are too low, and the cost of building materials in Haiti is too high. Instead, the migrant, if he succeeds in saving money abroad, makes two to five voyages before he can accumulate the materials and money he needs.

Because his net savings from the Dominican Republic are typically small, the returnee commonly invests in livestock at home to get secondary earnings from his *Sêdomêg* money. People in the Cayes-Jacmel and Cap Rouge areas raise animals mainly for sale, and they slaughter and consume animals at home only for important ceremonies of the Voodoo cult. Livestock's natural reproductive capacity and its complementarity with agriculture—i.e., consuming crop residues and fertilizing the soil with droppings—make it an attractive investment. Animal husbandry has long helped adolescents in rural Haiti get a start in life. It has also been a means by which adult men and women save up for major purchases and insure themselves against the expenses of ceremonial/health crisis management.

Even so, reinvestment in livestock runs a risk of failure through mortality or theft. The migrant generally balances this risk by dividing his savings between livestock and direct purchase of target goods. Upon returning home, a young man saving to build a house might, for instance, spend U.S.$30 on corrugated metal roofing and reinvest $15 in livestock. "After you return," an elderly returnee asked rhetorically, "if you are left with [only] a little money, what do you do? You buy a goat with it. When there were pigs, you bought a 50 gourdes [U.S.$10] pig, you bought a 75 gourdes [$15] pig: you stretched your little money. If luck was with you, fever did not kill it; that little pig could grow and make little ones. Later, if it got big, you put it in a pen, and you fattened it. Well, that pig, if you sold it, there were pigs here which even sold for $100, 400 gourdes ($80). In the end, it's the same *Sêdomêg* money still at work there." Another moderately successful migrant also emphasized the necessity of "putting the *Sêdomêg* money to work":

> You do not return from *Sêdomêg*, and, say, build a house, and furnish it, and marry all in one stroke. No! It is not done like that. *Sêdomêg* money does not give enough for that.
>
> What might happen is that you left *Sêdomêg* and bought a pig or a couple of piglets. The pig might lead to a cow. You could go to *Sêdomêg* again. You return with a little money. You mix it with money from a pig you sold and buy wood to saw for the house. After that, you make another voyage, you sell the cow, you sell a pig, you buy metal roofing, and raise the frame of the house. After yet another voyage, if God wills it, you may put the craftsmen to finish building the house.
>
> You sell livestock, you make gardens, you make voyages to *Sêdomêg*, you mix it all together. It is like that. You struggle for your livelihood [*U'ap chache lavi-a*]. If I had not put the *Sêdomêg* money to work, I would not in the end have been able to do anything with it at all.

Of 89 seasonal voyages described in the personal histories of male returnees in Rocheteau and Cabrouette, only 55 (about 62 percent) yielded a surplus that was invested in Haiti. If one considers that many local investments fail to yield a profit, it seems likely that less than half of these voyages yielded the migrant any material gain, beyond subsidizing consumption in the short term. Yet, because most migrants make several voyages, their chances of eventually getting something of lasting value out of their Dominican money are probably better than half. About 55 percent of male returnees (17 of 31) can trace some tangible benefit—commonly, a house, cattle, or land—to seed money brought home from the Dominican Republic. Others can no longer say which of their assets might have sprung from foreign-earned capital. Only about 29 percent of returnees (9 of 31) state unequivocally that they gained nothing of lasting value from the Dominican Republic.

For many men, the first stage of their migratory careers, when they struggle to accumulate the material resources they might need to enter adulthood, is followed closely by a second stage. After building a house and establishing a conjugal union, 20 of 27 returnees (about 70 percent) emigrated again. They made one or more further seasonal voyages to the Dominican Republic to earn money to buy seed, livestock, and, ultimately, land or to buy household necessities, make house repairs, and pay for their children's education. Collective misfortunes, such as drought and storm damage, have also led mature men to emigrate. Among recent disasters, the worst occurred in 1966, when Hurricane Ines hit the area. In the aftermath of Ines, as many as 40 to 50 percent of the able-bodied men who were present in Rocheteau and Cabrouette emigrated to the Dominican Republic, seeking money to replace the dwellings, seed, and animals lost in the storm.

Yet local people agree that, barring catastrophic misfortune, men "put *Sêdomêg* to rest," that is, cease migrating, once they gain relatively secure means of earning a living in Haiti. Most Haitian *braceros* cease migrating well before retirement age, rather than circulating perennially between the two countries for most of their working lives (see appendix B). Of 91 male migrants over 35 in Rocheteau and Cabrouette, only 13 (about 14 percent) have made 10 or more seasonal voyages to the Dominican Republic. One Rocheteau man observed, in a skeptical tone, "Ah! The *Sêdomêg* thing, my dear, if a person is obliged to go, you go, but if you had work to do at home, you could sit tight. If you had a little place to plant four banana trees, you could stay put rather than go."

For many, the chances of dying in the Dominican Republic or of failing to save enough money to return to Haiti seem too great to merit making the voyage, if they already have the means at home to sustain a growing household at minimal standards of living. Men and women with money to spare are much more likely to lend that money at interest for another person's voyage than to use it to emigrate to the Dominican Republic themselves.

Producing a surplus beyond culturally defined subsistence needs is a necessary condition for peasant livelihoods to be perpetuated from one generation to the next. Before a new generation can be accommodated on the land, new dwellings must be built and furnished, land and other assets for producing a livelihood must be acquired, and funds for putting those assets into production must be accumulated. In rural Haiti, young men bear much of the responsibility for producing this fund, but they encounter serious obstacles in the low productivity of agriculture and the lack of alternative sources of income for poorer people in their home areas. Many go as cane workers to the neighboring Dominican Republic in an effort to earn the money they need. Yet migrant money alone rarely suffices. *Sêdomêg* money must be put to work at home to make up the shortfall.

These observations have implications for our understanding of labor circulation. Any version of equilibrium theory that takes only income levels into consideration and ignores issues of income security is unlikely to recognize that these migrants might rationally remain committed to their home places in Haiti. The migrants who adapt best maintain strong ties with their home areas in rural Haiti. Most do not stay long in the Dominican Republic but return home, invest any savings in housing and agriculture, and ultimately settle into nonmigratory life-styles in Haiti. They hold fast to customary modes of livelihood in Haiti not out of unthinking conservatism but out of a recognition of economic advantages in doing so, within sometimes violent constraints on their freedom of choice. Subsistence-crop cultivation and ties of kinship in Haiti may offer most migrants a more secure basis for survival than working for pitifully low wages in the cane fields of the Dominican Republic. The savings men bring back from the Dominican Republic, meager as these are, are commonly put to use at home in ways that subsidize local employment in food production and marketing. Through these economic maneuvers, rural Haitians try to adapt labor circulation to the goals of meeting present needs and assuring future subsistence at home.

One of the most vexing questions is how to make sense of the migrants' attitudes toward risk. It may seem paradoxical that the men who emigrate as cane workers to the Dominican Republic combine extreme poverty with a willingness to run certain fairly high risks. For instance, the risk of failing to meet savings goals is quite high: the migrant often returns with little or nothing to show for his work in the Dominican Republic—or worse, he may fail to return at all. Accepting risks like these seems odd if one considers that these migrants are without a doubt the poorest of Haiti's international migrants. One might sooner expect migrants as poor as these to be particularly averse to risk because they stand so close to the brink of total destitution.

At the same time, some of the other risks of emigrating as a cane worker are quite low. For anyone "willing" to cross the border for pay and conditions of work as awful as those on the sugar estates, the risk of unemployment in the Dominican Republic is practically nil. The same may be said for the risk of being turned away at the international frontier: for the duration of the cane harvest, at least, all able-bodied entrants are welcome. Surely, the low risk of unemployment is one of the conditions that make emigration to the sugar estates possible for impoverished Haitians. It may be significant in this regard that migrants and returnees often temper their condemnations of the mistreatment they suffer in the Dominican Republic by saying, "At least they have a place for us *nâ pâyòl.*"

I hypothesize that some of the anomalies in the foregoing picture might be resolved by disaggregating risk into short-, medium-, and long-term components. Each step in the process of emigration and return might be understandable as the least risky option available in its particular time frame. In the short term, the risk of unemployment is lower across the border than at home. And, while it is true that the cane cutter generally works at a caloric deficit, it is also probable, barring lengthy disability, that he will not starve much more in the Dominican Republic than he would at home.

His medium-term prospects are also clearly favored by going to the sugar estates. There is a great risk of coming away from the cane harvest with nothing. Yet this may seem preferable to the near certainty of continued frustration faced by peasants who strive to ascend from the bottom of the socioeconomic heap in Haiti. In the long term, by contrast, risk aversion may strongly encourage the *bracero* to renew his commitment to home. Staying indefinitely on the sugar estates generally means depending on meager and uncertain wages for one's livelihood, far from one's kin. It is easy to see why returning to Haiti, pursuing a diversified subsistence strategy, and resuming one's place in kin-based and neighborhood networks of reciprocity at home might seem a less risky option. Whether or not my reasoning is correct in its details, all this suggests that it might be more accurate in this case to speak of multiple risks, rather than *the* risk of emigrating. Bringing to light more evidence about how these migrants perceive and weigh risk might make possible informative comparisons with other migrants worldwide.

5

The Impact on the Home Area

It would be too simple to conclude that labor circulation has a positive impact on the lives of people in Cayes-Jacmel and Cap Rouge, just because *Sêdomêg* money has helped men there build homes and improve peasant livelihoods. Just as migration generally involves people other than the individual migrant him/herself, so the impact of migration on the home area is more than the sum of individual outcomes of emigration. Students of migration agree that labor exports may have both negative and positive effects on migrant source areas. On the one hand, emigration may in some cases deprive local production units of needed labor. It certainly diminishes local self-sufficiency and may foster lasting dependence on outside wages. On the other hand, emigration may at times provide employment for labor that might otherwise go idle, and it generally channels capital, in the form of migrant remittances, to economically depressed home places.

I cannot pretend to judge conclusively whether the overall impact of emigration on the economy of rural southeastern Haiti has been positive or negative. In this chapter, I instead examine a few more specific aspects of the problem. I weigh evidence concerning the impact of labor circulation on inequalities of wealth in the migrants' places of origin. I discuss whether *Sêdomêg* money has been an agent of economic innovation in rural southeastern Haiti. Finally, I consider certain implications for the migrant source areas of increased dependence on external labor markets, taking as a case study recent downturns in migrant earnings and their effects on people in the Cayes-Jacmel and Cap Rouge areas.

"Not All the Fingers Have the Same Length"

Accurate data on land ownership and other indicators of wealth could not be obtained in the field to test for covariance with measures of migratory behavior. People in the Cayes-Jacmel and Cap Rouge areas distinguish relatively wealthy (*grâ nèg*), poor (*malerè*), and very poor (*pòv nèt*) categories of people. Yet Rocheteau and Cabrouette residents rarely let slip such judgments in my presence and could not be drawn to place a neighbor in any but the middle rank, *malerè*.

Yet, even without quantitative economic data or an accurate ranking by wealth, migrants' personal histories reflect differing socioeconomic backgrounds and recount diverse migratory experiences. The three personal histories that follow are each in some way atypical of the migrant population as a whole. Part of the point I wish to make is precisely that no one migrant career is in all significant respects "typical" because not one but several types of migrant careers exist.

It should have suggested something to me that I was first introduced to Joseph Pierre-Louis on a local footpath, as he was returning from taking a cow to pasture and going to one of his fields. He seemed one of the most active of the men I interviewed in Rocheteau. Joseph speaks with the assurance of a man who knows that his word counts for something among his neighbors. This befits his status as a leader of one of the older and wealthier families in Rocheteau and its surrounding *katye*. Even so, Joseph does not seem to be wealthy, even by rural Haitian standards. It is only relative to poorer neighbors that he could be considered fortunate. He is perhaps better described as a "middle peasant," poor but not desperately disadvantaged.

His story begins in 1964, the year his father died. Then only 20, Joseph was the only son old enough to have cultivated gardens of his own, and it was to him that his mother turned for help in managing the land his father left behind. These holdings were relatively large, and, within a year, Joseph had put aside enough money to build his own small wattle-and-daub house in his parents' yard.

Two years later, in the aftermath of Hurricane Ines, he took his first and only trip to the Dominican Republic. As he explains, "After the cyclone passed, everybody got up and left because of the hunger which befell the area, after Ines. Well, when I looked and saw I was the only young man who was staying, ah! I wouldn't stay! I, too, went to *Sêdomêg*." In his absence, his mother took care of the family's agricultural holdings. Upon returning, Joseph found that his mother had set aside money for him from the sale of garden produce (U.S.$80), greater than what he had brought from the Dominican Republic ($50). "The corn, beans, taro, ginger they sold for me brought even more money than *Sêdomêg* did."

Joseph was happy with the earnings from his gardens, but he was not yet satisfied that he wanted to remain a farmer. After distributing most of his *Sêdomêg* money to relatives and friends, he took what was left to go spend some time with relatives in Haiti's capital city, Port-au-Prince. It took 10 weeks before he found a job there, weaving ornamental palm-leaf covers around small bottles, at the pay rate of U.S.$3 per gross. Joseph found that he could not finish enough bottles per day even to feed himself in the city. After a few weeks, he quit this job and returned to Cap Rouge. In the end, all he had to show for having emigrated was a radio he had won in a raffle in the Dominican Republic. This he later sold in order to buy a cupboard (which he still owns).

Within a year of his return to Cap Rouge, Joseph married. In the next few years, he handed over two parcels of his father's land to his younger brother and continued to sharecrop land belonging to each of his five sisters. As the economic leader of his family, he bore much of the cost of formal education and of ceremonial/health crisis management for his siblings, nephews, and nieces. The largest single family project he financed was his brother's attempt to emigrate to Venezuela. For this, Joseph raised U.S.$300 by selling two cows and a horse, and he borrowed another $600. The money was mostly lost when authorities in Curaçao detained his brother as an illegal entrant and deported him to Haiti.

In spite of his family burdens, Joseph prospered during the 1970s from his garden produce and livestock husbandry. One visible sign of this prosperity is the nearly one *carreau* (roughly 1.45 hectare) of land he has added to his inheritance through purchase. This includes a spring-watered, carefully terraced parcel of nine *"centièmes"* (0.09 *carreau*), on which he grows the prized *mazôbèl* variety of taro. He owns at least 10 other small parcels scattered throughout the local area. Another indicator of his prosperity is the four-room house where he has lived with his wife and children since 1979. It is the only stone house in Rocheteau, and, in building it, Joseph incurred costs of over U.S.$1,600.

Since the early 1980s, Joseph's economic fortunes have stagnated. He has been unable to complete the ceiling of wooden planks in his house and is hard pressed to pay school fees for his six children. He once again harbors hopes of emigrating, this time to the United States or Canada.

Joseph's history highlights the fact that not all Dominican Republic migrants are equally constrained by poverty. Migrant cane workers do not all come from the poorer strata of rural society. On the contrary, in spite of unequal access to land, men from middle and lower peasant families seem equally prone to make at least one voyage to the Dominican Republic in their youth. As Joseph himself explained, "Not all the fingers [of the hand] have the same length. The little one goes *nâ pâyòl,*" he pointed to his pinkie finger, "but this one goes, too," he said, pointing to his thumb. "Each goes to resolve his own problems, [which vary] according to the means he has. Some have less property than others. Some have more children to feed. Some need materials to build a house. Some need to buy livestock. Some need to pay debts. But, regardless of what they need, they all seek to resolve their problems *nâ pâyòl.*"

What commonly distinguishes the migratory histories of poorer and richer men is not simply whether or not they have ever emigrated. It is, rather, the *number* of voyages they make before settling into a non-migratory livelihood. Few men who enjoy relatively abundant access to family land in young adulthood make many voyages to the Dominican Republic, but men who lack enough land on which to subsist commonly make four or more trips.

Men whose parents are relatively "wealthy" in land, if they emigrate, may go only to earn money for a house or to experience life on their own in a foreign land before taking on the responsibilities of adulthood. "The *pâyòl* money gave me a beginning, only a beginning," one man said. He made three voyages in the late 1950s before settling for good in Rocheteau: "There was no work, and I wanted to take a little step forward, understand? I lacked a house, I lacked other things, so I went in order to acquire them. But when I got them, I began to work [in Haiti] with what little I had gotten in *Sêdomêg.* I did not go again. I found instead another way here: I buy animals, I raise them. That gave me an asset so that I did not need to go anymore."

For a man of a less prosperous background, by contrast, circulation may be not just a beginning but a way of life. After he succeeds in building a house, a man from a land-poor family might make several more voyages to survive the squeeze on subsistence brought to bear on the young household by low farm incomes and the birth of dependent children. But the correlation between number of voyages and land poverty seems to be far from perfect. Contrary to what one might expect, men from the poorest backgrounds are not necessarily the most persistent migrants, as the next personal history exemplifies.

Ti Bo Charles cuts quite a different figure from Joseph Pierre-Louis. Whereas Joseph is of average height and solidly built, Ti Bo is tall and lanky. Joseph walks and talks with an air of authority; Ti Bo is stooped, soft-spoken, even laconic, but shows flashes of cutting humor. Joseph may be poor by North American standards, but one need not search for relative terms to say that Ti Bo is poor. The bare wattle walls of his small house and the malnutrition-distended bellies of his young children indicate his situation more eloquently than words. For him, how to survive from day to day until the next rainy season and, when that comes, how to get a crop in the ground are perennial worries, not uncertainties that occur only in famine years.

In 1975, at age 16, Ti Bo first tried to emigrate to the Dominican Republic. With U.S.$15, borrowed at 100 percent interest, he caught a bus from Cayes-Jacmel to the official recruitment center in Croix-des-Bouquets. "Batons!" he exclaims, gesturing as if swinging a club. "The Tontons Macoutes were killing people under their batons." (This was the Macoutes' style of "crowd control.") Unable to stand his ground before the Macoutes and lacking enough money to bribe his way into the recruiting center, he failed to get a place in the *okazyô*. After being turned away at Croix-des-Bouquets, he returned to Cabrouette and hired out on a fishing boat to try to earn enough money to pay back his debt. This was hard work at low pay and often took him away from home for days at a time. (His mother, even though single, could get by in his absence because Ti Bo's older brother farmed for her.) After nearly a year, Ti Bo was able to repay his loan.

He immediately borrowed money again for a trip to the Dominican Republic, this time *âba fil*. "At that time," he recalls, "I was very young. I was hardly 18. I didn't control myself. I saw everybody going to *Sêdomêg*. I went, too. [Once there], I earned my money, I partied, I went on a spree, but, in the end, I gained nothing [from it]." It was only after his second trip as a cane cutter to the Dominican Republic, in 1977–78, that he cleared enough money to buy some nylon fishing line, fishhooks, and traps and began fishing on his own account. At that same time, he began buying materials for a house and entered union with a local young woman. They took up residence in his mother's house. Later that year, his older brother went to the Dominican Republic for the first time, and Ti Bo took over the work of farming for his mother.

By 1980, he had raised the frame of a house, but for some time afterward he was unable to get any further. In 1981, he decided to try his luck in the Dominican Republic again. There, he saved over RD$200. He spent almost RD$100 on a suitcase, pots and cooking utensils, and clothing for himself and for his wife and mother at home. Some friends who spoke better Spanish than he exchanged the rest of his money, which yielded only U.S.$30. This was hardly enough to repay the debt he took to finance his voyage. He was disappointed at how little was left, but he does not know if he was cheated in the exchange.

When he departed for the Dominican Republic, Ti Bo left his wife with a baby daughter and pregnant with another child. By the time he returned, the first child had died and the next had been born. After repaying the funeral costs, they were worse off financially than before he left the country. Following that trip, he decided, for the sake of the children and his mother, not to emigrate again. When we spoke in early 1987, he, his wife, and their children had recently moved into their own house, unfinished though it was. "If it was not for the garden," he says, "I would not survive. When I leave the garden, if I did not go to the sea, I would not eat. I eat, I drink, but my work gives me nothing more. I have nothing."

Men from land-poor families often decide to abandon the migrant route after one or two voyages. In some households, bad luck at home always seems to follow good fortune abroad, which leads to discouragement. If drought, storm damage, severe illness, or death strikes the migrant's family in his absence, the greater part of his savings may go toward repaying the debts his wife or other family members incur to meet those emergency needs. The wife of another three-time Dominican Republic migrant explained, "The man does not have luck. Each time he goes, he returns with some money, but he always finds illness in the house or a death. In '83, he went to *Sêdomêg*, and when he returned he found me very ill. He had a niece, too, who became sick. The money slipped through his hands [i.e., for remedies]. That finally discouraged him. He saw that it yielded him nothing, because each time he left, he returned to find a big expense. . . . He decided not to go again." Bastien (1951, 155–56) tells of a similar case in his monograph on rural Haitian household and family structure, based on his fieldwork in the late 1940s in the Marbial Valley, not far from Cap Rouge:

> We met in Marbial an exceptional informant, who had worked in Cuba and Santo Domingo, and saved enough dollars to make himself a respectable place in the Valley; but, upon his return, the illness, then the deaths, of his parents destroyed his plans. Like a good son, he spent his savings on the funerals. He then rented out his inheritance (33 *centièmes carreau*), and went to earn a living in Port-au-Prince. First, he worked as a servant and gardener in a bourgeois household, earning two dollars a month. Later, he was hired in public works at 30 cents a day. Being a physically strong man, he later became a stevedore in the docks. This job he abandoned for that of "chained ox," or porter, for a Cap Haïtien trucking company. After three years of struggle, he thought: "Here, one could die of hunger, and nobody would care. . . . If I fall ill, who will nurse me? If I die suddenly, who will bury me? Better to be poor with one's own family. . . ."
> He returned to Marbial to farm his 33 *centièmes carreau*. (my translation)

Economic risk may sooner dissuade the very poor from emigrating than their wealthier neighbors. Because they stand closer to the brink of total destitution, poor peasants may be more easily put off emigrating by the risk of losing what little they have after an unsuccessful trip to the Dominican Republic. Emigration may also pose a greater threat to household stability among poorer folk. In the event that the migrant brings back nothing, or worse, if he fails to return or send home money, he may stand little chance of holding his *plasaj* together for long. At this point, rather than putting herself and the children through further hardship, the wife of a particularly unsuccessful migrant may begin considering her alternatives to continuing their union. Even though many of the very poor emigrate often, these risks may dissuade others from emigrating repeatedly. Conversely, coming from a relatively well-to-do family does not guarantee that a man will make only one or two seasonal trips before settling down in Haiti, as the following case exemplifies.

A few hundred meters from Joseph's house, down the main path leading to Cayes-Jacmel, live Dieusibon Mésuzière, his wife, Philomène, and their six children. Dieusibon is an exception to the rule that associates emigration to *Sêdomêg* with below-average schooling. He was only one or two years from finishing secondary school when he left school and took his first voyage to the Dominican Republic. He has crossed the border so often—13 times—that, when asked how many voyages he has made, he has to stop for a moment and count the trips year by year. Dieusibon regrets not finishing his schooling, but thinks that even with a secondary school degree he probably would not have achieved upward mobility. His parents, even though not among the poorer folk locally, lacked connections to anyone who could have helped him get a good job.

Like Joseph, Dieusibon made his first voyage to the Dominican Republic in 1966, at the age of 22, when he signed onto an official *okazyô* (recruitment voyage), together with his older brother and a maternal uncle. At that time, though he had already planted gardens of his own, he was still a dependent member of his parents' household. Like many other local men that year, he wanted money to buy seed after Hurricane Ines. Also, he wanted to begin building a house for Philomène, with whom he had "already spoken." From that first voyage, he brought back U.S.$160, of which he spent $45 on metal roofing, invested another quarter or so in seed and livestock, and gave away most of the remainder in small quantities to relatives and friends. Upon his return, he and Philomène became engaged to marry.

For the next three years, official recruitment was suspended. Not wishing to cross the border *âba fil*, Dieusibon did not go to the Dominican Republic. Even so, during those years, with money from the sale of livestock and garden produce, he raised the frame and the roof of a house and wrapped it with wattle. Before he remigrated to the Dominican Republic, he and Philomène moved into the house.

A second voyage, in 1970–71, netted him U.S.$220. With this, he plastered the walls of the house with daub, whitewashed them, bought wooden planks for the ceiling and cement for the floor, and paid craftsmen to do the skilled labor. Soon afterward, he and Philomène married, and their first child was born.

In the 14 years from 1971 to 1985, Dieusibon made a further 11 voyages to the Dominican Republic, each except the final one with the official *okazyô*. From these voyages, he never came back with less than U.S.$80. He attributes the unusual regularity with which he accumulated good savings in the cane harvest to hard work, frugal living, and the support of his harvest companions. He made each trip with two to five companions, drawn from a small group of local men. In the Dominican Republic, these companions shared the same room, pooled money for food expenses, divided cooking duties, and even helped guard one another's savings against theft.

Back in Haiti, money from his third voyage enabled Dieusibon to buy a parcel of 15 *centièmes* from his father for U.S.$160. This parcel included the site on which Dieusibon had already built his house. Part of the proceeds of his fourth and fifth voyages went toward buying household furnishings, including a wooden bed, table, cupboard, and chairs. In 1975, the savings of his sixth trip were spent mostly on food during an islandwide drought. From each of three subsequent voyages, he brought home enough money to buy a small parcel of land. All three parcels were bought at favorable prices from relatives. The four parcels of land he has bought add up to about one-half *carreau* (0.7 hectare). Much of the rest of his *Sêdomêg* money went toward house repairs and clothing and school fees for his children.

Besides the land he has bought, Dieusibon has held two parcels in sharecrop since before his first voyage and he works some of his father's and his father-in-law's land. He wants to expand his agricultural holdings further, and he urgently needs to make a number of house repairs, including installing a new roof. Yet, since the harvest of 1984–85, he has been dissuaded from emigrating again. The exchange rate between the Dominican peso and Haitian gourde has deteriorated, and the real wages for cutting cane have dropped. Dieusibon is also an enthusiastic adherent to the popular Catholic church, Ti Legliz, which, through its Creole language monthly, *Bon Nouvèl,* has advised Haitians against further seasonal migration as cane workers to the Dominican Republic.

Dieusibon's case shows that belonging to a family that has land does not always mean that a man can get rights to use enough of that land in his youth to support a wife and children. A young man might be in line to inherit several parcels of land but only be granted immediate access to one or two, which leaves him for the moment almost as badly off as a son of a land-poor family. The contrast between the histories of Joseph and Dieusibon suggests that, among men from middle peasant families, the age at which interviewees receive their full inheritance from father or mother may determine the number of voyages they will make before settling permanently in Haiti. A son of middle peasants who receives a full share of his inheritance at an early age will make fewer voyages than a man of similar age and status background who gets access to only one or two small parcels of land in his youth. Similarly, the number of voyages a man makes may depend on whether his parents' estate is divided among many heirs or few.

Dieusibon's history suggests also that, in the life histories of men from middle peasant backgrounds, *purchasing* family land may be as important as inheriting family land. In the Cayes-Jacmel and Cap Rouge areas, as elsewhere in Haiti, peasants observe the custom of *vât pwoteje*, wherein the first option to buy land is reserved for relatives, and they will defend this principle even to the point of bringing legal suit against family members who disregard it. Through *vât pwoteje*, a young man from a family that has land for sale can use his *Sêdomêg* money to buy choice parcels from his parents or other relatives, generally at below-market prices. Land in *vât pwoteje* is available scarcely, if at all, to men from land-poor families. Land tends thus to remain in the hands of a single inheritance group as a result of customary practice as well as uneven distribution of wealth.[1]

THE IMPACT ON THE HOME AREA

In rural areas of poor countries throughout the world, a number of negative trends are observed to coexist with high rates of emigration. These include technical stagnation, growing socioeconomic inequality, disruption of production units, removal of land from cultivation of subsistence foodstuffs, and increasing consumption of foreign imports (Rhoades 1978; Rubenstein 1983). It is observed, further, that repatriated migrant savings tend to be squandered on urban manufactures and are often invested in ways that generate little employment locally (Kayser 1972; King and Strachan 1980; papers in Kubat 1984). At times, migrant money has just "enabled migrants to raise their standard of living to a level which can only be maintained through recurrent migration" (Reichert 1981, 63; also Griffith 1986). Only a few recent empirical studies find reason for optimism concerning the impact of emigration, remittances, and return on migrant source areas (Griffiths 1979; McArthur 1979; Simmons 1984; Stahl and Arnold 1986; Gmelch 1987).

At first glance, it might seem that the investment of *Sêdomêg* money in Haiti refutes the pessimism of social researchers concerning the economic impact of emigration and remittances on labor-exporting rural areas. Emigration to the sugar estates does *not* result in a declining intensity of land use. Nor does it reduce food production or increase dependence on imports in the Cayes-Jacmel and Cap Rouge areas. The personal histories of *Sêdomêg* returnees suggest, on the contrary, that peripheral migrants may be more inclined than returnees from the highly industrialized countries to invest their money in labor-intensive agriculture at home.

Yet, to observe that *Sêdomêg* money is spent productively is not necessarily to say that it has been an agent of development of the kind rural Haiti needs. There is no sign that *Sêdomêg* money has made possible agricultural innovation in the Cayes-Jacmel and Cap Rouge areas. Returnees farm the land with the same range of techniques and seem to plant more or less the same combinations of cultigens as others do locally. Further, because of its circularity, emigration to the Dominican Republic has probably done much less to relieve demographic pressure than other more permanent and urban-oriented streams of population mobility. Even at levels of relatively permanent male emigration of 15 to 25 percent, emigration to the Dominican Republic may scarcely abate the intensity of land use in the migrants' home areas. This is because returnees generally work the land more intensively than they did before emigrating. The money Haitian cane workers bring home from the Dominican Republic commonly allows them to rent land and to purchase productive inputs that they lacked. High-intensity land use is encouraged further by the Haitian norm that local land should be made available for local people to farm, rather than left idle just because its owner is absent. In short, the main impact of labor circulation on agriculture in rural southeastern Haiti has probably been to sustain farming of the area's erosion-prone slopes at its already high levels of intensity. It is questionable whether this is entirely a good result, if not accompanied by improved soil conservation measures, of which I found no evidence.

Labor circulation also seems to favor the reproduction of local disparities of wealth. In spite of increasing the income of many poorer men, emigration to the Dominican Republic seemingly does little to level inequalities of wealth between different families and branches of families locally. In the general vicinity of the *katye* where I did fieldwork, a handful of men are reputed to have used *Sêdomêg* money to climb from backgrounds of poverty to the status of "*grâ nèg*" (i.e., "wealthy" peasants). They have accumulated relatively large herds of cattle in Haiti on the basis of their repatriated savings. Most of these men are unusual in having risen from the rank of cane cutter while on the sugar estates, to take better-paid jobs as company foremen, self-employed craftsmen, and traders. These men also had the advantage of returning home before the 1980s, when economic conditions in Haiti were more favorable than today. Yet the degree of upward mobility enjoyed by these men is exceptional among *Sêdomêg* returnees. Few returning cane workers achieve freedom from want or gain effective economic independence from wealthier people in the home area. Most returnees bring home savings that are too small to invest in activities more profitable than labor-intensive agriculture. Risk also dissuades poor returnees from abandoning cultivation of the food staples they eat.

Also, a large chunk of migrant savings goes immediately into the hands of richer local people as repayment of debts, largely taken to finance migration, plus interest of 50 to 100 percent. Most lenders are relatively prosperous farmers or traders. Others are merchants or coffee brokers in the town of Cayes-Jacmel and the city of Jacmel. Debt repayment is not the only way migrant savings are transferred to wealthier people locally. If the returnee wishes, for example, to invest in a calf, to purchase wood for the frame of a house, or to buy or rent a parcel of land, he will probably make this transaction not with someone as poor as he is but with a neighbor who owns cattle, wood trees, or land in relative abundance. Through sales and rentals to returning migrants, the relatively well-off capture a healthy share of the *Sêdomêg* money that enters the area each year.

On balance, labor circulation seems to have permitted, even favored, the continuity of peasant social and economic institutions. Wealth inequalities have been preserved among the peasants of the Cayes-Jacmel and Cap Rouge areas but have not been amplified to the extreme of creating distinct capitalist and laboring classes among the source population. Emigration has not trapped individuals in lifetimes of dependence on migrant wages and has not brought about disinvestment in small-scale, labor-intensive agriculture at home. Yet neither has it raised the general standard of living of the source population to a level where emigration is no longer necessary for the young. On the contrary, circulation has become a key element in the perpetuation of peasant livelihoods from one generation to the next. In short, *Sêdomêg* money has probably helped reproduce a peasant way of life in the major migrant source areas, both through what it has done and what it has failed to do for the migrants and their kin.

It is not that labor circulation is part of an unchanging cycle of social reproduction in rural southeastern Haiti. On the contrary, the area's continuing dependence on outside incomes, at a period of increasing hardship on both sides of the island, gives particular cause for concern. Shrinking migrant savings have coincided with a turn for the worse in Haiti's agrarian crisis. These trends may now pose one of the greatest threats ever to the reproduction of a peasant way of life in the Cayes-Jacmel and Cap Rouge area.

THE TWIN CRISES

Be it as migrant laborers or as small-scale agricultural producers, the people of Cayes-Jacmel and Cap Rouge are earning sharply reduced incomes, when compared to the cost of the goods they must buy from the outside world. This is to some degree a continuation of long-standing trends. For example, since the withdrawal of the American occupiers in 1934, Haitian coffee production has declined on a per capita basis, and the producer's share of the returns from coffee exports has dropped. "During the 1950's," DeWind and Kinley (1988, 89–90) report, "62.3 percent of the returns from coffee exports went to the peasant producers, while 15.9 percent was divided between the coffee exporters and *spéculateurs* [middlemen]. [Export duties took the remaining 21.8 percent.] Since [then], . . . coffee merchants have managed to increase their share of coffee revenues to an average of 24.2 percent [and the government has raised its take to an average of 30.3 percent], while the peasant producers' share has dropped to an average of 45.5 percent. . . . As a result, coffee production, which averaged 35 thousand tons per year in the 1950's, has gradually dropped to an average of 34.2 thousand tons in the 1960's, and to 32.4 thousand tons since 1970." Since 1987, the collapse of the international coffee market has only worsened this picture. And coffee is only the most prominent export to have declined since the Second World War. Sisal hemp production for export has virtually disappeared, and Haiti has lost its position as a leading exporter of many essential oils (Trouillot 1990, 212). In 1987, even HASCO, Haiti's only sugar exporter, went out of business, after having lost much of the Haitian market to contraband sugar from the Dominican Republic.

Perhaps the most serious blow to peasant livelihoods has been the eradication of the island's entire pig population. From 1980 to 1983, the Haitian and Dominican governments, with the encouragement of international aid agencies, slaughtered all the pigs to stop the spread to the American continent of an African swine fever that had appeared in Hispaniola. The pig eradication cut a major link in the chain of reinvestment that had enabled peasants to expand their assets gradually from a meager base of migrant savings to the purchase of large livestock, building materials, and even land. "Since we lost pig husbandry," said one farmer, "our very breath has left us." The local strain of pig suited peasant needs well because it subsisted on a wide range of abundant feeds and waste products, and it reproduced itself more rapidly than any other variety of livestock raised in Haiti. No other type of livestock production has picked up the dynamism formerly associated with swine production. Even in 1987, four years after the slaughter, pigs were not available to peasant farmers at prices most could afford to pay. Immediately prior to the slaughter, piglets sold in Cayes-Jacmel for U.S.$10–$20; in 1987, piglets of North American varieties introduced to replace the native swine sold for U.S.$100–$120.[2]

Price inflation in building materials and land in Haiti has taken a further toll on local standards of living. In 1967, as local people recall, the cost of building a typical two-room, wattle-and-daub dwelling, with thatched roof and dirt floor, was roughly U.S.$250; the price of a comparable house with corrugated metal roof and concrete floor was about $325. By 1987, the cost of building the same dwellings had risen by about 125 to 130 percent, to roughly $550 and $715, respectively. The price of wood made up a large part of that increase. From 1947 to 1987, the local price of wooden posts and planks increased by 400 to 700 percent. The price of land rose comparably: 150 percent, between 1967 and 1987; 400 percent, between 1947 and 1987. Even more rapid inflation marked the general cost of living in Haiti during the 1970s and 1980s. "If we take as a base (100) fiscal year 1975–76," Trouillot (1990, 214) writes, "the general cost of living went from 53.07 in 1969–70 to 151.02 in 1980–81, to 206.98 in 1984–85."

To a worsening economic situation has been added the problem of declining migrant incomes. No one has yet documented changes in wage levels and cost of living of cane workers over the length of the twentieth century. Yet a 50-year periodicity is evident in the evolution of cane cutters' wages. Troughs in real wages occurred in the 1880s, 1930s, and 1980s, and peaks arrived in the 1910s and 1960s. The latest trend has been sharply downwards. Since 1970, the real incomes of cane cutters have fallen dramatically. In real terms, as of 1990, cane cutters were paid only 31 percent of what they had earned in 1969 (Báez Evertsz 1986, 182; 1992, 122). *Braceros* of the mid-1960s to mid-1970s typically cleared U.S.$50 to $200 from the cane harvest, after expenditures on personal and household goods in the Dominican Republic. At that time, Haitian *braceros* received none of the end-of-harvest payments to which they were entitled under the contract their government signed with the CEA. Yet, by putting aside money from their daily wages, they commonly saved a much higher fraction of their earnings than is possible today. As recently as the late 1970s, a returning migrant could even on rare occasions buy a small parcel of land with the cash he brought home from the Dominican cane harvest. In 1981, by contrast, Murphy (1986, 267) found that "the average contract worker . . . was returning to Haiti with a couple pairs of pants, a shirt, a cooking pot, and U.S.$56.58 after more than six months of work." Since 1981, a greater than tenfold drop in the value of the Dominican peso relative to the U.S. dollar has reduced migrant savings even further, the Haitian currency being tied to the American at a rate of five gourdes to one dollar.

Today, nearly every unfinished house in the highland Cap Rouge area holds a story of hopes left unfulfilled by recent Dominican sugarcane harvests. In spite of trying times in Haiti, the combination of unfavorable investment conditions at home and reduced earnings abroad has discouraged many veteran migrants from going again to the Dominican Republic. Today, fewer men over the age of 30 go to the Dominican Republic than went in the 1960s and 1970s (see appendix B). Corten (1986, 256) notes that, between 1970 and 1981, the number of cane workers under the age of 30 rose from 44.8 percent to 71.5 percent of the total sample he interviewed in the Dominican Republic. The migrant of today seems to be on average younger, poorer, and less experienced than migrants of decades past.

In many ways, the present situation resembles the crisis of the late 1930s. Today, as in the 1930s,

(1) the real wages of cane workers in the Dominican Republic have dropped by more than half, when compared to their levels of a decade or two earlier;

(2) officially regulated recruitment in Haiti has been suspended;

(3) the cane harvest depends largely on the labor of *âba fil* entrants, yet men in rural Haiti, especially veteran cane workers, are increasingly reluctant to emigrate to the sugar estates;

(4) the Dominican security forces and sugar producers have escalated forced relocation of Haitian men from non-sugar-producing areas of the Dominican Republic to the sugar estates, and the civil rights situation has deteriorated for Haitian working people in the Dominican Republic generally;

(5) thousands of Haitians have been forced to return to their country from the Dominican Republic (i.e., fleeing the *corte,* in 1937, and via forced repatriation, in 1991), and tension has increased between the Haitian and Dominican governments concerning the treatment accorded Haitians in the Dominican Republic.

The crisis of today differs from that of the 1930s in at least two important ways. First, in 1937, the Trujillo regime was willing to risk international condemnation by slaughtering Haitians by the thousands on Dominican territory. Today, official violence on such a scale seems unlikely to recur, even if the most xenophobic extreme of the Dominican political spectrum were once more to take power. The government is too eager to maintain good international publicity (on which hinges, among other things, the lucrative tourist industry) for ethnic-purification measures as extreme as Trujillo's *corte* even to be contemplated in official circles. The second obvious difference is the further deterioration in the economic situation in rural Haiti. Today, withdrawing onto parents' farms in Haiti is a viable option for proportionately fewer young men than it was a half-century ago.

It is too soon to say whether the present crisis will be followed by a partial recovery in cane cutters' earnings or whether it foreshadows the transformation or breakdown of the migratory labor system. The personal histories of recent migrants lead me to believe that most migrants still go to the Dominican Republic for reasons other than immediate relief from hunger. Even so, recent trends give little reason for optimism. Haitian cane workers today face particularly daunting conditions, when compared to earlier cohorts of Dominican Republic migrants. It remains to be seen what the social and economic impact will be in southeastern Haiti if incomes from temporary labor in the Dominican Republic deteriorate further, and progressively more young men find themselves without the means to marry "on time."

In summary, a broad variety of experiences and outcomes characterize the migration histories of men from the Cayes-Jacmel and Cap Rouge areas. These histories suggest that it is peasants who are not desperately disadvantaged, rather than the very poor, who circulate most persistently. This is in keeping with the principle that the people who are most likely to emigrate from rural areas are the "rather poor . . . rather than, in general, the very poorest" (Connell et al. 1976, 197). Yet personal histories do not always coincide with economic backgrounds. They may instead be shaped by the vagaries of particular households' demographic histories, such as the number of children and the age at which those children receive the bulk of their inheritance from their parents. These findings are consistent with a conclusion reached by earlier ethnographers, that patterns of wealth distribution in village Haiti are determined jointly by the developmental cycle of domestic groups and by enduring inequalities between families (G. F. Murray 1977; Smucker 1982).

My findings do not suggest that emigration leads inevitably to rural breakdown. The temporary adoption of a proletarian life-style in neighboring countries by the men of southeastern Haiti has not hastened the demise of a peasant way of life in that area. In fact, labor circulation has probably aided the survival of this life-style. Contrary to what researchers have commonly observed in other economically depressed, labor-exporting regions, emigration to the sugar estates has neither encouraged people to abandon agriculture nor fostered lifelong dependence on migrant workers' wages in southeastern Haiti.

Even so, it would be a mistake to idealize the impact of emigration in rural Haiti. There, as elsewhere in the Third World, migrants returning home with small amounts of capital are unlikely as a group to go far toward righting long-standing regional trade imbalances. If emigration to the Dominican Republic has favored the reproduction of customary livelihoods in southeastern Haiti, it has done so partly because it favors stagnation over innovation. *Sêdomêg* money has seemingly not made possible any new way of making a living in the migrants' home areas. The nonfarm investments typically made by Haitians returning from North America lie beyond the reach of Dominican Republic returnees. Nor can Dominican returnees afford to make major improvements in agricultural technology with their savings. Continuing poverty ties most returnees to the land, and risk dissuades them from abandoning livelihoods based on the cultivation and sale of subsistence crops. In spite of helping many poorer men get a start in life, *Sêdomêg* money neither stimulates economic innovation nor diminishes structural economic dependence in rural southeastern Haiti.

I hypothesize that internationally the only migrants who are generally willing to invest in labor-intensive smallholder agriculture at home may be those who have the most limited economic alternatives (e.g., the very poor and people from particularly isolated rural areas). Rather than investing in agriculture, wealthier returnees prefer putting their money into more lucrative investments, often of the kind decried by social researchers as destructive of local economic autonomy (e.g., modern housing, bars, family shops, trucks, and buses). Relatively powerless and economically insecure migrants, such as the Haitian *braceros,* may often be incapable of doing much more with their savings than bolstering endangered customary sources of livelihood in their home areas. The present example does not so much refute the alleged negative effects of labor exports as confirm the limited potential of migrant remittances as a motor of sustainable economic growth.

6

Migrants and Stay-at-Homes: Women and Labor Circulation

Far fewer Haitian women than men go to the Dominican sugar estates. Of people over 35 from the rural neighborhoods of Rocheteau and Cabrouette in southeastern Haiti, only 10 percent of women versus 66 percent of men have made a trip of any kind to the Dominican Republic. Two-thirds of these women traveled to the Dominican Republic in search of employment, or went there in the company of, or to rejoin, a spouse or adult guardian. One-third crossed the border only briefly to buy trade goods. Yet it is only in relative terms that female emigration to the Dominican Republic is small. Tens of thousands of Haitian women reside in the sugar *bateyes* and other agricultural towns where most of the Haitian population of the Dominican Republic is found.

As a consequence of the relatively few Haitian women who live in the *batey* of Yerba Buena, and the even lower number who return to the *katye* of Rocheteau and Cabrouette, my data about migrant women draws from a smaller pool of informants than my information concerning migrant men. Adding to my uncertainty is the fact that previous anthropological studies of rural Haiti have analyzed the female life cycle less thoroughly than that of the male. Little is known for sure about how women's ways of earning a living tend to evolve over the life course, or what makes some women stand a better chance of economic success than others. Until more is known about these things, we will be badly prepared to say why some women emigrate to the Dominican Republic, while others stay at home.

Much also remains to be learned about the situation of women in the sugar *bateyes*. From an early time, novels, poems, journalistic pieces, and other elite representations of sugar's place in Dominican society have high-lighted the starkness and brutality of life in the *bateyes,* but done little to illuminate how people survive there.[1] It is only recently that social research-ers have begun to remedy this neglect by expanding the frame of analysis to include the *batey* population as a whole, rather than looking only at the immigrant male segment of it (Newton 1980; Sabbagh Khoury and Tavárez García 1983; Bobea and Guzmán C. 1985; Báez Evertsz 1986; Moya Pons et al. 1986; Jansen and Millán 1991).

Remunerative employment for women is scarce on the sugar estates. Nearly everyone who works for pay on the sugar estates either works for the sugar companies or sells goods and services to company employees and their dependents. The companies hire an overwhelmingly male work force and offer relatively few income-generating opportunities to women on the sugar estates. This scarcely encourages Haitian women to emigrate there.

If one also considers that Dominican women more commonly depend on their mates for support than women in Haiti, it seems puzzling that even a few Haitian women would be willing to leave home for the sugar estates. I try to shed light on women's reasons for entering into the sexu-ally discriminatory environment of the *bateyes,* and I describe some of their ways of coping with life there. A question that has been central to many previous studies of women migrants (Morokvasic 1984, 891–96) is whether emigrating increases women's economic independence and improves the material and social condition of their lives or places women in new situa-tions of dependence, with which they may be little prepared to cope. Fol-lowing this line of inquiry, I also examine evidence concerning the impact of seasonal, male emigration on the women who stay at home in the Cayes-Jacmel and Cap Rouge area. Labor circulation can be conceptualized as a form of capitalist incorporation at a distance, allowing the question whether it, like other more direct and enduring forms of incorporation, tends to bring fewer benefits to women than to men.

HAITIAN WOMEN ON THE SUGAR ESTATES
OF THE DOMINICAN REPUBLIC

It is widely thought in the Dominican Republic that women on the sugar estates are an economic burden on their men. This is hardly what I ob-served in Yerba Buena. Of women 15 and older in Yerba Buena, at least 55 percent (101 of 184) earn money in petty commerce and/or occasional do-mestic service.[2] Levels of economic activity are even higher among Haitian women in Yerba Buena. Of the 24 Haitian women who maintain perma-nent residence there, 19 (about 79 percent) earn incomes of their own rather than depending solely on the support of husbands and grown children. Four of these women (about 17 percent) are single and support themselves with their own cash earnings. Nor do women who reside permanently in the *bateyes* necessarily depend on a man for access to company housing. After the harvest is over, a single Haitian woman who stays on in a *batey* of the CEA may obtain housing individually from local company bosses, in exchange for a small cash gratuity.

The provision of sexual services for pay to Haitian men and the sale of cooked food to cane workers in the fields are virtual monopolies of Haitian women. Yet Haitian women in Yerba Buena do not sell to Haitian men alone. As much or more of their independently earned income comes from the sale of goods and services to Dominicans and Haitian-Dominicans. Dominican nationals have more buying power at their disposal, and they demand a wider range of services than the Haitians. Nearly all economically active Haitian women who can understand and make themselves understood in the Spanish language try to tap into this market. Doing laundry and other occasional domestic labor, preparing sweets, frying snack foods, and retailing charcoal, fruit, and sundries from their doorsteps or along the roadside are among the activities through which Haitian women generate incomes in Yerba Buena.

Even so, women on the sugar estates do not often earn enough either to gain effective economic independence from men or to make a lasting improvement in their standards of living. Given the pitifully low incomes most Haitians earn on the sugar estates, it is necessary that all able members of the household work for money, including women and children. Even during harvest time, the income of an adult male cane worker is generally too low and unstable to support a family alone (Bobea and Guzmán C. 1985, 142–45; Báez Evertsz 1986, 311). Women and children must also earn money to put food on the table after the company paycheck has run out and to tide the household over on days when the male wage earner cannot work because of illness or injury or when he is idled by a breakdown in the factory or by a bottleneck in the transport of cane from field to mill (Sabbagh Khoury and Tavárez García 1983, 49–53; Bobea and Guzmán C. 1985, 126). The situation gets even worse when the agricultural calendar turns from harvest to dead season. Women are no more able than men to avoid the seasonal swings in activity in the *batey* economy. Men's wages determine the amount of money that circulates locally. This sets the level of demand for women's informal commerce (Bobea and Guzmán C. 1985, 130–31).

In spite of their special involvement with domestic labor, women play a relatively small role in providing domestic services to the *braceros*, during these men's sojourn on the sugar estates.[3] The *braceros* are too poorly paid to afford many domestic services, and they generally seek to avoid unnecessary expenses. *Braceros* do not often hire domestic labor or take wives in the *bateyes;* instead, they personally do most of the domestic tasks that Haitians consider to be women's and children's work. As individuals or in small groups of housemates, they gather their own fuelwood and water, purchase household necessities, prepare the main meal of the day, and do their own laundry and housekeeping. Generally, the *braceros* only turn to women for two services, which they consider impossible to provide for themselves: cooked food in their places of work, which men's long hours of labor prevent them from preparing themselves, and sexual gratification. The *braceros* provide themselves with most other daily necessities or, quite often, do without these at physical and emotional cost.

It would therefore be a mistake to think that the role of Haitian women on the sugar estates is chiefly to assure the daily reproduction of the labor of the seasonal migrants. Migrant women secure only a small fraction of their incomes by capturing the wages of the *braceros*. And the *braceros* are not so bound by their gender roles that they feel they cannot do tasks that in Haiti are regarded as women's work.

On the other hand, it would be equally wrong to conclude that within the ambit of the migratory labor system women's domestic labor is trivial. By my observation, self-provisioning of domestic labor does not make solitary male cane workers regard the services they get from women as insignificant or nonessential. Nor do the sugar companies lightly dismiss the value of women's services. On the contrary, during the cane harvest, agents of the CEA pay for Haitian women to be transported to the sugar estates on the same buses that carry male seasonal migrants, and company guards may impede these women from leaving the *bateyes*, by force, if necessary. Women generally do not work in the cane fields, but, as one company boss put it, "Where there are men, there must be women."

Âba fil has always been the only way for ordinary Haitian women and children to enter the Dominican Republic. My interviews suggest that proportionately fewer women than men fall into official custody after crossing the border. Even so, many women also turn themselves in to Dominican authorities at border garrisons, or they are arrested by soldiers or police at checkpoints further inside the Dominican Republic. Upon arriving on the sugar estates, the women receive much the same treatment as the men. Each new arrival, man or woman, is given a food ration and issued a thin foam mattress on which to sleep. Whether or not she was transported to the *batey* by the company, any Haitian woman whom company guards identify to be a seasonal migrant may be prevented from abandoning her *batey*. Women are more reluctant than men to sneak out of their *bateyes* through the cane fields under cover of darkness, out of fear of being raped or killed as they pass through isolated places. Women are reputed to be easier to stop from abandoning their *bateyes* than men because they stick too much to the main roads in their escape attempts.

Yet, in at least one crucial way, the company treats migrant women differently than migrant men. A single Haitian woman who is new to the *batey* is not allowed to live on her own or to share a room with other single women in the *braceros'* barracks. She must either stay with any friends, relatives, or fellow villagers she might find in the *batey* or take up union with a man just to get a roof over her head. In spite of women's varied economic activities, company bosses do not recognize that a migrant woman might have an independent economic identity and might wish to play a role in the *batey* other than wife or prostitute.

It is not clear what advantage the CEA gets from having Haitian women shipped to its estates. It is possible that women's paid or unpaid domestic labor enables the sugar companies to extract a greater profit from the cane worker by making him spend more money, work harder, and stay longer on the estates than he would in a single-sex environment. Yet there is reason to suspect that this might be too neat an explanation. Certainly, the abysmally low productivity of the Haitian *braceros* when compared to cane cutters in other countries does not suggest that the sugar companies are very concerned with optimizing the cane cutter's output (ONAPLAN 1981a, 44; Báez Evertsz 1986, 232–49; Moya Pons et al. 1986, 291–99; Murphy 1991, 59–61). Cane growers' harvest labor strategy might be more accurately summarized as, "Round up as many Haitians as you can, and assume that hunger will make them work."

From the bosses' point of view, the value of women may sooner be that they help hold the *braceros* in place. It may be recalled that, on sugar estates throughout the country, CEA bosses and private growers implement a range of coercive labor control practices in an attempt to slow the leakage of labor from their properties. Yet cane growers do not make common cause to stem the migrants' mobility. Rather, each local production unit stands in competition for labor with others of its kind. Growers often attempt to take advantage of the dissatisfaction of *braceros* on neighboring estates by sending out agents to "steal" Haitians from their neighbors. Local company bosses are keenly aware that nearby growers are attempting such ploys, because they themselves are using the same techniques to try to persuade Haitians on other estates to come to their own *bateyes*. Short of increasing pay or improving conditions of employment, each employer is willing to accommodate what he understands to be the preferences of the workers, in order to "keep the Haitians happy."

Company bosses regard women as an indispensable means toward this end. In the opinion of company officials, a *batey* without women will not take long to become a *batey* without men. The presence of women in the *bateyes* is one of the "carrots" by which the cane growers hope to persuade "their" Haitians to stay. They work this in tandem with a "stick"—armed surveillance and the threat of violence—by which they mean to dissuade the Haitians they have from moving elsewhere. In short, from the bosses' point of view, the transport of Haitian women to the sugar estates may be not an indirect way of getting the *braceros* to work harder but simply a means of persuading those men to stay put.

Certain facts contradict the bosses' impression that Haitian women must be forcibly relocated to the *bateyes*. For example, most of the Haitian women I met in Yerba Buena and its surrounding *bateyes* were not taken there by the authorities but found their own way there. That most women in Yerba Buena are gainfully employed in activities other than sex work also belies the bosses' opinion that women have only one important reason to be on the sugar estates, to be the sexual partners of men. Yet, in the bosses' eyes, the more Haitian women who enter their *bateyes*, the better. And, in the end, it is the bosses who demand the forced transport of Haitian women to the *bateyes*, and it is what the bosses think that counts.

TYPES OF MIGRANTS

The women who emigrate to the Dominican Republic from the Cayes-Jacmel and Cap Rouge areas may be placed in three categories: (1) international traders, (2) trailing spouses and children, and (3) single women. That observable differences in migratory behavior can be related to women's marital status perhaps reflects the increased sexual discrimination and dependence on men that women experience when they leave Haiti and enter the Dominican Republic.

The traders buy goods in the Dominican capital, Santo Domingo, and take these to Haiti to be sold at a profit. They may also carry smaller quantities of merchandise from Haiti to sell in the Dominican Republic. Without having done a survey of the traders, I cannot say for sure how many women move up to international trade after coming to the Dominican Republic as simple migrants.[4] The large capital requirements of international trade might prevent much mobility of this kind from taking place. Of 27 women emigrants from the neighborhoods of Rocheteau and Cabrouette in southeastern Haiti, none had gone to the Dominican Republic as traders after having first emigrated there for another reason. In my year in Yerba Buena, I met only one specialist in international trade, a woman who was visiting relatives for a few days. This suggests that the traders and the women who end up on the sugar estates are largely distinct groups.

Considerable overlap exists between the other two categories of female emigrants, single women and trailing spouses and children. This is because a woman commonly emigrates under more than one status in her lifetime. Some women enter the Dominican Republic for the first time with a husband, break up with him there or after they return to Haiti, and emigrate again while single. Conversely, some single women take a husband while in the Dominican Republic, return to Haiti, and later remigrate with their spouses. Single migrants seem to predominate. Of 29 female migrants whose personal histories I recorded, 20 (about 69 percent) emigrated for the first time when young and single.

Remarkably, of these 29 women, *none* had ever left a current conjugal partner behind in Haiti when she emigrated. Instead, the women either broke up with their husbands sometime before leaving home, or went to the Dominican Republic with, or to rejoin, a spouse or adult guardian. For women, in total contrast with men, going to the Dominican Republic seems to be incompatible with maintaining union with a spouse who remains in Haiti. It is probably a rare man who would accept his wife emigrating on her own to the Dominican Republic, knowing the strong chance that she will take a new man there.[5]

Women's personal histories reveal, further, that single migrants typically leave Haiti for the first time soon after the breakup of a conjugal union in Haiti. Of the 20 interviewees who first emigrated when single, 14 (70 percent) had split from their husbands in the 6 months before they left Haiti, and 18 (90 percent) had done so in the 12 months before. The other two had never been in conjugal union before emigrating. Of course, marital instability is far from the sole determinant of women's decisions to leave home. Each year, many Haitian women leave conjugal union, but very few, relatively speaking, decide to emigrate to the Dominican Republic. It may be that conjugal breakup leads to emigration if it follows upon such unfortunate turns of fate as the loss of trading capital or a breakdown in family and neighborhood support in time of need. In other cases, a woman's decision to go to the Dominican Republic may itself lead to breakup.

Only a few migrants' wives choose to follow their husbands to the Dominican Republic. From the small number of interviews I had with women who accompanied their husbands, I cannot generalize about these women's motivations for emigrating. Their personal histories suggest that these reasons are diverse. One woman had her mother as well as her husband in the Dominican Republic, and, in emigrating, she largely sought her mother's support in caring for her sick toddler. Two women had emigrated on their own and established independent means of earning a living in the Dominican Republic before entering union with their migrant husbands. Three, by contrast, claimed to have depended so heavily on their husbands for support that they could not make a living on their own in Haiti. One left Haiti with her husband and two children to escape attack by sorcery. If nothing else, these examples suggest that the label of "trailing spouse" is not always appropriate for these women. When a woman decides to accompany her migrant husband, she does not necessarily do so simply to make his life easier or because she depends on him for support. She may, rather, decide to emigrate for reasons that relate to her own independent goals. And, as their relatively high level of economic activity in Yerba Buena suggests, Haitian women in the Dominican Republic may not be as dependent on men as outside observers have tended to conclude.

THE MIGRANTS' BACKGROUNDS AND MOTIVATIONS

In deciding whether or not to emigrate, women seem to exercise about as much personal autonomy as men. None of the women I interviewed spoke of consulting with older relatives about emigrating or of searching for approval for the trip among the extended family, as is generally the case among men and women who emigrate to North America. A few even said they decided to go on the spur of the moment, with the encouragement of friends or strangers who were on their way to the border.

In spite of this personal autonomy, certain evidence suggests that women, more often than men, leave home in response to daunting personal circumstances. Women may often go to the Dominican Republic more as a possible interim solution to their economic problems than as a strategy of petty accumulation over the medium to long term.

Women's migration goals are usually less clearly defined than men's. When asked what final factor made them decide to go to the Dominican Republic, most do not mention a particular goal but point to bad personal economic circumstances. Others say they were convinced to go by friends or kinfolk who told them stories about good jobs and money that could be gotten on the Dominican side of the border. One woman told me, "It is like I wanted to get to know the country [the Dominican Republic]. They [two male friends] were talking to me about the country, saying the country was very good. They were people who had just left the country, they were telling me that. I went to see if it really was good." Another woman said, "People were telling me '*Sêdomêg, Sêdomêg, Sêdomêg!* There is a place which has more money!'" She chuckled. "'Money?' I asked. They answered, 'Money multiplies (*Lajâ fè pitit*)!' I said——." A woman bystander interjected, "A lie, yes, my brother!" A third woman added, "A big lie, yes." The interviewee concluded, "I said, 'I want to see that country!'" The three women then laughed heartily.

The vagueness of women's migration goals is matched by their uncertainty concerning employment prospects in the Dominican Republic. Most say that, before leaving Haiti, they had little idea of what kind of work they would do in the Dominican Republic, and they claim to have had no plan for job-hunting other than to see what they could find when they got there.

One recent arrival, Simone Morancy, was typical of many in having decided to emigrate not with a fixed plan but with an attitude of flexibility in the face of what might come. She entered the Dominican Republic in November 1985, at age 20, with a male cousin, whose employer in the Dominican frontier town of Pedernales had asked him to find a woman to employ as a domestic servant. She was persuaded to go because she wanted to save up for false teeth, which are bought more cheaply in the Dominican Republic than in Haiti. She had broken up with her first husband, the father of her three children, five months before deciding to leave Haiti. She left one child in the care of its godmother and two with a paternal aunt. After only two months, she gave up the job in Pedernales because it did not pay enough for her to save any money. She then joined a group of labor recruits who had just entered the country *âba fil* and were being trucked by the CEA to Yerba Buena. The day she arrived there, knowing no one, she took up union with a *viejo*. When we spoke, she had not yet saved any money but hoped to earn enough to return to Haiti the following year.

As impoverished Haitians, female emigrants face many of the same forms of discrimination as male emigrants do, but, as women, they confront prejudices particular to their gender. In particular, popular opinion links female migration to the Dominican Republic with involvement in prostitution, and women risk a heavy social stigma when they decide to emigrate. Given that this prejudice exists, it seems likely that some of the women I interviewed may have been less than forthright about the reasons why they went to the sugar estates. Interviews with well-informed local people suggest that most Haitian women in Yerba Buena do *not* work as prostitutes. Even so, some of the women who denied having plans for finding employment in the Dominican Republic may have been trying to conceal having emigrated with the intent of working as a prostitute. Others, in saying that intolerable hardship drove them from home, may have been seeking an excuse for having gone to such a notorious destination for prostitutes as *Sêdomêg*. A woman who enters prostitution just because it pays better than any other work she can find will be condemned by most Haitian peasants. Yet very many would condone the choice if she faced hardship and had no other viable means of support (Lowenthal 1987, 81). For this reason, even if a woman had gone to the Dominican Republic with the idea of working as a prostitute, she might give lip service to her society's sexual mores by implying that she only went there out of desperation.[6]

It is quite possible that many Haitian women who have worked as prostitutes in the Dominican Republic knew exactly what they were getting into when they left home, and they understandably decline to admit this publicly. Even so, it is still questionable whether a Haitian woman often gains much in personal autonomy or economic power by working as a prostitute on the sugar estates. I doubt very much that moving to the sugar estates often gives a Haitian woman greater scope for independence and self-assertion than she would have at home. The circumstances of Haitian women's lives in the *bateyes* indicate that the deprivation and limited freedom of choice they describe are real. Prostitution may pay better than whatever other work they can find, but it rarely seems to give women in the *bateyes* either freedom from want or economic independence from men.

SURVIVAL STRATEGIES

Women generally travel to the Dominican Republic with one or more friends, relatives, or neighbors. Most often, upon arriving at their destination, these companions find the first-time migrant a place to sleep and help her find work in the *batey*—as a part-time domestic or a wayside vendor, for instance—with the understanding that she will contribute what she can toward household expenses. Of the 29 personal history interviewees, 19 (about 66 percent) stayed with friends or relatives upon arriving in the Dominican Republic.

Less commonly, a single woman will arrive in a *batey* where she has no friends or kinfolk. In this circumstance, the woman almost always takes up union with a cane worker immediately upon arrival. This happened to all seven of the interviewees who emigrated when single and did not settle with relatives or friends. It is therefore possible that the woman migrant seeks the aid of friends and kinfolk not just as a means of ensuring survival. She may also thereby seek to preserve some freedom to choose when, with whom, and under what terms she will take up union with a man.

Yet the presence of relatives in the Dominican Republic is by no means a guarantee of support. Eight of 29 interviewees (about 24 percent) experienced a breakdown of the kinship network in migrating. Four of these women did not know if or where they had relatives in the Dominican Republic. Three knew where their relatives were, but they were prevented from joining them when Dominican authorities took them to distant *bateyes* and/or prohibited them from traveling further to meet up with their people. One recent arrival had an uncle in the nearby mill town of Santa Ana, but for reasons unknown to me she had not gone to see him. Even when the migrant's social support network is not disrupted, there may be severe limits on what friends and relatives can do to help a recent arrival. Even a woman who settles initially with friends or kinfolk is likely to move out within a few months and take up residence with a man. Of the interviewees who entered the country when single, 85 percent (17 of 20) took a husband in the Dominican Republic within six months after first arriving, and an astonishing *95 percent* (19 of 20) did so within a year. Most of these unions last no longer than a year or two and may be for some women an interim survival strategy.[7]

Migrant women's tendency to enter union soon after arriving in the Dominican Republic has at least one lasting consequence, the conception of offspring. Of the 21 personal history interviewees who had spent more than one year abroad, 20 had borne children while in the Dominican Republic, and the remaining woman had adopted a child there. These children, more than anything else, represent migrant women's investment in the future. Few Haitian women in the *bateyes* of the Dominican Republic could endure their lives of hardship and insecurity without the helping hands of their offspring and foster children. In addition, the prospect of receiving support in their old age from their children reassures many about the future. In the squalor of the sugar estates, there is of course no guarantee that their children will remain nearby or will be able to provide support when it is needed. Yet the experiences of the oldest Haitian women in Yerba Buena confirm the wisdom of the Haitian aphorism, "Children are wealth" ("*Pitit se richès*").

The life story of Clémence Jean-Philippe, the oldest woman whose personal history I recorded, exemplifies a pattern I saw in the histories of several nonreturning emigrants, male and female. From the perspective of marital status and residence history, her adult life can be divided into two contrasting parts. In early adulthood, she went through several unions with men and frequently changed residences, but after the age of 25 she stayed with the same mate and did not move from Yerba Buena. Between the ages of 8 (in 1915) and 25 (in 1932), Clémence experienced a remarkable sequence of turning points:

(1) In 1915, her father died;
(2) In 1918, she, her mother, and three siblings fled into the Dominican Republic to escape combat around the town of Thomassique during the U.S. Marines' campaign to suppress the Cacos rebellion in the Plateau Central;

(3) In the Dominican Republic, her mother entered union again with a Haitian man;

(4) In 1919, they moved to Barahona, in southwestern Dominican Republic, where forest was being cleared and an irrigation system was being dug for a new, American-owned sugar plantation;

(5) In the early 1920s, the family returned to Haiti;

(6) In Haiti, Clémence took up her first conjugal union and gave birth to her first child;

(7) In 1926, she, her husband, and her child remigrated to the Dominican Republic;

(8) Soon after, she met by chance relatives of her stepfather, living in Yerba Buena and its neighboring *bateyes;*

(9) She, her husband, and her child moved to Yerba Buena, where her second child was born;

(10) In 1929, her husband left to join his relatives in the La Romana area, while she decided to stay near her stepfather's family;

(11) She had two short-lived unions and gave birth to her third child;

(12) In 1932, she entered union with her last husband, Edner.

Clémence and Edner had eight children together, six living into adulthood. At the time of my fieldwork, they occupied two sparely furnished rooms of a wooden company barracks. Through frugal living and hard work, they had come to own a few head of cattle, and they lived relatively securely with the help of their children. A year earlier, Edner had delegated care of his livestock to his sons, but Clémence, in her seventy-eighth year, still made sweets for sale in the *batey.* Their door was almost always open to any of their many grandchildren who might be hungry. In my latest visit to Yerba Buena, I was saddened to learn that Clémence and Edner had died in 1991, he having passed on only a few months before she.

The second oldest woman in my interviews, Soisbénie Denis, left the town of Thiotte, in southeastern Haiti, in 1928 at age 17 with her first child to escape an abusive husband and to join her mother and older sister in the Dominican town of Elías Piña. Since the mid-1930s, she has lived in Yerba Buena or nearby *bateyes.* She reports having been in four unions between 1924 and the mid-1950s, but she has gone through much longer periods than Clémence without a husband.

Her three surviving offspring, two daughters, then a son, were born of different fathers at intervals of several years. After breaking up with her last husband, Soisbénie supported herself and her son with the help of her two grown daughters. Together, they engaged in petty commerce and cultivated tiny, rain-fed gardens on the margins of company cane fields.

Soisbénie's mother and older sister died several years ago, and her oldest daughter died recently. At the time we spoke, her son supported her out of his relatively high wages as a worker on the estate's railroad system. Yet she still earned her own money, in spite of frail health and failing eyesight, by buying charcoal wholesale and retailing it from her doorstep.

When they were young, Clémence and Soisbénie experienced upheavals and hardships much like those which women migrants go through today. In later life, by contrast, the support of their children and grandchildren has given these women a level of income security greater than they ever knew during their most active years. It would be an exaggeration to say that raising offspring from infancy to productive adulthood changes migrant women's tales of woe into success stories. Yet, for many, this may be one of the few sources of hope that remains intact after time in the *batey*.

THE WOMEN WHO STAY AT HOME

Since the 1970s, the situation of women who stay at home in systems of predominantly male labor migration has received increased scholarly attention. Most students of the issue have emphasized the impoverishment, loneliness, and extra drudgery women may suffer in the absence of their intimate partners (Mueller 1977; Sibisi 1977; Gordon 1981; Brown 1983; Islam and Ahmad 1984; Jetley 1984; Bernstein 1985; Griffith 1985; Unesco 1985; Savané 1986). Some have followed the lead of Schapera (1941, 279), who recognized the existence of these negative effects but suggested also that men's absence in migration could in some ways enhance female autonomy (Abbott 1976; Hay 1976; Sudarkasa 1977; Hayano 1979; Taylor 1984). Others have pointed out that the protracted absence of a man from the household is not universally regarded as unusual, and they have concluded that women experience no marked improvement or decline in status as a result of it (Moses 1977; Flores 1984; Paranakian 1984; Colfer 1985). Colin Murray (1981, chap. 7) stands out for having emphasized that the personal consequences of male labor migration for women in Lesotho are not uniform but vary from enhanced economic security to utter destitution. Sharp (1987) and Spiegel (1987) in separate essays and together (Sharp and Spiegel 1990) have elaborated the implications of Murray's conclusions in relation to women's ways of coping with irregular receipt of income from the absent worker.

These studies show that the effects of male labor migration on women's status vary considerably, worldwide and within particular societies. All these studies also share a recognition that the man who emigrates and the woman who stays at home may experience emigration and return differently. This is not just because one moves and the other stays at home, but because men's and women's interests do not always coincide.

More recently, there has been a growing recognition that many earlier analyses of domestic relations, including but not limited to those in migration studies, have been perhaps too quick to identify women's sphere of interests with the household. For example, the concept of "household strategy" of migration has drawn needed attention to gender relations but may have helped conceal the importance of women's ties to people outside the household. In a manner prefigured by anthropological critiques of the notion that the family household is a universal human institution (e.g., Fortes 1949; R. T. Smith 1956; Goody 1958; Solien 1960; M. G. Smith 1962), a new wave of domestic analysis has asked if it is accurate to assume that the household is *"the* unit . . . within which the reproduction of human labor, or of the individual, is assured" (Wong 1984, 56; also Guyer 1981; Sanjek 1982; Harris 1984; Collins 1986; Dwyer and Bruce 1988).

These questions are highly pertinent to the study of rural Haitian domestic relations. In rural Haiti, neither common ownership of property nor collective production is the basis of household cohesion. It is rare for an able adult to submerge his or her individual economic assets completely into joint funds of household production or consumption. Household incomes are not so much produced through collective effort as pooled from the contributions of individual members, out of their own independently managed funds. Conjugal partners who "live well" together consult each other on important financial decisions and may hold property jointly. But almost always husband and wife also maintain personal discretionary funds, and each retains the prerogative to earn and to keep much of his or her own income. Just as importantly, mobilizing personal networks of cooperation that reach beyond the boundaries of the household is essential to success in both men's specialty, farm management, and women's specialty, petty commerce.[8]

All this might be read—not inaccurately—as evidence of a certain kind of individualism. Yet these patterns of behavior also reflect what Lowenthal (1987, 273) has called a "de-emphasis of the conjugal bond in favor of that linking each parent, separately, to their respective progeny." This is one variant of the primacy of the consanguineal over the affinal tie in domestic relations observed throughout the Caribbean (Price 1971). The rural Haitian household might aptly be characterized as an intersection of individual survival strategies. Yet these strategies are not just formulated according to individual needs and preferences. They generally also take into account the welfare of the individual's parents, siblings, offspring, and other consanguines.

That said, it may seem odd that I have chosen to focus on the wives and children who stay at home, rather than giving equal attention to the effects of male emigration on the migrants' mothers, sisters, and other female kin. The impact of emigration on migrants' wives at home is obviously only one dimension of the consequences of separation for women in rural southeastern Haiti. Yet, without denying the importance of women's ties to emigrants as mothers, sisters, and daughters, there is reason to believe that when a man goes to the Dominican Republic, it may often change his wife's life more significantly than it changes the lives of his other female kin. This may be understood partly in terms of the differing repercussions of labor circulation for single and married men. The young, unmarried man bears the risks and reaps the rewards of migration primarily as an individual. His parents, siblings, and other relatives at home rarely expect him to bring them much money when he comes home. It is of little consequence to them whether he succeeds or fails in meeting his savings goals. What matters most to them is that he returns home well. For the married man, by contrast, failure in the Dominican Republic can easily destabilize his conjugal household in Haiti. Women's personal histories suggest that it is not uncommon for unions to dissolve after the migrant husband returns home penniless or fails to return at all. Conversely, if the migrant brings home money, any assets he may acquire out of his migrant savings are regarded as the joint property of both spouses, partly out of recognition of the woman's efforts to sustain the household in the migrant's absence.

Labor circulation may also bring about short-term changes in conjugal relations not often otherwise seen in rural Haiti. Even as it separates spouses, male emigration commonly leads the woman who stays at home to intensify her labor. More importantly, it may oblige her to surrender some of her own income-generating activities in order to manage her absent husband's agricultural holdings. Labor circulation, in common with more direct and enduring forms of capitalist incorporation, often leads thus to greater economic interdependence between spouses. This increased economic dependence may be one reason why many women come to oppose emigration openly.

"IT WAS I, A WOMAN, WHO HOED THE LAND"

In rural Haiti, even a child can summarize what is men's work and what is women's, by saying, "Men farm, and women do the marketing." This is a broad generalization, to which many exceptions apply, but it has the merit of making it clear that men's and women's conventional tasks are distinct but for the most part complementary. In rural Haitians' eyes, the relationship of husband and wife provides the ideal model of complementarity between the sexes, in which a man cultivates gardens for his wife, and a woman takes her husband's garden produce to market.

Rural Haitian men consider a whole range of tasks to be "women's work" and as such regard these tasks as quite simply beneath their dignity as adult males. Provision marketing, cleaning house, doing laundry, ironing, and cooking are all activities to which men are averse and for which they turn to their mothers, wives, daughters, or other kinswomen (Lowenthal 1984, 31, n. 8 and 32, n. 10). A woman, by contrast, through participation in Haiti's internal marketing system, can potentially earn a living entirely without the support of a man. According to Murray and Álvarez (1975, 121), "The internal market system . . . constitutes in effect a separate status system within which a woman can plan to 'move up in the world' somewhat independently of the particular economic position of her husband in their home community. . . . A woman is judged socially (and hence comes to judge herself) by the criterion of success in trade."

Besides the enhanced self-esteem and social status that may come through success in trade, a Haitian woman is often motivated to earn her own income in order to improve her household's standard of living and to further her children's schooling. Given the general poverty of rural Haiti, it is hardly surprising that the support a man offers his conjugal household often falls short of or scarcely surpasses household subsistence minima. If one adds to this the adaptiveness of economic autonomy in an environment of economic uncertainty and frequent marital instability, it is easy to see why a Haitian woman might be strongly motivated to maintain an independent source of income. If her union breaks up or if her husband becomes disabled, dies, or disappears, a woman may have to adapt quickly or else suffer a decline in her standard of living. By maintaining a fund of capital in trade, she acts to secure a potential means of subsisting independently of a man, if she so needs or desires.

A woman can realize the full degree of autonomy allowed her by Haitian society only if she develops her *own* means of earning an income apart from daily management of household finances (Lowenthal 1984, 19). Rural women's main avenue of independent economic attainment is itinerant trade (i.e., buying goods in one marketplace and selling them in another in order to profit from price discrepancies between locations). Not every woman can be a full-time trader: "full-time, relatively large-scale, professional market women (resellers or travelling intermediaries) are specialists, and their numbers are limited" (Lowenthal 1987, 55). Yet, in spite of this, many women still find it possible to sustain their households through trade. Lowenthal (1984, 31–32, n. 9) observes, "A significant minority of women in their thirties and forties deliberately opt out of the conjugal system . . . , either temporarily or entirely. They depend upon the labor of their adolescent sons, or upon wage labor, for the pursuit of limited agricultural production and devote their own time to commercial marketing activities. . . . They forego the kinds of reciprocity that conjugality entails in favor of personal independence and, when successful, are usually lauded by most other women for their achievement."

Another kind of household headed by single women is also common in the Cayes-Jacmel and Cap Rouge areas, that in which a migrant's wife temporarily assumes sole leadership in her husband's absence. Between October 1986 and March 1987, about 9 percent of men in conjugal union in the *katye* of Rocheteau and Cabrouette (6 of 69) departed on seasonal trips to the Dominican Republic. Five of the six wives left at home temporarily assumed leadership of their households in their husbands' absence. The sixth and youngest (age 22) remained in her in-laws' household when her husband departed. The retrospective testimony of 24 migrants' wives suggests that the woman assumes temporary leadership of the household in over 90 percent of married men's migration voyages. Unlike the female heads of households Lowenthal describes, the wives of absent *Sêdomêg* men often have neither a resident adult male at home to till the fields nor access to enough capital to set up a full-time trading venture. Migrants' wives generally attempt to sustain prior levels of agricultural production, rather than fall back on their trading skills, to hold their households together until their husbands return.

In her study of the impact of seasonal labor migration on household production in southern Peru, Collins (1988, 27) observes, "Seasonal absence is a potential problem when . . . its scheduling is beyond the control of those who understand (or respect) the demands of local production." Just so, in southeastern Haiti, coping with the seasonal absence of male heads of household can be difficult for the women who stay at home, because the spring planting season there (mid-January to mid-April) coincides with the sugarcane harvest in the Dominican Republic (December to June). To prepare their fields for planting, some men wait until March, April, or May before leaving for the Dominican Republic.[9] Yet, much more commonly, men leave in November or December, and their wives shoulder the bulk of the farm work. Of 39 men who had gone to the Dominican Republic at least once after establishing a conjugal union in Haiti, only 5 (about 13 percent) said that they customarily turned over management of their agricultural holdings to kinsmen while they were gone. The rest left farm management in their wives' hands.

Haitianist ethnographers disagree about the quantity of agricultural labor that women generally do (G. F. Murray 1977, 255). Yet most agree that women customarily perform relatively "light" tasks—sowing, harvesting, and processing—and rarely do the heaviest field labor, such as clearing weed-choked ground with a heavy-handled hoe or breaking up the soil with a pick (A. Métraux 1951, 88; R. Métraux 1952, 5; G. F. Murray 1977, 256–59; Smucker 1982, 116; Lowenthal 1987, 51). In preparing a field for planting, the underbrush is felled with hoes and machetes, left to dry, and then burned. Following the first heavy rains, the earth is broken with picks and hoes. Even though women may be seen at work in all these tasks, preparing the fields for planting is considered men's work. With the exception of building yam mounds, an exclusively male task, women's participation increases with each successive stage of cultivation: planting, weeding, harvesting, and processing. With the exception of a few cash crops, like coffee, the final step in the cropping cycle, merchandising the produce, is handled exclusively by women. Generally speaking, then, the control of garden produce falls to women as men's gardens mature (Lowenthal 1984, 18).

I did not record how much female labor went into each farm task. Yet my daily observation of work in the Cayes-Jacmel and Cap Rouge areas between late January and the end of March 1987 partly supports and partly contradicts this picture of Haitian women's participation in agriculture. Single female heads of household without exception recruit male assistance in the heaviest tasks of preparing fields for planting. These are tasks that even highly experienced farmers are loath to do alone. Yet, in the absence of a suitable man, women of the Cayes-Jacmel and Cap Rouge areas quite commonly maintain a continuous and intensive presence in the cultivation of the land. Definitive conclusions must await quantitative and comparative study. I can only hypothesize that the high prevalence of male seasonal emigration in southeastern Haiti may oblige many, if not most, women there to manage a relatively substantial agricultural holding at some point in their lives. Sidney Mintz (personal correspondence) suggests that this degree of participation in agriculture, far though it may be from women's experiences in other parts of Haiti, may well have typified the women "left behind" by male labor migration throughout the Caribbean during the late nineteenth and early twentieth centuries.

Often, the same low farm surpluses and lack of credit for agriculture that stimulate seasonal emigration in the first place also make it difficult for the woman who stays at home to raise enough money to hire farm labor. The typical migrant is too poor to leave anything by way of material assistance for his family besides the crops standing in his gardens for harvest from October through January. And the *bracero* rarely remits money to people at home, unless he stays on in the Dominican Republic beyond the end of the cane harvest.

Migrants' wives overcome much of their labor deficits not by hiring labor but through nonmonetary channels of recruitment. The relationships of reciprocal support that a woman builds in her roles as mother, household manager, and trader generally serve her well if and when it comes time for her to head her household singly. Solidarity between kinswomen is particularly instrumental to the survival of the migrant household. While a woman is at work in her household's gardens, female relatives and older children, especially daughters, take on many of the tasks of housekeeping, minding the children, and provision marketing in her stead.

The woman who stays at home fares less well in securing direct cooperation in farm labor. It is not that a woman is necessarily less capable than a man of recruiting unpaid farm labor from outside the household. By exchanging labor reciprocally and receiving free assistance from relatives and neighbors, the woman who stays at home is at least able to find help in the heaviest tasks of preparing her household's fields for planting. Even so, the woman who stays at home generally bears a much increased load of drudgery and stress as a result of taking on management of her absent husband's agricultural holdings. Interviews suggest that, in most migrant households, the woman personally shoulders the bulk of the garden labor and accepts a decline in farm output as an inevitable consequence of her husband's emigration. One woman lamented, "After the rocks take over the land completely, there is little you can do about it. You will not find anyone to lift the rocks for you, so it is you who must lift them yourself. Well, where you cannot lift a rock, you dig out a little bit of ground beside it, and put a little plant there. But a garden planted like that will not give much food in the end." "You do what you can," said another woman, "but your work does not yield as much as a man's work."

Interviews with migrants' wives also indicated that time conflicts between agriculture and domestic responsibilities cannot always be resolved by entrusting one or the other to another responsible person. An elderly woman, whose husband had made 16 seasonal voyages to the Dominican Republic, recalled, "The hardship (*mizè*) I went through when my husband was not there! It was I, a woman, who hoed the land. Before I went [to work in the gardens], I had to send the children to school. It was only when they went to school at seven o'clock that I could go to work, quite late. [After that late start,] the sun ate me up by midday there. Well, the day did not end with work in the gardens. When I left work, I had to feed the livestock, then find food for the children. They were not easy times, those."

In spite of the limitations on women's farm productivity, the gardens women plant sometimes save their households from starvation or from the humiliation of defaulting on a loan when their husbands fail to bring back money from the Dominican Republic. The same woman I quote immediately above recalled this about the aftermath of an unsuccessful voyage: "Well, when the mister [her husband] returned [from the Dominican Republic], he said he had injured his thumb and had not worked. He spent three months [there] without working. When he returned, the little work I, a woman, did, beat his work 10 times over! The little penny he brought home was not enough to pay back the people from whom he had borrowed money [to make the voyage]. In the end, hunger killed us all, but we had to sell what little grain we had, the little grain *I produced,* so that they would not take him before the law to make him repay the money."

When a woman takes on responsibility for managing her husband's agricultural holdings, she may also be insuring herself and her children against the risk that her husband will not return from the Dominican Republic. If a woman surrenders management of her husband's fields to one of his kinsmen, and her husband then fails to return, it may later be impossible for her to reclaim rights to that land for any children she has had with the missing man. Granted, most abandoned wives soon effectively renounce any claim to their missing husbands' land by marrying again or leaving the area with their children. Yet the case of one Rocheteau woman, Yolette Louis, twice abandoned by husbands who failed to return from the Dominican Republic, suggests that a woman may retain control of her absent husband's land and make a living on it on her own. Since Yolette's second husband left Haiti in the early 1970s, she has made a living by tending cattle for her neighbors and farming the land he left in her hands. Her neighbors regard her as particularly unlucky because she also lost twin brothers and her two sons to *Sêdomêg.* Her only remaining relatives are a single daughter and two grandchildren, who have a house in her yard. Hers is an exceptional case, but the fact that her daughter now stands to inherit her absent father's land may be traced to Yolette having managed that land in his absence.

Given the increased hardships they endure while their husbands are away, it is not surprising that many women talk about migration with bitterness. But there may be more to women's complaints than a demand that their double workday, in the home and gardens, be recognized as unfair. Women may also perceive that the high risk of failure in migration suits neither their households' income security nor their own economic autonomy, and they may question the value of their husbands' migrations accordingly.

THE RISKS AND REWARDS OF MIGRATION

Some women express the opinion that the rewards they get from their husbands' emigration do not justify the deprivation, risk, and extra labor they endure while their husbands are absent. As one Rocheteau woman concluded, "There were times when, instead of having gone to *Sêdomêg*, better he would have stayed here with me. When he left for *Sêdomêg*, he put me in a lot of problems. Better, then, that he had stayed, hoed his fields, made a garden for me. Even if you do not get a lot from it [the garden], God will not leave you without anything to live on out of it."

Women's apprehensions about migration may be occasioned not just by risk. They may also reflect concerns about how male emigration affects a woman's independent remunerative employment. A woman's responsibility for managing her husband's agricultural holdings in his absence is a direct impediment to participating in trade. As Gerald Murray (1977, 257) observes, "The full-time pursuit of . . . trading activities is incompatible with full-time tending of gardens." "This incompatibility," he explains, "stems on the one hand from competing time demands," and, even more significantly, from "the physical impossibility of being in two *places* at once. For trade entails not only a full commitment of time, but also extended *absenteeism*."

In this situation, if a woman's husband fails to clear a surplus from his migratory voyages, she effectively loses twice. First, her extra labor will have been spent in vain. Second, she will have forgone the opportunity to enhance her own independent means of earning an income through trade. It is therefore perhaps not surprising that many women come to question the wisdom of surrendering control over their economic fates even temporarily to their conjugal partners. One such woman, wife of a four-time seasonal migrant, recalled this about her husband's *Sêdomêg* money:

> He did not bring anything from *Sêdomêg* for *me* [*Li pa't pòt âyê sòt Sêdomêg pu mwê-mêm*]! If he had worked well, he would come [home], and say to his wife, "Here is what I made, here is what I brought for you." But he said *Sêdomêg* was not good for him.
>
> He picked himself up, and returned [to *Sêdomêg*] again, but it was always the same thing. Every voyage he made, he had a problem, and did not bring anything from *Sêdomêg* for *me*. I always went through hardships (*pase mizè*) here with the children when he went to *Sêdomêg*. He said *Sêdomêg* was not good for him again, and he put *Sêdomêg* to rest [i.e., ceased migrating]. He did not go again.
>
> After he did not go again, I see things are better for me, because he works, the children eat, I buy the food I need in the market. You see? He works, the children eat, I eat, too.

This woman's apprehensions about migration's risks are intertwined with concern about its all-too-frequent failure to supply the woman who stays at home with assets she can call her own. This may not be surprising in the light of earlier ethnographers' frequent indications that security and autonomy are linked goals for women in rural Haiti. My point is simply that men's seasonal migrations suit neither of these goals optimally and may often threaten both.

Statements of the kind I have quoted above suggest that many of the women who stay at home neither follow their husbands' lead unquestioningly nor hesitate to voice opposition to their husbands' emigration plans. Even so, it would be a distortion to suggest that women explicitly evaluate the real outcomes of migration against an ideal standard of equality. On the contrary, women's testimonies consistently project pragmatic assessments of migration's risks and rewards. No woman whose husband has successfully become a better provider on the basis of *Sêdomêg* money voices resentments about his having had a greater hand than she in steering the process that produced this good result. Also, even though it is the migrant's prerogative to decide how his savings will be put to use, a man who "lives well" with his wife will consult her about how he should invest any surplus. And it is recognized that a woman's domestic labor entitles her to joint ownership of any income-producing assets her husband might acquire out of his *Sêdomêg* money.

I would also caution against drawing overly gloomy conclusions about the impact of seasonal Dominican migration on relations of power in the rural Haitian household. Male labor migration creates few, if any, lasting relations of dependence among women in rural Haiti, unlike what happens, say, to wives of perennially absent migrants in South Africa, whose links within the household and roles in the general economy are of a different order.[10] After their husbands settle into nonmigratory lifestyles, "stay-at-homes" generally seem no less capable than other women of taking up itinerant trade and other kinds of independent commerce.

It is widely understood in feminist studies that economic independence for some women in society does not signify economic independence for all. In Haiti, for every woman who works full-time in trade, there is another who stays at home, cleans house, does the laundry, manages the domestic budget, and cares for the children. One lesson to be drawn from the experiences of Haitian women on the sugar estates of the Dominican Republic is that female emigration is not always a road to greater participation in the economic leadership roles open to women in Haiti. Whether they return to their consanguineal households in Haiti or form conjugal households in the

Dominican Republic, the women who go to the sugar estates rarely shed female support roles. Perhaps more importantly, the fact that most migrant women remain at the bottom of the economic heap after they go to the Dominican Republic suggests that they achieve only a very limited "independence" by emigrating. The hardship, injustice, and physical and economic insecurity they experience in the Dominican Republic show that this limited independence is often gained only at a high personal cost.

This condition probably differs little from that of the mainstream of working women in other poor countries of the tropics. Yet it does contrast with the relative autonomy generally understood to characterize the economic position of women in rural Haiti. Granted, the desperate situation of the relatively few women who emigrate to the sugar estates is not a valid indicator of the condition of women in rural Haiti generally. There is little doubt that Haitian society affords women opportunities for personal independence unsurpassed by any other Latin American society. But the experiences of this small emigrant minority are a reminder that, in Haiti, a woman, like a man, needs the support of others and access to capital before she can reach for the opportunities for economic attainment Haitian culture allows her.

The women who stay at home, almost always without the aid of remittances, bear a burden of deprivation, risk, and increased labor fully comparable to that of the male emigrant. For both the men who emigrate and the women and children who stay at home, labor circulation promises gain in the medium to long term, at the price of increased drudgery and deprivation in the short term. Male labor migration often brings tangible benefits to all household members: it subsidizes consumption and may expand assets for generating future incomes. Yet, to many women, the risks and hardships associated with labor circulation seem doubly problematic because their husbands' voyages often contribute little or nothing toward women's long-term goal of maintaining their own independent means of earning a living.

Depending on whose interests in the household or family are furthered and whose are sidetracked, labor circulation may take on different meanings for different individuals. When the emigrant's absence compels stay-at-homes to neglect their own independent remunerative activities, emigration may become not just a strategy of survival but a source of conflict in the household. Women's own evaluations of their husbands' migrations reflect this contradictory reality. Nearly all women agree that men emigrate not out of choice but out of economic necessity. But, after years of struggling seasonally to maintain their households in their husbands' absence, several seem to have concluded that migration no longer serves their own interests, and they oppose it openly.

7

Viejos and Congoses

In this chapter, I attempt to shed light on why some Haitian emigrants stay indefinitely in the Dominican Republic—"become *viejo*," as Haitians put it—rather than returning shortly, as the majority do, to Haiti. I also briefly assess how nonreturning emigrants cope (and commonly fail to cope) with poverty and economic insecurity on the sugar estates of the Dominican Republic.

As background to these concerns, it is first necessary to compare the "auspices" of emigration to the sugar estates with those of Haiti's rural-urban and overseas migration streams. I follow Tilly and Brown (1967, 142) in defining the auspices of migration to mean "the social structures which establish relationships between the migrant and the receiving community before he moves. We may say that an individual migrates under the auspices of kinship when his principal connections with the city of destination are through kinsmen, even if he comes desperately seeking a job. Likewise, we may say that he migrates under the auspices of work when the labor market or a particular firm provides the main organized relationship to the new community, even if he also has kinfolk there. Of course, he may migrate under several auspices at once, or under none at all." A thorough comparison of the behavior that typifies each group of migrants is not possible here, because I did not do systematic fieldwork with rural-urban migrants or overseas emigrants and their kinfolk in Haiti. The contrasts between these groups are many, and they merit more careful description and analysis than I am capable of at present. My field observations may even so be compared with the published findings of social researchers who have done fieldwork with Haitian migrants in North America and in Haitian cities. This comparison suggests that, as rural Haitians take divergent paths of geographical mobility, their patterns of behavior also tend to differ. Indeed, if one did not know they shared similar rural roots, one might think that the *braceros* held different family and community values than their neighbors who emigrate to the city or to countries *lòt bò lâmè*. That is, one might wrongly conclude that the *braceros* were "individualists," and the other migrants, "communitarians."

NETWORKS OF SOLIDARITY OF HAITIAN RURAL-URBAN MIGRANTS AND OVERSEAS EMIGRANTS

Several studies of Haitian rural-urban migrants and emigrants overseas show that these people commonly collaborate closely with people from home in relocating to and finding lodging and employment in their places of destination. These studies also document that the migrants, once resettled, dedicate much effort to enhancing the welfare of kith and kin in home and host areas. This behavior is fully consistent with the "group-oriented strategies" that ethnographers have observed among rural emigrants elsewhere around the world.[1]

Even though the initial decision to emigrate may be made most often by the migrant him/herself (Ahlers 1979, 86), it is perhaps correct to say that emigration to the city or to a country *lòt bò lâmè* is from its inception a "family project" (Laguerre 1978, 468–69). Usually, before an individual can emigrate, his or her decision "must receive the approval of other members of the extended family" (Laguerre 1984, 36). Members of the migrant's family also commonly mobilize far-flung ties of reciprocity to raise money for the project and to spread the risk of failure.[2]

Once at his or her destination, the migrant and the household of origin keep in frequent contact through letters, audio and video cassettes, and remittances. Migrants and people at home, in spite of geographical distance, remain active participants in each other's lives (Saint-Louis 1988; Charles 1990; Glick-Schiller and Fouron 1990). As Karen Richman observes concerning emigrants to North America from the Léogâne area of Haiti, "It was not uncommon for an emigrant to support children, spouse, parents, stepparents, siblings, half-siblings, nieces, and nephews. Single migrating men were expected to pool their resources with that of their parents. An often talked about issue was how to keep young men *lòt bò* from getting involved with foreign women who might compete with the family for rights to his wages. Competition between parents and spouses over emigrants' remittances provided motivations for much of the maneuvering and disputes to which I was privy. In one instance, the *chef de section* intervened to redistribute a remittance" (personal correspondence, 5 December 1989).[3] The migrant may also seek to fulfill obligations to people at home by sponsoring the migration of relatives to join him or her in the place of destination (Glick 1975; Locher 1978; Laguerre 1978; Laguerre 1984; Ahlers 1979; Buchanan 1980; Woldemikael 1980; Fjellman and Gladwin 1985).

The migrant's initial contacts in urban Haiti and countries *lòt bò lâmè* are most commonly kinfolk and fellow villagers. "Most Haitian households [in New York]," Laguerre (1984, 78) observes, "have included a friend or distant relative at some time during their history." Relatives and friends in places of destination not only help the migrant materially. They also provide psychological support and help the migrant to find his or her way around the unfamiliar surroundings of the host area. When the time comes to strike out on his/her own, the migrant not surprisingly tends to take up residence somewhere near these original contacts. As this process is repeated, it gives rise to clusters of interdependent migrant households and, on a larger scale, promotes the formation of Haitian ethnic neighborhoods (Glick 1975; Locher 1978; Ahlers 1979; D. I. Marshall 1979; Buchanan 1980; Woldemikael 1980; Laguerre 1984).

The Social Adaptations of Haitian Cane Workers in the Dominican Republic

A strikingly different picture emerges from examining the social adaptations of the Haitian *braceros*. With a Haitian population as large as 200,000 to 400,000 in the Dominican Republic, it might be expected that ties with kin and countryfolk would be a major mechanism whereby Haitians relocated to the neighboring country. Yet, upon arriving for the first time in the Dominican Republic, less than 5 percent of the migrants and returnees I interviewed joined relatives and friends who already lived on the sugar estates. And reliance on kin and fellow villagers who reside in the Dominican Republic does not seem to increase much with subsequent voyages. As noted in chapter 6, women more often than men move to the Dominican Republic under auspices of kinship and friendship. Yet it should be recalled that of every 10 migrants to the sugar estates only 1 is a woman. Therefore, in spite of the relatively high percentage of women who settle with people from home upon arriving in the Dominican Republic, the fraction of the total migrant population that relocates via ties with kin and countryfolk is small, perhaps less than 10 percent.

Tangled lines of communication may go part way toward explaining this low level of migration via ties with fellow countryfolk. Excepting certain veteran *braceros* who return to the same *batey* year after year, the migrant generally does not know ahead of time where he will work in the Dominican Republic. Without postal facilities or telephone within easy reach, the recent arrival usually has no way of rapidly notifying people in Haiti or relatives in the Dominican Republic of where he has taken residence. Nor is a messenger often available to carry a message home. Even when a neighbor is heading back to the home area, the migrant commonly has no money to spare and may feel too ashamed to send a message without any money for his people at home. In short, conditions for renewing contact with relatives in Haiti are generally not favorable until the end-of-harvest bonus comes through and the migrants begin returning to Haiti.

On the Dominican side of the border, Haitian men are probably not so much barred from joining their contacts as reluctant to seek out the support of relatives, fellow villagers, and friends who may already be on the sugar estates. The male migrant often knows the names of the *bateyes* and towns where he might find kinfolk, fellow villagers, and previous acquaintances who are long-time residents of the Dominican Republic. He may even visit some of these people occasionally. Yet he generally chooses not to take up residence with these contacts after entering the Dominican Republic. Instead, the male migrant usually prefers to stick with the companions with whom he left Haiti. This loyalty to travel companions may have much to do with Haitian cane workers' extreme dependence on the sugar companies and their subordinate position in Dominican society.

In most Third World migrations, housing and employment are the areas of material concern where kin and fellow countryfolk can do most to help the newly arrived migrant. On the sugar estates, by contrast, these are areas in which the migrants have quite limited freedom of maneuver. Haitians in the *bateyes*, of course, greet visiting relatives with open arms. But with scarcely enough room to lodge their own immediate families, and with few income-generating activities of their own in which to employ new arrivals, they rarely take the initiative to recruit relatives or friends from home to join them on the sugar estates. Conversely, the newly arrived Haitian man knows he is unlikely to find either cheaper housing or better-paid employment through relatives than he would get on his own from the sugar companies. The vast majority of Haitians who reside permanently on the estates inhabit the same kind of dilapidated, overcrowded barracks as those in which the CEA houses the seasonal migrants, free of charge. A lack of alternative employment in and around the sugar estates makes it difficult also to find a newly arrived kinsman remunerative work, other than in the cane fields. This is especially true of the estates of the southeast, where sugarcane dominates the landscape. On the Santa Ana estate, the company holds a grip on employment that verges on absolute monopoly. Over 90 percent (176 of 192) of all economically active men in the *batey* of Yerba Buena derive most of their yearly income from working for the CEA. Among Haitian men, the level of dependence is more pronounced. And in the smaller *bateyes satélites*, the company's domination is even more extreme.

It may also be significant that Haitian seasonal migrants regard the material deprivation they experience in the Dominican Republic as a source of shame. Even though they might speak freely of their hardships after returning to Haiti, I sense that few, if any, migrants would want many kinfolk and fellow villagers to witness their plight. The days when they lack the money or time to prepare a hot meal are not the ones they would want people from home to see. The *braceros* largely limit their visits with nearby friends and relatives to payday weekends, when they can put a good face on their situation by taking a Sunday afternoon off, donning their good clothes, and perhaps sharing out salty, fried snacks and a small bottle of rum.

The first one or two evenings after a new group of *braceros* arrives in the *batey*, their barracks are crowded with *batey* residents. *Viejos* go there seeking news about their home places in Haiti, other local men go around to check out any women in the group, and other residents just drop by to join the crowd. After this, few permanent residents of the *batey* set foot often in the *braceros'* barracks, which they say are too filthy and crowded to linger around in their leisure hours. The temporary residence of the *braceros* is an obstacle to establishing relations of trust with permanent residents. Most residents think there is little point in striking up friendships with people who, as one Dominican woman put it, "may get up and go from one day to the next." *Batey* residents generally also hold the opinion that it is not they but the company which should materially assist the seasonal migrants it brings to the area. The *braceros* have the further disadvantage of arriving at the end of the long dead season on the sugar estates, when most *batey* residents are scarcely able to provide enough nourishment for themselves, let alone share what they have with dozens of temporary workers. Aside from regular but brief contacts at work, *braceros* generally mix with *batey* residents only by seeking out the company of *viejos* in the *viejos'* own quarters. These contacts with *batey* people, limited as they are, may be enough to convince the migrant to try to return to the same *batey* in subsequent voyages, even if it means embarking on a long and possibly futile journey from another *batey* to which company officials have transported him. Yet most of the voluntary recruits whom I interviewed in Yerba Buena and its surrounding *bateyes* had never resided there in any previous year.

The isolation of the *bracero* extends to the formal organizations established to protect workers' rights. The ranks of the CEA's dominant labor unions exclude all cane cutters, regardless of nationality (Murphy 1986, 362–63). On the CEA estates, the seasonal migrant instead has many of his dealings with the company hierarchy through a company employee called the *capataz de braceros* (*bracero* foreman).[4] In spite of being called a foreman, the *capataz de braceros* does not regularly supervise work. He is instead responsible for an unspecified range of tasks involved in maintaining discipline among the seasonal migrants. For example, he is expected to do what he can to prevent his recruits from abandoning the *batey*, and he is often called upon to persuade the *braceros* to work on Sunday or do other unwelcome tasks the bosses deem necessary. In return, Haitian *capataces de braceros* may communicate *braceros'* complaints and requests to the bosses, and otherwise function as the seasonal migrants' main avenue of contact with company officials above the level of workplace foremen. Given how deeply involved the *capataz de braceros* is in the company's practices of labor control, it is perhaps surprising that joking and good-humored banter typifies relations between a *capataz* and "his *congoses*." Often, the relationship between *capataz* and *bracero* takes an aspect of informal patronage. In return for a small gratuity, for instance, the *capataz* may intercede with a higher-ranking foreman, the *capataz de corte*, to secure an assignment to a "good" field of cane for one of his recruits. Yet no one holds any illusions about where the *capataz's* ultimate loyalty lies. When push comes to shove, he will favor the interests of his employer, the sugar company.

In the face of their isolation on the sugar estates, the only source of support most *braceros* have is one another. When in need of assistance, the *bracero* generally turns to travel and work companions, rather than soliciting aid from host country employers or any relatives or fellow villagers who might live on the sugar estates. Next to his own strength and resolve, it is his peers who provide the *bracero* with his strongest guarantee of survival on Dominican soil.

PEER-BASED NETWORKS AMONG SEASONAL MIGRANTS TO THE SUGAR ESTATES

More than once, in the Cayes-Jacmel and Cap Rouge areas, I witnessed a local person inquire about the health or whereabouts of a neighbor, only to be surprised to learn that a member of the household had left for *Sêdomêg*. A man who is contemplating a voyage to the Dominican Republic almost always keeps his intention to leave a secret. The emigrant will reveal his travel plans to at most a handful of trusted relatives and friends. Men keep this veil of secrecy around their travel plans to protect themselves from possible outside interference. Because undocumented passage across the border is officially prohibited, an enemy who knows the migrant's intended date and route of departure might bring the local authorities down on him. As a result, relatives and friends are an irreplaceable source of information for the first-time migrant. It is only from them that the neophyte can learn about good routes to follow into the Dominican Republic and obtain the names of people who may be of assistance along the way. It is most often with a sibling, a cousin, an uncle, or another close relative who has already been to the Dominican Republic that a young man will make his first migration voyage. Subsequent trips are less often made with relatives because the migrant may come to find other men more compatible as roommates and work partners.

Travel companions generally remain together for at least part of the harvest, and often they stay together until they return to Haiti. At times, companions are picked up along the way. There seems to be more trust between fellow villagers than between companions who come from different places in Haiti. In spite of this, Haitians in Yerba Buena and its surrounding *bateyes* do not congregate with large numbers of fellow villagers, as happens commonly in other Third World migrations. Most migrants leave their places of origin in Haiti in small groups, which travel independently and without knowledge of the plans of others. Fellow villagers tend thus to be scattered among *bateyes* around the country. It is only when a large group of men is recruited at the same time and place in Haiti that many fellow villagers may arrive together in the same *batey*.

Generally, the men who share a room buy food together and take turns cooking meals, which saves time and money. One group of five men even made a habit of giving their money for safekeeping to one companion, so that they would not ordinarily have much money in their pockets to spend. Cooperation among the *braceros* is equally important in the cane fields. All but the most inexperienced *braceros* cut cane on their own. Yet reciprocal exchanges of labor speed the manual lifting and loading of cane onto carts for transport to company weigh stations. It is not unusual to see a *bracero*, a *viejo*, a *capataz de braceros*, and a Dominican low-level employee share a moment of leisure after work around the same dominoes table. Yet, even in their leisure, *braceros* tend to spend more time in one another's company than with the *batey*'s year-round residents. Rather than join the drinkers and strollers who gather most evenings in front of the *batey*'s dry-goods store, most *braceros* prefer to stay near their *barracones* and share a cigarette and some conversation with other Haitians. On moonlit nights, impromptu musical combos often stay up past midnight in front of the *braceros'* barracks, singing pop tunes from Haiti and the Dominican Republic and scratching out rhythms with whatever improvised instruments fall to hand, say, a discarded bottle cap scraped against the concrete floor and drums fashioned from large, empty tins and discarded five-gallon plastic containers.

Trust between harvest companions is, of course, not unlimited. It is apparently not rare for a man to abuse the confidence of his companions by absconding with their money, *incentivo* receipts, and other valued possessions. Before they even set foot on Dominican soil, young men have heard enough stories of the treachery of harvest companions to know that, in the end, each man is responsible for himself in the Dominican Republic. The words of one young returnee, quoted in chapter 4, bear repeating in this context, "It is your wrist (i.e., your own strength) which is your mother and father *nâ pâyòl*."

Yet when the *bracero*'s own strength fails, he usually has nothing to fall back on but the support of his work companions. When sick or injured, *braceros* are at times denied access to medical care. Rarely do they get the social security benefits to which Dominican law entitles them and for which they pay 2.5 percent of their wages. Roommates are therefore the only source of security against temporary disability on which a migrant can rely. When a man is too sick or too badly injured to work, his roommates and other *braceros* chip in to make sure that he is at least fed. This support has saved many from starving during extended periods of disability.

Migrants cooperate not just by lending one another tangible assistance. They also share information and introduce one another to potentially useful acquaintances. In the Dominican Republic's sugar industry, the quantity and, above all, the quality of the sugarcane in a particular area may be important determinants of the cane cutter's income. These attributes may vary considerably in time and space. A *batey* may begin the harvest with good cane but be left by harvest's end with only bad cane. And *braceros* distinguish different estates and the *bateyes* of any one estate by the quality of the cane grown there. For the *braceros*, picking up their belongings and moving to another *batey* can spell the difference between success and failure in meeting their harvest savings goals.

Yet information transmission among seasonal migrants is a far cry from the freewheeling, efficient marketplace of data that has been found to characterize migrant networks elsewhere in the Third World. Migrants tend to keep secret any information they may have about work opportunities in other parts of the Dominican Republic, particularly when it comes to laying real plans for departure. The main reason for discretion is the surveillance that company officials keep over the *braceros*. This surveillance may be hidden as well as open. *Capataces de braceros*, for instance, may secretly pay certain *braceros* for information about any unusual activities taking place in the *braceros'* barracks. On the basis of such information, the *capataces* do not often succeed in preventing *braceros* from abandoning the *batey*. But the distrust that company surveillance sows among the *braceros* is a real barrier to sharing information about job opportunities elsewhere and may thus slow the leakage of harvest laborers from the estate.

Even when information is given freely, it is not always reliable. At the beginning of the harvest and again sometime around April or May, sugar estate managers commonly become anxious about labor shortages. At these times, company bosses and independent cane growers (*colonos*) send out Haitians in their employ as agents to "steal" *braceros* from other estates. Such an agent, under cover as a *bracero*, ingratiates himself with the real *braceros* and tries to "turn their heads" by describing his own *batey* as a place with tall, heavy canes, good housing, many friendly women, and benevolent bosses (Murphy 1986, 194, 248). Inevitably, some men are dissatisfied enough with their present *batey* to be willing to seek out better opportunities elsewhere. The proximity of five estates in the San Pedro de Macorís area makes it relatively easy for a group of young, unattached laborers to sneak away at night through deserted cane alleys and pastures to a prearranged rendezvous point, where a truck from another estate or *colono* will be waiting to pick them up. More often than not, when they arrive at the new place, the "friend" who persuaded them to move is revealed to be a lackey of the top local boss, the better pay and conditions they had anticipated do not materialize, and they are left wiser if not wealthier for their trouble.

In short, it seems that Haitian cane workers in the Dominican Republic cooperate with fellow countrypeople in fewer and more restricted ways, when compared to Haitian rural-urban migrants and emigrants *lòt bò lâmè*. Their social ties fall short of "making emigration a reliable and relatively risk-free economic resource," as Massey (1988, 398) claims for the networks of Mexican immigrants in the United States. Yet, within the limits that poverty, economic dependence, and official oppression place on their ability to adapt socially, the seasonal migrants' practice of relying on peers for support works pretty well as a means of getting by on the sugar estates. Relying on peers provides a shaky safety net at best, but it is a form of cooperation that can withstand frequent changes of residence and costs little in time or money to sustain. It gives many the minimal guarantee of survival they need in order to take the risk of emigrating as cane workers. And most migrants need only depend on the support of their work companions for the three to nine months of a typical *Sêdomêg* sojourn, after which they return to whatever security their land, family, and neighbors in Haiti may have to offer.

Perhaps the most serious pitfall of depending on peers for mutual support is that such a network is only good for as long as one's peers are around to lend assistance. At harvest's end, most migrants gravitate back to Haiti. Those who stay behind in the Dominican Republic face the uncertainty of how they will get by without the circle of work companions to whom they have so far turned for support and cooperation.

"Doubling *nâ Pâyòl*"

Each year, on average, perhaps 10 percent of the men who emigrate as cane cutters do not return to Haiti but stay in the Dominican Republic through the dead season and into the cane harvest of the subsequent year. Haitians call this yearlong extension of the migrant voyage "doubling in the Dominican Republic." Staying on the sugar estates after the harvest is over seems to be not so much a strategy of emigration as the *failure* of a strategy of return. With few exceptions, the migrants and returnees who had at some point "doubled" say they stayed on not because income opportunities in the Dominican Republic encouraged them to stay. They remained, rather, because circumstances prevented them from returning to Haiti as they had wanted. According to men's personal histories, doubling results most often from failing to earn enough money to return, or from losing, being dispossessed of, or spending their savings. It is important to note that a misfortune of this kind does not always keep a man from returning to Haiti. Many do return after having such a bad turn of luck, even though it may mean taking home no savings to speak of. Others are left without even the money to pay their return passage. Others still do not consider it worth the expense to return to Haiti, only to remigrate the following year. A man's obligations to people in Haiti, of course, weigh heavily in his decision to stay or to return. Yet it is not rare for a man with a wife and children in Haiti to double in the Dominican Republic. In this case, the migrant remits whatever he can and sends home instructions about how to meet outstanding debts and other expenses in his absence.

Changes in the organization of work from harvest to dead season encourage the man who doubles *nâ pâyòl* to widen his contacts with local residents. Even though the volume of employment shrinks during the dead season, the number of employers increases. This is because much cane work at this time is subcontracted to *batey* residents and because *batey* residents sometimes hire labor in their private gardens. This may bring the *bracero* into work-related affiliations with many more *batey* residents than during the cane harvest.

Striking up ties with local residents may make it possible for the man who doubles *nâ pâyòl* to survive. Yet it rarely enables him to avoid a big drop in income during the dead season. It is difficult to arrive at a precise estimate of how much cane workers' incomes decline during the dead season. Employment is occasional, and piece rates for weeding, applying fertilizer, and other field tasks may vary widely, even for men working at the same time in adjacent fields (Moya Pons et al. 1986, 237–38). Investigators who have asked cane workers themselves to estimate their monthly earnings have arrived at disparate figures for the dead-season income drop, ranging from about 10 percent (Báez Evertsz 1986, 322) to more than 40 percent (Bobea and Guzmán C. 1986, 157, 166). What is certain is that as the dead season nears its end the availability of company employment falls from little to none. Residents survive the final, hungriest weeks of the dead season on what little credit they can scrounge from local shopkeepers and on the produce of their tiny, rain-fed gardens.

Better employment prospects during the dead season are to be found off the sugar estates. Many Dominicans have the impression that the use of Haitian labor is spreading into new regions and economic activities (ONAPLAN 1981b; Grasmuck 1982; Caroit 1992; Ferguson 1992, 90–91). Dominican coffee, cotton, tobacco, citrus, rice, bean, and cattle producers presently employ Haitians at wages higher than those the sugar industry pays (ONAPLAN 1981b, 25–28). The city also beckons to the Haitian immigrant with a variety of informal employment opportunities. Báez Evertsz (1986, 149) nicely illustrates the wage gap between the city and the sugar estates by observing that even a child shoeblack in the city of Santo Domingo generally earns more per day than an adult cane cutter does. Urban employers hire Haitians only for jobs that Dominican workers reject as being too badly paid for the effort. For instance, Haitian men hold a virtual monopoly on pick and shovel work in the Dominican capital. This work pays relatively well by the day but is only available occasionally, and it may be even more gruelling than cutting cane. Lower but steadier incomes are available in the city to those who work as porters, lottery ticket sellers, and ambulant vendors of fruits and vegetables. Haitian women find employment off the sugar estates mainly as domestic workers, petty traders, and wayside vendors.

With available information, it is difficult to say how many Haitians leave the Dominican Republic's sugar estates to take advantage of wage opportunities elsewhere in the country. It is known that relatively few Haitians circulate seasonally between the sugar estates and non-sugar-producing areas of the country. Those who stay on in the Dominican Republic tend either to stay put or to abandon the estates for good, rather than shuttling back and forth between sugar- and non-sugar-producing areas (Báez Evertsz 1986, 321). In Yerba Buena, for example, during the dead season of 1985, only 10 of the 58 economically active Haitian adult male permanent residents (about 17 percent) left the *batey* for longer than a week to work elsewhere.[5]

Given the improvements in pay, housing, and conditions of work that can be found on the outside, it must be asked why so many Haitians remain on the estates. As much as any other factor, it may be social isolation which keeps Haitian immigrants there. In Yerba Buena, when asked why they do not move elsewhere, most long-time Haitian residents respond that they would not even know where to go, because they know no one who lives outside the country's sugar-producing areas. Of Haitian residents of Yerba Buena between the ages of 15 and 65, only about 32 percent (22 of 69) report that they or their spouse know of a relative or friend who lives in a Dominican city. Among solitary men and women, the proportion is even smaller, about 21 percent (6 of 29). Even on the less isolated Barahona estate in southwestern Dominican Republic, Dore Cabral (1987, 65) found that only a little more than 40 percent of people of Haitian ancestry had relatives outside the sugar *bateyes*. Networks of fellow countryfolk, of course, exist among Haitians who reside off the sugar estates. Yet, perhaps as a result of having immigrated outside the auspices of kinship, those Haitians who remain on the estates often seem not to be well connected with those networks.

"BECOMING *Viejo*"

For some, doubling in the Dominican Republic is only a temporary setback to their initial strategies of returning to Haiti and investing their *Sêdomêg* money in housing and agriculture at home. But, by my estimate, the majority of the men who double in any given year will end up spending most of their adult lives in the Dominican Republic, rather than settling into a nonmigratory livelihood in Haiti. I should repeat here that, by my estimate, as many as one-third of the men who emigrate as cane workers from the Cayes-Jacmel and Cap Rouge area end up returning only infrequently, if they return at all.

The Spanish term "*viejo*" is a word Haitians use also to denote a man who maintains a permanent residence in the Dominican Republic. A man "becomes *viejo*" when he stays in the Dominican Republic longer than two consecutive cane harvests and the intervening dead season (i.e., 18 months or longer). Obviously, "becoming *viejo*" is related to the concept of "doubling *nâ pâyòl*." A man becomes *viejo* once his stay in the Dominican Republic exceeds what could reasonably be considered to be doubling his planned sojourn of one harvest season.

Keeping a residence in the Dominican Republic does not necessarily prevent a *viejo* from also maintaining a residence in Haiti, to which he may periodically return. Some *viejos*, especially those who move up a bit on the company job ladder, visit their places of origin in Haiti regularly. They invest in housing and livestock at home, and they remit small sums of money to family members, with an eye toward someday returning for good. Yet most return only rarely, if ever, and remit only slightly more often. Many say it would cause them shame to send home a message without any money for their kinfolk. It may be thus that many gradually lose touch with their relatives in Haiti. In a random sample of Haitians who reside permanently in Yerba Buena, only 35 percent of men (11 of 32) and 61 percent of women (10 of 17) reported having exchanged messages during the previous 12 months with people at home in Haiti. After many years abroad, contact with people at home may diminish to the point where the migrant no longer knows which, if any, of his or her relatives are still alive. Many nonreturning migrants say their people at home have "forgotten" them, and they are unsure that they would find a household willing to take them in, were they to return to Haiti.[6]

Many nonreturning migrants say they would be afraid or ashamed to return home without any money to hand out as gifts to relatives and neighbors. Yet the shame of which these *viejos* speak is not a feeling that universally prohibits return: each year many seasonal migrants return to Haiti with little or no savings. Even if shame does keep some men from going home, it must be a rare individual who never receives a small cash windfall. Not all men, of course, have the stamina for heavy field labor, and not all are frugal with their earnings. But, if by no other means than by winning the local numbers game, which most *viejos* play religiously, nearly *every* emigrant at some point gets his or her hands on a lump sum of money, comparable to the savings with which most seasonal migrants are willing to return. This raises doubts that the immobility of most *viejos* stems from an inability to acquire enough money to pay for return passage, with something left over to distribute as gifts to people at home.

Another possible explanation is that *viejos* choose to stay because their economic prospects seem better in the Dominican Republic than in Haiti. They either earn more on the sugar estates than the average Haitian cane worker does or they have even less access to productive property in Haiti than the average migrant and are therefore less strongly pulled to return home.

A few Haitian men choose to stay in the Dominican Republic because they are promoted to jobs that pay better than cane work, typically as low- or middle-level foremen in the cane fields. Even though their company salaries are usually seasonal, some of these men never leave their *bateyes* for more than a few weeks at a time, out of fear that they might be replaced in their jobs while gone. Those who stay in the *bateyes* year-round get secondary incomes by setting up family shops, farming subsistence plots, and raising poultry, goats, and cattle. Their wives often earn independent incomes through petty commerce. The duration of their residence in the Dominican Republic may easily surpass 10 years, but those who move up the company job ladder tend eventually to return permanently to Haiti.

Yet most *viejos* never work as salaried employees, even on a seasonal basis. Ethnic Dominicans, men of mixed ancestry, and second- and third-generation Haitians may rise in the company hierarchy under the patronage of an influential godparent (Murphy 1986, 417–18). Few Haitians benefit from similar patronage. Haitian nationals instead remain mostly in day labor and piece work, the worst paid, most physically punishing, and least secure jobs in the industry. Of 58 economically active *viejos* in Yerba Buena, 52 (about 90 percent) receive wages only as piece workers and day laborers, 5 are salaried company employees for part of the year, and 1 is an evangelical minister and self-employed trader. In short, it is not because they have achieved upward mobility that most *viejos* remain on the sugar estates.

Even though *viejos'* material prospects in the Dominican Republic are dim, it is possible that for many their economic situation might be better than it would be in Haiti. In spite of suffering backbreaking labor and chronic economic insecurity, the poorest migrants might conceivably consider their economic opportunities in the Dominican Republic to be better overall than in Haiti. Or the poorest might need to accumulate a larger sum of money than what the average migrant saves before they can return home to Haiti with any hope of establishing a viable livelihood. Either way, it may be the neediest emigrants who run the greatest risk of not returning from the Dominican Republic.

The existing information on this question is inconclusive. Data from the personal histories of *viejos* in Yerba Buena does not suggest that most had been destitute in Haiti. Half (16 of 32) either owned two or more parcels of land or had a skill by which they could support themselves in Haiti. Only 12.5 percent (4 of 32) inherited or stood to inherit less than one-quarter *carreau* (about 0.4 hectare) of land from their families. Also, Báez Evertsz's (1986, 101–3) survey of Haitian cane workers in the Dominican Republic reveals no significant difference between seasonal and nonreturning emigrants in the amounts of land they report owning in Haiti. Therefore, even though it makes sense that nonreturning emigrants might tend to come from poorer-than-average backgrounds, this remains an unsubstantiated hypothesis.

It is possible, finally, that many *viejos* might have had no choice about staying in the Dominican Republic but got stuck there after being barred from reentering Haiti. Between 1963 and 1966, Haitian president François Duvalier forbade all movement across the border, on pain of death, in order to obstruct an expected invasion of anti-Duvalierist rebels. It is not that Haitians sought refuge from Duvalierist oppression by going to the sugar estates of the Dominican Republic. Rather, thousands who had gone to the sugar estates for purposes of economic attainment prior to 1963 *remained* in the Dominican Republic out of a well-founded fear of persecution if they returned home. Among *viejos* interviewed in Yerba Buena, a surprising *59 percent* (19 of 32) left Haiti during the first six years of the Duvalier regime, from 1957 to 1962. This number of permanent immigrants outweighs that of the next highest six-year period (1972 to 1977, when 4 of the 32 *viejos* entered the country) by almost five to one. Similarly, of 21 returnees in southeastern Haiti who had experienced an absence from Haiti of 18 months or longer, 12 (about 57 percent) first "became *viejo*" when they spent the years between 1962 and 1967 in the Dominican Republic. Of course, it may be that both Yerba Buena and the Cayes-Jacmel/Cap Rouge areas are unusual in this regard. Only survey data from a representative sample of *bateyes* can provide a reliable estimate of how many Haitian immigrants got stuck on the sugar estates during Duvalier's blockade of 1963 to 1966. Such data might also make it possible to estimate more accurately what the average rate of permanent emigration has been in "normal" years, when movement across the border has not been disrupted.[7]

SEARCHING FOR SECURITY

Of all the social relationships that a *viejo* can strike up, conjugal union and fatherhood undoubtedly hold the greatest possibilities for enhancing his security. Besides the benefits of cooperating as a family in making a living, it is the opportunity to have children of their own that *viejos* value most highly in conjugal union. *Batey* men are wont to remark that, whereas "the single man gets by any which way," a man with a wife and children must struggle to give his progeny even minimally adequate food, clothing, and schooling. Even so, few men with family responsibilities would willingly trade their burden for the freedom of a solitary man. The forlorn figures of those older *viejos* who have no kinfolk to support them, who survive only out of the charity of others, are hardly enviable examples of what might await a man who lives alone. A man who raises children into productive adulthood, on the other hand, can look forward to the day when one or more of his children might be able to lend him support.

Granted, living alone does not necessarily deny a *viejo* all access to the comforts of family life. Even though solitary *viejos* are rarely happy in the Dominican Republic, neither are they often alone in adversity. Solitary Haitians in Yerba Buena regularly exchange visits, workdays, and servings of cooked food with their neighbors. Some even attach themselves to family households as fictive kin. If a solitary man or woman falls ill, neighbors and friends gather round to see that he or she is fed and cared for. When he or she dies, these people can be depended on to arrange for a wake and burial.

Yet, generally, once he is past his physical prime, the cane worker's only hope of long-term economic security is that his children may find better-paying jobs than he did. Even though discrimination still hounds Haitians after two or three generations in the Dominican Republic (Dore Cabral 1987), it is not necessarily unrealistic for a man to anticipate filial support in his later years. Surprisingly, the occupational profile of second- and third-generation Haitian men in Yerba Buena more closely resembles that of ethnic Dominicans than of first-generation Haitian immigrants (see table 8). Even this small degree of economic betterment may assist Haitians of the second generation in providing support to their elderly parents.

Many *viejos* who are now single have gone through one or more short-lived unions during their time in the Dominican Republic. Yet, in spite of the many advantages of forming a family household, roughly half (34 of 67) of the Haitian men who reside permanently in Yerba Buena live alone. Of those *viejos* who earn the greater part of their incomes through day labor and piece work, only 38 percent (20 of 52) have wives. Most solitary *viejos* remain single not because they cannot afford a wife but because the unbalanced sex ratio of the *bateyes* puts the odds of finding a wife against them. Among permanent residents of Yerba Buena, for instance, there are 128 men for every 100 women (236 men versus 184 women). Among Haitian residents, the sexual imbalance is even more pronounced, there being about 279 men per 100 women (67 men versus 24 women). In a place as poor as a Dominican *batey*, it is not surprising that the poorest men, the Haitian cane workers, should be those least likely to attract and hold onto a wife. And not just poverty but social isolation may be an obstacle to forming a lasting union. This is because the value of a conjugal union to a *batey* dweller may reside in part in the contacts with third parties—the prospective spouse's kinfolk and friends—to which it opens access. A woman is likely to find union with a man who has many relatives at hand more desirable than living with an individual who is alone in the country.

Over time, the migrant's connections to Haiti become more tenuous, and the value of relationships with people in the *batey* grows comparatively greater. Yet, against all evidence on the contrary, *viejos* cling to the hope of returning someday to Haiti and refuse to consider the Dominican Republic their home. This may be largely because no nonreturning emigrant, not even among the men and women who have been in the Dominican Republic for decades, seems ever to have consciously *decided* to stay permanently. Rather, they seem to have simply put off returning to Haiti until next year, over and over again. Only those who with age have grown too frail to travel admit that they will never go back.

Table 8

Occupational Profile of Economically Active Men in Yerba Buena,
by Ethnic/Generational Status, 1986

Occupational Category	Haitians	Second- and Third-generation Haitians[a]	Ethnic Dominicans
Agricultural piece work and day labor	52 (90 %)	16 (33 %)	17 (20 %)
Salaried employment	5 (9 %)	26 (54 %)	61 (71 %)
Self–employed	1 (2 %)	6 (13 %)	9 (10 %)
Total	58 (101 %)[b]	48 (100 %)	87 (101 %)[b]

Source: Based on a census of the *batey's* year–round residents. Data excludes second- and third-generation descendants of immigrants from islands of the Lesser Antilles.

[a]Includes 10 men of mixed Haitian and Dominican ancestry.

[b]Rounding error.

"[M]igration under the auspices of kinship," Tilly and Brown (1967, 142–43) write, "seems to be most common among groups which have the least skill in dealing with impersonal urban institutions like markets, bureaucracies, and communication systems, or the most uncertain relationships to those institutions. . . . [W]ithin the categories particularly inclined to migrate under the auspices of kinship, individuals who do *not* do so more commonly suffer personal disruption when they move." This principle is borne out all too clearly by the example of the Haitian *braceros.* The rural poor who do not migrate under the auspices of kinship are particularly vulnerable to the negative consequences of geographical displacement. The large number of men who go to the Dominican Republic as seasonal migrants and never return to Haiti, having died or gotten "stuck" abroad, gives silent testimony to the unusually high risks to which this migration exposes its participants. The data is lacking with which to say whether Haitian *braceros* fall short of their migration goals more or less often than Haiti's rural-urban migrants and emigrants to North America. But, with the possible exception of boat emigrants to South Florida, the *braceros* suffer personal catastrophe—destitution, physical disability, social isolation, and early death—seemingly much more often than any other major category of Haitian migrants. These dangers have many sources, among which the disrespect shown for the immigrants' basic rights by the Dominican Republic's sugar producers and state authorities must rank first. Yet there can be little doubt that the risks are made worse because the particular circumstances of this migration tend to isolate Haitian men from their kin.

The "individualism" of Haitian cane workers is an outcome not of choice but of systemic constraints. They take an individualized approach to economic attainment not because they prefer this but because pooling material assets with kin and countryfolk is neither necessary nor easily sustainable under the conditions that prevail on the sugar estates. On the one hand, relocating to the Dominican Republic costs little, and finding lodging and employment on the sugar estates is relatively easy. Therefore, a group-oriented strategy of attainment is not as urgent as it is in emigration to the city and to countries overseas. On the other hand, collaborating strategically with kin and countryfolk also seems to be more difficult for the *braceros* than it is for Haitian rural-urban migrants and emigrants overseas. The major obstacles to enacting a group-oriented strategy of attainment on the sugar estates include the brevity of the *braceros'* stay in the Dominican Republic, the limited scope for popular economic initiative permitted by the sugar companies, and the isolation of many sugar *bateyes* from non-sugar-producing areas of the Dominican Republic.

Recent trends do not justify optimism that reforms—such as improving the migrants' terms and conditions of employment, or relaxing restrictions on their freedom to move about the country at harvest time—may soon be instituted to mitigate the poverty of Haitians on the sugar estates. On the contrary, there are signs that CEA administrators have responded to the potential unreliability of their supply of labor from Haiti by recurring to forced recruitment more frequently than in the years immediately before 1986. This hardly bodes well for the Haitians who reside permanently in the Dominican Republic. As on previous occasions when the flow of seasonal immigrant laborers to the sugar estates has faltered, it is the nonreturning emigrants who are likely to bear a disproportionate share of the industry's costs of adjustment.

8

Migration in Global Perspective

The movement of men and women between homeplaces in rural Haiti and the sugar estates of the Dominican Republic illustrates clearly the inadequacy of voluntarist conceptualizations of migration. The hand that distant powerholders have had in promoting and guiding labor circulation shows how misleading it may be to suppose that migratory behavior is determined solely by the individuals who move and the families who send members abroad. Rather, the case of Haiti confirms the historical-structuralist premise that the "internal imbalancing" of subordinate populations by dominant interests has set migration in motion in many parts of the Third World (Portes and Walton 1981, chap. 2). Decades of open and disguised taxation and other forms of exploitation have impoverished the free peasantry and stifled its innovative potential. This has set the stage for rural Haitians to begin emigrating in large numbers to neighboring countries.

That said, it would be a distortion to suggest that Haiti took this path of development simply because powerful interests or a higher capitalist logic dictated that it do so. Haiti's relations with the world's great powers fit no scheme of historical inevitability. Haitian independence was in its time perhaps the greatest slap in the face ever given to European colonialism by a subordinate people of the tropics. Following independence, out of the ashes of the colonial plantation system, the Haitian people reconstructed a village society, based on self-employment in small-scale farming, fishing, crafts production, and trade. While never turning their backs entirely on the world market, Haitians, to a degree unsurpassed among postplantation societies of the Antilles, achieved independence from having to work the land of large proprietors for wages.

Haitian leaders only reluctantly accepted that theirs would be a nation of free peasants. The Haitian government neglected production of subsistence crops, when not taking measures to undermine it, and repeatedly tried to encourage large-scale export agriculture. From the earliest days of Haitian independence to the present, the country's rulers and powerful outsiders would have been only too happy to transform the country's landscape into a checkerboard of monocrop agricultural estates. The reasons why these designs have nearly all come to grief are complex. Immediately after the Revolution, the freed people had the power to resist any new form of economic subordination envisioned for them by Haitian leaders. Before long, merchants, bureaucrats, and military officers came to regard trade with and governance of the rural masses as their meal ticket, and they joined the peasantry in opposing the reimposition of plantation agriculture. The opposition of Haitian rulers to foreign investment also favored ordinary Haitians' aspirations to greater economic autonomy.

Today's Haitian land tenure system, gender- and age-based divisions of occupations, and patterns of socioeconomic inequality are largely products of this history of struggle and accommodation among Haiti's social classes. All these aspects of the Haitian social structure in turn may play a part in determining the who, when, and how of migration. Had any one of these structural factors developed differently, it might have transformed the entire migratory system. Imagine for a moment that Haitian peasant land tenure and customs governing the transmission of wealth from old to young had been less adaptive to scarcity. If, for example, the dominant tendency of the land market and inheritance customs had been to concentrate family land in the hands of one or two heirs, rather than to give all male heirs at least a foothold on the land, then surely fewer emigrants would have been able to return and accommodate themselves on the land. In this circumstance, the majority of migrants might have aimed to relocate permanently, rather than follow a circular pattern of mobility. In time, the entry into the Dominican Republic of large numbers of would-be settlers from Haiti might have obviated the importation of labor by the sugar companies or eventuated strict official measures in the Dominican Republic to curb further immigration. Either way, not only immigration patterns and policies but agricultural labor relations in the Dominican Republic's sugar industry might have been transformed. In short, the Haitian case suggests that not only the designs of distant powerholders but the structure of migrants' societies of origin may determine how people on the margins of the world economic order come to participate in external markets.

Emigration to the sugar estates of the Dominican Republic is a conscious attempt on the part of the migrants, first, to extract a profit from selling their labor in external markets and, second, to return shortly with that profit to the relative security of their homeplaces in Haiti. Circulation may thus be an inherently contradictory strategy. Through it, Haitian men can enhance the security of their livelihoods at home only by first putting their very lives at risk on the sugar estates of the Dominican Republic. How migrants and nonmigrants prioritize and cope with the different kinds of risk involved in crossing the border as cane workers is a matter about which one would like to know more. Enough is known to say that emigration is not in this case the relatively reliable and risk-free economic resource it is accepted to be in some Third World migrations. Economic and physical insecurity may be a condition that Haitian *braceros* share with many others caught up in peripheral migration streams elsewhere in the world today.

Emigration to the sugar estates of the Dominican Republic is not part of an unchanging cycle of social reproduction but a source of income vulnerable to cyclical economic downturns. One of the more sobering observations of my fieldwork is that rural circuits of petty accumulation, which make possible the conversion of migrant money to subsistence resources, have seriously degraded since the 1970s. This seems to have been largely a result of the swine eradication and the slow but perhaps no less damaging erosion of peasants' terms of trade with the outside world. On the Dominican side of the border, shrinking real wages for cane workers and the deteriorating value of the peso vis-à-vis the Haitian gourde have made it perhaps more difficult than ever for *braceros* to bring back money to Haiti. The steep fall in the real value of *Sêdomêg* money during the 1970s and 1980s and the suspension of official recruitment in Haiti after 1986 have discouraged many veteran cane cutters from going to the Dominican Republic again. As on all earlier occasions when the flow of labor from Haiti has faltered, the Dominican authorities have escalated forced recruitment of Haitians in non-sugar-producing areas of the country. Written and oral history indicate that in the past the real wages and civil rights accorded Haitian immigrants have undergone similar cyclical downturns, most notably during the 1930s. Only time will tell if, as in past crises, cane workers' wages may recover some of their lost value.

If greater freedom of mobility, the right of free association, and better terms and conditions of labor were gained by Haitians in the Dominican Republic, this would doubtless mark a great improvement in the *bracero's* condition. Yet, even if this were achieved, only half the battle for a more decent living for these workers would be won. What channels Haitian labor to the sugar estates is a combination of official coercion and economic need. Most *braceros* cross the border of their own volition, knowing what coercive and exploitative terms and conditions of employment likely await them on the other side. In effect, they consent to enter temporarily into a state of unfreedom. For brevity's sake, I must leave it for another occasion to explore the implications of this terrible reality for the study of systems of domination in the Caribbean after emancipation, as well as its broader meaning for our understanding of poverty under capitalism. Suffice it to add that the *braceros* have so little freedom to choose if and how they will emigrate that their "decision" to cross the border implies not so much free choice as coerced consent. The coercion to which they are subjected is not mainly legal/physical but economic. It is perhaps not too much to say that these migrants are deprived of a basic human liberty the moment their economic circumstances leave them no choice but to cross the border. The international community has already recognized freedom from poverty as a basic human right. Yet this right is too often forgotten, even when, as in this case, dire need opens the door to further human rights abuses. The case at hand is thus perhaps an unusually clear example of the link between economic empowerment and the protection of individual freedoms.

Someday, perhaps soon, the emigration of Haitian men and women to the sugar estates of the Dominican Republic will come to an end. Whether it ends as a victory or as a defeat for the people of rural southeastern Haiti will likely depend on whether more viable bases than *Sêdomêg* money can still be created for the reproduction of rural livelihoods. A challenge to development professionals is to support new rural circuits of petty accumulation, especially those that permit the participation of the young and the land-poor.

Proposed remedies to Haiti's agrarian crisis differ according to the observer's understanding of how Haiti entered its present impasse. Discussions of Haiti's agrarian problems tend to draw circles around one implicit question: would things get better or worse if Haiti were to host the development of large, capital-intensive agricultural estates, rather than remain a nation of smallholder agriculturalists? This is an old controversy, as old probably as the Republic of Haiti itself. Yet the question is still very much alive, as is shown by recent USAID/World Bank proposals to clear much of the Haitian countryside of its human inhabitants and replace them with stands of fruit trees and winter vegetables as a means of reversing the island's economic decline and averting its ecological collapse.

In spite of disappointing results during the 1980s, USAID and the World Bank continue to advocate capital-intensive export agriculture and the assembly industry as the cure for Haiti's economic woes. These international agencies cling to the idea that Haiti's only hope lies in a drastic transformation, from a predominantly rural economy, oriented toward supplying internal markets, to one that is urban and export-oriented. According to DeWind and Kinley (1988, 58–59), "In total, AID proposes to shift 30 percent of all cultivated land from the production of food for local consumption to the production of export crops. AID advisors anticipate that such a drastic reorientation of agriculture will cause a decline in income and nutritional status, especially for small farmers and peasants. These problems are expected to last at least until export earnings reach a level high enough to pay for the import of foods no longer produced in Haiti. . . . Even if the transition to export agriculture is successful, AID anticipates a 'massive' displacement of peasant farmers and migration to urban centers."

Admittedly, rural Haiti is perhaps poorer now than it has ever been. There is good reason to be pessimistic about the chances of repairing the damage that has been done to the country's agrarian ecology and economy. And there is a crying need to employ more Haitians in work other than tilling the soil. But with plans such as USAID's for the transition to non-farm employment, it is hard to decide whether action or inaction is the more frightening prospect. For most poorer Haitians, it is questionable whether embarking aggressively on an urban- and export-oriented path of development, as USAID and the World Bank recommend, would be better than continuing under the neglect and exploitation Haitians have endured for decades. The vision that these international organizations have for Haiti's future resembles the reality that Haitians experience today on the sugar estates of the Dominican Republic. Most jobs in Haitian agroindustry would be seasonal, pay a pittance, teach few useful skills, and offer little or no long-term security benefits. That three generations of Haitian peripheral migrants have preferred returning home to staying on the Dominican sugar estates suggests that a rural proletarian life-style under conditions such as these holds few lasting attractions, even for the very poor. Willing as they are to supplement farm incomes with off-farm wage labor, Haiti's rural poor mostly do not consider reliance on meager wages to be a better bet for the future than self-employment in food production. It is not that independence from emigration to the Dominican Republic may be achieved via a return to a rural autarchy that almost surely never existed in the first place. Rural Haitians have always sought to maintain a symbiosis between production for profit and the attainment of food security. My point is that, whatever form this symbiosis takes, the fate of most Haitians will remain linked for some time to come to smallholder agriculture and its associated petty commerce. Development plans that propose to sidestep these sectors will be unlikely to empower Haiti's people to find sustainable solutions to their problems.

As an expatriate researcher, I will not presume to make recommendations to Dominicans and Haitians about how they might solve the civil rights and economic development problems that surround the employment of Haitians as cane workers in the Dominican Republic. Let me only point out again that individuals and organizations in both countries and internationally are already exerting pressure on the Dominican, Haitian, and U.S. governments to see to it that Haitian workers are granted fair treatment in the Dominican Republic. The work of these advocates of Haitian workers' rights should be given full support.

That said, certain questions may be raised about the tactics used in this case by international human rights organizations. Human rights advocates have perhaps too often aimed at making a splash in the international news media by denouncing the mistreatment of the Haitian *braceros* as a new form of slavery, and they have too rarely intervened directly on the migrants' behalf in the Dominican Republic itself. Human rights monitor groups would, of course, be remiss in their responsibility to inform the public if they failed to publicize disturbing trends in the labor recruitment and employment practices of the Dominican sugar industry. Yet it is not at all certain that "[a]ny attempt to exhaust local remedies [in the Dominican Republic] would be futile," as the Lawyers Committee for Human Rights (1991b, 4) asserts. Legal recourse has not been exhausted. On the contrary, it has hardly, if ever, been attempted. Legislation should be put forward, and court action initiated in the Dominican Republic, to try to get the Dominican authorities to stop deporting people of Haitian ancestry without legal proceedings and to bar the forced relocation of undocumented immigrants to CEA estates.

The forced repatriations of 1991 have also made it painfully clear that international media attacks on the Dominican government may elicit a painful backlash against Haitians in the Dominican Republic. This is not an excuse for silence. To remain silent now would in effect be giving in to a kind of hostage taking. Through its deportation campaign of 1991, the Balaguer regime has served notice that it will tolerate the presence of Haitians in non-sugar-producing areas of the country only so long as it gets little adverse publicity for forcibly relocating many of those immigrants during the cane harvest. In the face of this implied threat, the only viable response is to continue independent monitoring and publicity of the situation of Haitian workers in the Dominican Republic. Even so, it is incumbent on organizations like the Lawyers Committee and Americas Watch to be aware that their publicity may have adverse consequences for the people they aim to help and to prepare for this eventuality in any way possible. Measures should be taken on the ground to mitigate the foreseeable adverse consequences. This might not be possible in a totalitarian state, but it *is* possible in the Dominican Republic, which boasts a growing record of democratic pluralism and hosts a thriving community association movement. For instance, international human rights organizations could support efforts to provide legal representation to Haitian detainees, while continuing to exert pressure for change on all governments implicated in the migratory labor system. Such a proactive role may signify a departure from the proven methods of human rights pressure groups. Yet to refuse this role is virtually to ensure that Haitian immigrants will be the real casualties in any future war of words between the Balaguer government and international human rights organizations.

Without wishing to preach to either side of this debate, I believe that two more points should be taken into consideration in current discussions about the Haitian presence in the Dominican Republic. The first is that the emigration of Haitian men as cane workers to the Dominican Republic has always been predominantly a short-term, circular movement of people. Given that the prevalence of migration surpasses 40 percent among adults in some parts of southeastern Haiti, one of the most remarkable things about this migration is that there are not many more Haitians in the Dominican Republic than the half-million or so which the most reliable estimates indicate there are today. This is, of course, because most of those who have emigrated have soon returned and ultimately settled into nonmigratory life-styles in Haiti. Until convincing evidence emerges on the contrary, it should be assumed that this migration is still mainly circular. (Let me repeat that, to obtain results that reliably represent the entire migrant population, surveys done on the Dominican side of the border must always correct for the tendency of host-area samples to overrepresent long-term emigrants.) Gloom-and-doom scenarios have proven unreliable as predictors of trends in migrant behavior in the past and should be regarded with skepticism today. The idea that hungry Haitians are poised in their hundreds of thousands to overrun the Dominican Republic is as unsubstantiated by fact today as it was 50 years ago.

The second point to which I want to draw attention might seem at first glance to contradict the first point. This is that the Haitian population of the Dominican Republic (as opposed to the total migrant population, including returnees in Haiti) is probably made up mostly of people who have no definite plans for returning soon to Haiti. The finding that most of the immigrants remain in the host country for only a few months at a time should not be taken to mean that most Haitians now in the Dominican Republic are brief sojourners. It would be a mistake to think that Haitians in the Dominican Republic are people for whom few human services need to be provided, because they can always return in time of need to their villages of origin. There is, rather, a sizable population of Haitians on the sugar estates who have lost contact with people in their places of origin in Haiti. Even though most of these people might deny it vehemently, the Dominican Republic is for all practical purposes their home. Barring massive induced repatriation, most will probably remain in the Dominican Republic for life. In today's climate of fiscal austerity and widespread economic hardship, it is understandable that the Dominican government might be reluctant to extend more services to Haitian nationals residing on its territory. Nongovernmental relief and community development organizations might usefully expand their work with this particularly neglected and vulnerable segment of the Dominican population.

Concerning U.S. policy, I can make a few more specific observations. U.S. law attaches five labor rights conditions to trade benefits under the government's Generalized System of Preferences. These include "the right of association, the right to organize and bargain collectively, a prohibition on the use of any form of forced or compulsory labor, a minimum age for the employment of children, and acceptable conditions of work with respect to minimum wages, hours of work and occupational safety and health" (Americas Watch 1990, 65). It should be clear to any impartial observer that the Dominican Republic's treatment of Haitian cane workers flagrantly contravenes all five conditions. In principle, as provided for by the law, the U.S. Trade Representative should be called on to devise a program of progressive sanctions against the Dominican Republic, to bring home to the Dominican authorities America's concern for Haitian workers' rights.

Unfortunately, an important weakness in the American legislation makes it hard for me at this time to advocate trade sanctions against the Dominican Republic. The labor rights conditions I cite above enshrine individual rights which any democratic regime should strive to respect. Yet any concept of *collective responsibility* is alien to the legislation. U.S. trade sanctions, under the existing law, cannot punish Dominican leaders and sugar company managers for neglecting their historic responsibility toward the Haitians whose labor has for so long sustained the Dominican sugar industry. As a result, the threat of U.S. trade sanctions would carry with it certain dangers for Haitians in the Dominican Republic. Specifically, if trade sanctions appeared imminent, the Dominican authorities might conclude that the easiest way out of their "Haitian problem" would be simply to get rid of the Haitian immigrant population, once and for all. In the event, Dominican sugar production would fall sharply, and tens of thousands of Dominicans would lose their sugar-related jobs. Yet, with trade sanctions looming, Dominican leaders might regard this outcome as the lesser of two evils facing the country. It need hardly be spelled out that the sudden repatriation of Haitians in their tens of thousands, not to mention the inevitable *de-patriation* of Haitian-Dominicans in unknown numbers, would cause nothing short of massive disruption among Haitian populations on either side of the border. In short, U.S. trade sanctions are a more powerful but potentially much clumsier instrument of pressure than the international publicity and direct advocacy that human rights pressure groups and Dominican nongovernmental organizations might be able to carry out together.

Sadly, the racism that barred America's gates to immigrants of color for much of the nineteenth and twentieth centuries is not dead. Nor has U.S. immigration policy toward Latin America and the Caribbean yet abandoned the old double standard that automatically classifies only those fleeing communist regimes as refugees. Regardless of how acute Haiti's poverty may get, American pity is unlikely to translate into official preference for Haitian immigrants. A brief, one-time opening along the lines of the Haitian boat exodus of 1980 would be more likely. A sudden, massive increase in the arrival on American shores and the interception at sea of undocumented Haitian immigrants might once more be followed (after much avoidable anguish and loss of life) by a court order permitting the detainees to stay in the country legally. Such an exodus would involve mainly those Haitians who can respond most quickly to the opportunity to emigrate: town dwellers, relatively rich peasants, and people who live near ports of embarkation of boats headed for Florida (Buchanan 1981; Allman and Richman 1985). It would select many fewer people like those who emigrate to the Dominican Republic: the rural poor, who live in places far from ports of exit to the United States.

A *"bracero"* program, similar to that which recruits Jamaicans for work in the United States as sugarcane cutters and apple pickers, might draw more migrants from the poorer strata of rural society. In southeastern Haiti, a *bracero* program would find a practically inexhaustible supply of eager workers with experience in agricultural wage labor. Each worker could support several family members back home with his American wages. Yet high official fees for documents, plus kickbacks to administrators, might easily elevate the price of entry into this type of program beyond the means of those who could benefit most from it. Also, U.S. employers seem satisfied with the seasonal farm labor scheme as it exists, and they might be unhappy switching from a Jamaican to a Haitian labor supply. Even if this were not the case, it would hardly be fair to deprive needy Jamaicans of an important supplement to their incomes just to benefit marginally poorer Haitians. Only a decision to admit more Caribbean islanders into the United States as guest workers might provide a practical means of extending access to First World wages to greater numbers of poor Haitians than at present. It need hardly be added that the political and economic climate in the United States today hardly favors such a shift in policy. In short, there is little hope that increased U.S.-bound emigration, permanent or temporary, legal or undocumented, may soon provide a viable alternative to the Dominican Republic for the people of rural southeastern Haiti.

Yet, regardless of how hard it may be to muster the will, the means, and the imagination for a workable solution, it is too late for the United States to turn its back on the problem now. One need go no further than a few well documented facts of history to establish the direct role played by European and North American interests in creating the migratory labor system. In the late nineteenth and early twentieth centuries, European and North American capital underwrote the rapid growth of the Dominican sugar industry. In the 1890s, European and North American sugar barons initiated the migratory labor system by paying for workers to be recruited in the Leewards. After 1915, the U.S. military rulers of Haiti and the Dominican Republic took the first official steps to regulate the recruitment, transport, and employment of Haitian *braceros.* The departing U.S. occupiers established armed forces and structures of central authority on both sides of the island, institutions that subsequently helped repressive rulers manipulate the migratory labor system as a means of personal enrichment. At one time or another during the twentieth century, Great Britain, Canada, and the United States have each been the main consumer of Dominican sugar. And, if the reproduction of rural livelihoods in southeastern Haiti is in danger today, it is partly because of the instability of recent years in international markets for coffee and sugar, a situation for which the unfair trading practices of the north are largely to blame.

Peripheral migrants are by definition those who do *not* show up on the north's doorstep. The only visible link between the ordinary American and the cane worker in the Dominican Republic may be that portion of the sugar the northerner eats which is produced in the Dominican Republic. Sugar—pure and crystalline—bears no record of the human activity that went into its manufacture. It is hard for the consumer to visualize the cost in divided families, workplace injuries, and malnutrition-related deaths occasioned by the production of this commodity. To care about the plight of sugar's unseen producers is therefore perhaps too much to ask of the citizens of the highly industrialized countries. Yet peripheral migrants, like their neighbors who emigrate to the First World, are the products of changes wrought in their home societies by a European/North American–dominated global order. Not a reaction of guilt but a recognition of responsibility should activate the concern of Europeans and North Americans for those Haitians and others who leave homes in the south to produce commodities for export to the north.

Postscript: An Afterthought on Method

My fieldwork in Haiti and the Dominican Republic combined descriptive ethnography, personal history interviews with migrants and returnees, and, as specific data needs became apparent in the course of research, more focused and quantitative surveys. Village-level fieldwork of this kind, in addition to its recognized qualities of "holism" and "depth of focus," may bring to the study of labor circulation advantages of a "harder," quantifiable variety.

First, it is clear that community-based fieldwork may help overcome certain "shortcomings in data systems," which have hampered the study of circulation within the periphery: "[T]he migrational movements actually analyzed are usually those that happen to cross census or political boundaries and that intercept the time intervals used by census enumerators. In effect, a considerable fraction of territorial mobility goes unrecorded" (Zelinsky 1971, 226). Field studies at the village and neighborhood levels may be highly sensitive instruments for determining the prevalence and spatial-temporal patterns of short-term population movements.

Going further, I would suggest that, in gathering socioeconomic data with Haitians on the sugar estates, community-based fieldwork may offer solutions to several potential problems with conventional social survey techniques. My highly localized samples in no way obviate broad-based sample surveys, which I lacked the time and resources to carry out myself. Even so, certain of my fieldwork experiences may serve as cautionary examples to subsequent survey researchers. In at least three ways, the survey procedures I used in Haiti and the Dominican Republic differed from most previous studies of Haitian migrant cane workers.

First, I had the chance to gather information systematically not just with migrants in the Dominican Republic but also with returnees and migrants' kinfolk in Haiti. Random samples of Haitians in the *bateyes* will always overrepresent nonreturning emigrants, just as home area samples will over-represent returnees. To obtain a reliable picture of the entire migrant *and* returnee population, surveys must correct for this locational bias. One way of doing this is the kind of survey I carried out in Rocheteau and Cabrouette, which attempted to elicit basic information on absentees from family members left behind in the home area.

A second important feature of my survey procedures was that I did my interviews in Haitian Creole and thus did not need to select respondents, as some previous surveys have, on the basis of their ability to speak Spanish. The advantages of this in terms of eliciting reliable, detailed responses should be obvious. It also bears noting that the least experienced migrants are those least fluent in Spanish. Surveys that exclude people who do not speak Spanish are therefore likely to underrepresent less experienced migrants.

Third, I ensured randomness by selecting respondents, using a random numbers table, from complete lists of the residents of the fieldwork sites. This point may seem banal, but I think in the present case it deserves particular emphasis. My experience suggests that one cannot arrive at a representative sample of Haitians in a particular *batey* by, say, interviewing the first willing Haitian man or woman one encounters, and then asking to interview the resident(s) of every *n*th dwelling thereafter. This and all other blind sampling techniques rarely yield representative samples because only a nonrepresentative sample of the *batey* population makes itself available to be interviewed by a stranger. Those Haitians who speak Spanish most fluently, who come from urban areas in Haiti, who have lived in the Dominican Republic the longest, and who have the strongest ties to Dominicans are the first to come forward to see what the freshly arrived sample survey enumerator is up to. Those who feel less sure of their rights, because they do not speak Spanish, have only weak ties to Dominicans, etc., are disproportionately likely to conceal themselves from the outsider.

A further problem with random surveys administered by outsiders is the difficulty of determining accurately who is a Haitian national. In my field surveys in the Dominican Republic, only the discreet assistance of local people, whose trust I had gained through my extended residence in Yerba Buena, saved me from making gross errors concerning the nationality and ethnic background of residents. When asked to identify their place of birth/ethnic background in a survey format, even under assurances of confidentiality, many Haitian nationals attempted to represent themselves as second-generation immigrants, and many Haitian-Dominicans concealed their Haitian ancestry. Clearly, a survey researcher without previous ties to people in the *batey* would run a huge risk of confusing Haitian nationals with Haitian-Dominicans and of omitting many Haitian-Dominicans from analysis entirely. Misleading correlative data on socioeconomic attainment and ethnicity might thereby result.

For reasons such as these, a broad-based survey does not always produce a more representative sample than community-based ethnographic fieldwork. Just the opposite may hold true if the population one is studying is made up largely of undocumented immigrants and if survey designers and fieldworkers do not take into account the suspicion with which a survey is likely to be greeted among such a population.

Just as important as sampling procedure is the nonquantifiable factor of the reliability of the survey instrument. In this regard, the personal history interview technique I used merits particular attention. The personal history interviews sought to elicit individual respondents' retrospective accounts of personal experiences in three areas. First, it charted year-by-year changes in residence, mobility, work, marital history, and family formation. Second, for each instance of migration, it asked the motivations for moving and enquired about the uses to which any resulting savings were put. Third, it recorded land tenure and livestock holding at turning points in the life course, e.g., first migration, entry into first conjugal union, birth of first child, the death or retirement of a parent. The purpose of organizing the interviews in this way was to relate individuals' migratory behavior to socioeconomic status across the life course. Recall error was minimized by the use of a system of data-gathering modeled after the "partial" life history method of the Monterrey (Mexico) Mobility Study (Balán et al. 1969). In the interviews themselves, without sacrificing systematic data collection, I tried to set a natural, conversational style of dialogue, open to information other than that directly sought. An interview schedule was prepared as an aid to memory rather than as a formal questionnaire (the text of this schedule is reproduced in appendix A). My local assistants and I often asked questions not on the schedule, in response to emerging details in the histories of particular individuals.

I found that interviews with Haitian migrants produce remarkably different responses concerning individuals' reasons for migrating, depending on whether one poses questions in a synchronic or in a life history mode. "It is hunger," "hardship [*mizè*]," "we are barefoot [in Haiti] and we are naked," "our country is no good," "the country is collapsing," "we find the *pàyòl* country [the Dominican Republic] better than ours": these typify the answers migrants give when asked synchronic, standardized questions about their reasons for emigrating, such as, "Why did you come to the Dominican

Republic?" These responses show no sign of the commitment to home evident in the personal histories of most migrants but portray emigration instead as a response to invidious comparisons between home and host areas.

Interviewees respond very differently when asked for an account of personal experiences in a life story format. "To buy myself some clothing," "to buy wood for a house," "to repair storm damage," "to buy livestock," "to pay for my father's funeral": these typify men's responses when asked to recall what led them to leave home at a particular point in their lives, such as, "In your *n*th trip *nâ pâyòl,* what circumstance or final thing made you decide to go?" In other words, the same respondents who portray emigration as a flight from Haiti's poverty when asked synchronic questions about their reasons for leaving home tend to represent emigration as a purposeful sojourn abroad when asked questions situated in a life story context. It is well known to students of oral history that interviewees tend to give normative responses to atemporal, decontextualized questions and responses grounded in personal experience to questions that refer to a particular time and place in their lives. It is perhaps not surprising that this effect should also be observed in migration histories.

Admittedly, migrants' stated reasons for leaving home may present an incomplete, even distorted, representation of the forces that lead people to emigrate. Anthropologists have long recognized the danger of relying heavily on migrants' own ex post facto assessments of why they leave home. A. I. Richards (1954), Gulliver (1957), and Mitchell (1959), for example, point out that migrants' conscious motivations commonly reflect only a small part of the pressures that impinge on the decision whether or not to emigrate. What tends to stand out in migrants' personal narratives are the immediate "last straw" causes of departure—e.g., an argument with a significant relative or local notable, or a specific personal financial crisis—"rather than the cumulative effects of hopes and fears which are probably the real cause of pushing a man to leave his home" (Richards 1954, 65).

Yet the partial life history method I used differs from the conventional migrant survey, in that it seeks information about the personal *outcomes* of migration as well as asking interviewees what led them to leave home. What people do with repatriated migrant savings may be an important corrective to interviewees' stated reasons for migrating. This is because the way that people use migrant money is determined not just by their conscious intentions but by constraints of which they may not even be completely aware. This is the sense in which I understand Richards' (1954, 65–66) opinion that "the whole level of interpretation reached [in migrant surveys] could [be] greatly improved," if it were possible to check "what people said against what they *did*" (my emphasis). In keeping with this idea, I consistently strive to take migrants' stated motivations *and* histories of behavior as my guide to interpreting the role played by labor circulation in the lives of people in rural southeastern Haiti.

Finally, the likeness between the images of despair evoked by many earlier investigators and the migrants' own normative responses concerning the reasons why they emigrate is too close to let go without further discussion. Specifically, I wonder if the image of emigration as flight might not hold certain unremarked meanings for rural Haitians. A brief look at how rural Haitians often talk about migration may provide clues to these meanings. "*Mizè*," derived from the French "*misère*," is perhaps the word that recurs most often in Haitians' own generalizations about the conditions that lead them to leave home. No one English word adequately captures its meaning, which bundles concepts of poverty, hardship, and suffering. Examining the speech contexts in which "*mizè*" arises may shed light on its meaning in relation to migration. For example, in an exploratory interview in highland Rocheteau, two women voiced the following brief caveat against what they seemed to feel was an overemphasis that others in our conversation had placed on material gain as a reason for going to the Dominican Republic. First woman: "It is not to say that it is out of avarice [*âbisyô*] that you go. It is not out of greed [*pu tâdâs*] that you go." Second woman interrupts: "It's *mizè*, it's *mizè!*" By contrasting avarice and greed with *mizè*, it is clear that these two women sought to remind me that emigration is for them not a matter of choice but an economic necessity.

This was not an isolated incident. Rather, it seemed that interviewees were often at pains to make sure that I would not mistake their pursuit of material goals through emigration as evidence that they enjoyed material sufficiency or acted out of unconstrained acquisitiveness. Broadly, this suggests that Haitians' representations of emigration as a flight from poverty at home have a *rhetorical* as well as a literal meaning. The purpose of these statements is perhaps as much to persuade as to inform. Specifically, by identifying constraint rather than choice as the basic condition under which the decision to emigrate is taken, talk of *mizè* points to factors beyond local people's control as the ultimate causes of emigration. Its intent may therefore be partly to prompt the listener to ask who and what are responsible for Haiti's failure to provide its people with adequate means of reproducing their livelihoods at home. Haitians may thus interpret talk of *mizè* not just as evidence of deprivation but as a way of airing grievances of an ultimately political character.[1]

Whether my reading is on target or not, there is no doubt that, at the time I did my fieldwork, the rhetoric of *mizè* concealed considerably more than it revealed to me about what motivates Haitians to emigrate. Indeed, in my eyes, talk of *mizè* seemed at times almost calculated to confuse, as the following exchange, taken from another exploratory interview tape-recorded in highland southeastern Haiti, may illustrate:

> Author (S.M.): "I would like us to talk about what needs oblige Haitians to go *nâ pâyòl*."
>
> Jean, a former migrant: "Well, their circumstances are not good here."
>
> S.M.: "Explain that to me in more detail, please."
>
> Jean: "Yes, you do not have money, you must go look for money."
>
> Bonne, his wife: "There is nothing to do in the country!"
>
> Jean, impassively: "There is nothing to do in the country."
>
> S.M.: "Does that mean there is no work to be done in the country?"
>
> Bonne: "There is no work! If you are hungry, you must take to the bush, go *nâ pâyòl*, endure hardship [*pase mizè*]!"
>
> Jean: "If you need a cow, you will not buy it here. It is over there [to the Dominican Republic] you must go to make money . . . to come home and buy it."
>
> Bonne: "There is nothing to do!"
>
> Jean: "When you come back, if you need a house, you have nothing here to make it. Over there you must go . . . to make money to come home and make it."
>
> S.M.: "Would you say that it was hunger which led you [to go] *nâ pâyòl?*"
>
> Jean: "No, not hunger . . ."
>
> Willis, a neighbor, prompts in a whisper: "*Mizè, mizè!*"
>
> S.M.: "Or was it money you needed?"
>
> Jean: "Money."
>
> Willis, speaking up now: "*Mizè* itself!"
>
> Bonne, emphatically: "*Mizè.*"
>
> S.M., confused: "*Mizè?*"
>
> Jean, impassively: "*Mizè*, money; *mizè.*"
>
> Bonne: "*Mizè* and deprivation."
>
> Jean repeats: "*Mizè*, deprivation."
>
> Bonne, with growing emotion: "This deprivation of Haiti is killing us completely. We will not have anything at all one day, at all, at all. This little one [the small girl at her feet] is perishing under the deprivation. It is killing her completely. We have nothing, you see?"

Taking my experiences in Haiti and the Dominican Republic as a guide, it seems likely that previous investigators have often had conversations of this kind when interviewing Haitians on the Dominican side of the border. Except with people who had become friends, I found that inquiries about the reasons why someone had left Haiti could not be sustained for long without talk of *mizè* coming to the fore.

A synchronic and decontextualized line of questioning would have been likely to elicit only responses couched in the rhetoric of *mizè* or something like it. This would have left me with little reason to suspect that any motives other than immediate relief from hunger lead Haitians to go to the Dominican Republic. The deprivation of which migrants, returnees, and stay-at-homes speak is real. This deprivation finds expression in talk of *mizè*. Yet talk of *mizè* also tends to conceal the purposeful, calculated dimension of Haitians' migratory behavior.

These observations suggest that, in evaluating the reliability of interview data in migration studies, the suitability of the questions asked and the quality of the responses given should be considered to be as important as the statistical significance of the results. Of what use, after all, is statistically impeccable data based on dubious answers given to inappropriate questions? The search for quantitative rigor has perhaps led students of migration to draw too rigid a line between method and theory and to reduce methodology to questions of sampling and data processing procedures. The theory that informs the questions you ask also determines the range of answers you may get. Or, put another way, "Ask a misinformed question, and get a misleading answer."

It might be added, by conclusion, that what suggested the partial life history to me as a potentially useful method was not my own insight but my reading of earlier ethnographies of rural Haiti (particularly, G. F. Murray 1977, and Smucker 1982). This is not to downplay the importance of fieldwork. On the contrary, that my theoretical approach is rooted in earlier empirical research confirms that, in determining the "right" questions to ask, there is no substitute for knowledge derived from extended, firsthand observation of the migrants' ways of life.

Appendix A. Migration History Interview Schedule, Haiti, 1987

1. Nâ ki ane u te fèt?
   In what year were you born?
   - pa kônê
   - not known
   → 1a. Ki laj u kuniyea?
   What age are you now?
   - p.k.
   - n.k.
   → 1b. Su ki prezidâ u te fèt?
   Under what president were you born?
   1c. Lè u te gê kêz'â kôsa, lè u te gwo jèn mun, kilès ki te prezidâ?
   When you were about 15 years old, who was president at the time?

2. Ki kote u mun?
   Where were you born?
   - (IF BORN ELSEWHERE)
   → 2a. Kumâ u vin rete [place name]?
   How did you come to live in [place name]?
   2b. Nâ ki ane u te vin rete [place name]?
   In what year did you come to live in [place name]?

3.   Ki travay u fè?
     What is your work?

┌   kiltivatè   ┌   lòt travay
│   farmer   │   other work
└─▷ Eske u kôn fè kòb ak kenêpòt lòt └─▷ Eske u fè jadê ak fòs–u tu?
     travay tu, tâku tayè/kutiryè   Do you farm, too?
     ubyê chapât/komès, bagay kôsa?
     Do you earn money with any other
     work, too, such as tailoring or
     carpentry/commerce?
     wi
     yes
┌   nô
│   no
└─▷ 3a.   Ak kilès u pwoteje u pi plis, ak lakilti ubyê ak lòt metye–u?
            On which do you rely more, farming or your other work?

4.   Lè u te ti mun, eske u te ale lekòl?
     When you were a child, did you go to school?
┌   wi
│   yes
│   nô
│   no
└─▷ 4a.   Ki klas u fin fè nèt lekòl?
            What grade did you finish in school?

5.   Nâ ki ane u te môte nâ pâyòl premye fwa?
     In what year did you go to the Dominican Republic for the first time?
┌   p.k.
│   n.k.
└─▷ 5a.   Su ki laj u te môte nâ pâyòl premye fwa?
            At what age did you go to the Dominican Republic for the first
            time?

6.   Sa'k te fè u deside ale premye fwa? (Savledi, ki sikôstâs ubyê ki
     dènye bagay ki te fè u deside ale?)
     What made you decide to go the first time? (That is, what circum-
     stance or what final thing made you decide to go?)

7. Âvâ u te fè premye vwayaj nâ pâyòl, eske u te gê tâ reskôsab tèt–u nèt ubyê u te su kôt mun tuju?
   Before your first trip to the Dominican Republic, were you yet on your own, or were you still dependent on others?

8. Eske parâ–u te dakò pu u ale nâ pâyòl ubyê yo pa't dakò pu u ale?
   Were your relatives in favor of your going to the Dominican Republic, or against it?

(Q.9 FOR MEN ONLY)
9. Âvâ u fè premye vwayaj nâ pâyòl, eske u te kôn fè jadê pu kôt–u deja?
   Before your first trip to the Dominican Republic, had you yet planted gardens of your own?

10. Âvâ u fè premye vwayaj–u, eske u te gê madâm/mari deja?
    Before you made your first trip, had you already had a wife/husband?

(Q.11 FOR MEN ONLY)
11. Âvâ u fè premye vwayaj–u, eske u te gê tâ bati kay deja?
    Before your first trip, had you yet built a house?
    - wi
      yes
      nô
      no
    → 11a. Nâ ki ane u te bati kay–la?
         In what year did you build the house?
      11b. Plasmâ kote u te bati kay–la, su ki dwa li te ye?
         The site where you built the house, under what terms did you occupy it?
      11c. Ki jâ u te fè pu bati kay–la?
         How were you able to afford to build the house?

(REPEAT QQ.12–28 FOR EACH TRIP TO THE DOMINICAN REPUBLIC)
12. N° vwayaj–la, nâ ki mwa u te môte nâ pâyòl?
    In your *n*th trip, in what month did you leave for the Dominican Republic?

13. Sa'k te fè u deside ale nâ pâyòl n° fwa?
    What made you decide to go to the Dominican Republic the *n*th time?

14. Kumâ u te fè n° vwayaj–la, nâ imigrasyô, nâ okazyô ubyê âba fil?
    How did you make the *n*th voyage: in official recruitment, other
    recruitment, or clandestine passage?

    nâ okazyô
    in recruitment
    âba fil
    clandestine passage

    → 14a. Kote u te prâ okazyô–â?
        From where did you take the recruitment voyage?
      14b. Eske u te blije peye pu gê ô plas nâ okazyô–â?
        Were you obliged to pay for a place in the recruitment?

15. Eske u te môte nâ pâyòl ak kôpayèl ubyê pu kôt–u?
    Did you travel with companions or alone?

    ak kôpayèl
    with companions
    pu kôt–li
    alone

    → 15a. Kôpayèl–u, sa yo te ye pu u?
        Your companions, how were you related to them?
      15b. Eske u te pase lasaf ak mêm kôpayèl–yo?
        Did you spend the cane harvest with the same companions?

16. N° fwa u môte nâ pâyòl, lè u t'ap kite Ayiti, eske u te pote ô lajâ avèk
    u pu u fè vwayaj–la?
    The *n*th time you went to the Dominican Republic, when you were
    leaving Haiti, did you carry any money with you for the voyage?

    wi
    yes
    nô
    no

    → 16a. Kôbê lajâ kôsa u te kab pote avèk u?
        Approximately how much money did you take with you?

17. Ki sa u te fè pu u jwên kòb pu u te pati?
    How were you able to find the money to go?

18. Se eskôt u te fè?
    Did you borrow money on interest?

    wi
    yes
    nô
    no

    └─> 18a. Kôbê kòb u te eskôte kôsa?
             How much money did you borrow, more or less?
         18b. Kôbê mun–nâ te fè u peye su sa u te prete–a?
             How much did the lender make you pay back, beyond what
             you borrowed?

19. N° fwa u môte nâ pâyòl, eske'u te kite jadê?
    The *n*th time you went to the Dominican Republic, did you leave any
    gardens behind?

    wi
    yes
    nô
    no

    └─> 19a. Nâ mê ki mun?
             In whose hands?
         19b. Nâ ki kôdisyô u te kite'l nâ mê–ni?
             Under what terms did you leave it in their hands?

20. N° vwayaj–la, ki travay u te fè nâ pâyòl?
    In the *n*th trip, what work did you do in the Dominican Republic?

21. Nâ n° vwayaj–u, etâ nâ pâyòl, eske u te gê tâ voye lajâ ba mun
    ân'Ayiti?
    In your *n*th trip, while in the Dominican Republic, did you ever send
    money to people in Haiti?

    wi
    yes
    nô
    no

    └─> 21a. Ba ki mun u te voye lajâ?
             To whom did you send money?
         21b. Kôbê kòb kôsa u te kab voye ba yo?
             Approximately how much money did you send them?

22.   N° vwayaj–la, ki lè u te vin retunê lakay–u âkò?
      In your *n*th trip, when did you return home again?
      22a.   Nâ ki mwa u te desân ân'Ayiti?
             In what month did you return to Haiti?

23.   N° vwayaj–la, lè u t'ap kite Sêdomêg, kôbê lajâ dominikê kôsa u te
      kab pote avè u?
      In your *n*th trip, when you were leaving the Dominican Republic,
      how much Dominican money, approximately, did you carry with you?
      23a.   Lè sa, pu kôbê kòb lajâ dominikê–â te châje?
             At that time, what was the exchange rate for Dominican
             money?
      23b.   Apre u châje kòb–la, kôbê dola kôsa ki te rete pu u?
             After you exchanged the money, about how many dollars re-
             mained for you?

(Q.24 FOR CONTRACT BRACEROS)
24.   N° fwa u desân ân'Ayiti, eske u te tuche kòb nâ fwôkyè–a?
      The *n*th time you returned to Haiti, did you receive money at the
      frontier?
      ┌─ wi
      │ yes
      │ nô
      │ no
      └─> 24a.   Kôbê kòb kôsa u te tuche nâ fwôkyè–a?
                 About how much money did you receive at the frontier?

25.   Nâ n° vwayaj–u, eske u te rive lakay–u ak tut lajâ–â ubyê u te depâse
      ladân nâ wut ubyê mun te prâ kòb nâ mê–u?
      In your *n*th trip, did you arrive home with all the money, or did you
      spend some en route, or did someone take money from you?
      25a.   Ki kote u te depâse kòb/yo te prâ kòb nâ mê–u?
             Where did you spend money/they take money from you?
      25b.   Kôbê u depâse/yo kite nâ mê–u?
             How much did you spend/they take from you?

26.   Lajâ u te sòti Sêdomêg nâ n° vwayaj–u, ki sa u te petèt fè avè'l kôsa?
      What did you do with the money you brought from the Dominican
      Republic?

27. Lajâ u te sòti Sêdomêg nâ n° vwayaj–u, eske u te petèt fè êterè avè'l ki la tuju?

    Did you invest the money from your nth trip to the Dominican Republic in a way which yielded you some lasting benefit?

    wi
    yes
    nô
    no

    ⤷ 27a. Ki sa u te petèt fè ak benefis [name of investment] te bay u?
         What did you do with the profits [name of investment] gave you?

28. Apre u fè n° vwayaj–la, lè u t'ap môte nâ pâyòl âkò, eske se te tudêku ubyê u te kite dat pase? Nâ ki ane u te môte nâ pâyòl âkò?

    After you nth trip, did you go back to the Dominican Republic again right away, or did some time go by? In what year did you go back again?

(REPEAT QQ.12–28 FOR THE NEXT TRIP.)

29. Lè u t'ap môte nâ pâyòl premye fwa, eske u te gê fâmiy nâ tè Sêdomêg?
    When you first went to the Dominican Republic, did you have any relatives there?

    wi
    yes
    nô
    no

    ⤷ 29a. Mun u te gêyê nâ pâyòl–yo, sa yo te ye pu u?
         The people you had in the Dominican Republic, how were they related to you?

    29b. Eske u jâm kôtre avè yo nâ pâyòl?
         Did you ever meet up with them in the Dominican Republic?

30. Depi u môte nâ pâyòl premye fwa, eske u gê fâmiy ki môte apre u?
    Since you first went to the Dominican Republic, has any relative of yours gone, too?

    wi
    yes
    nô
    no

    ⤷ 30a. Mun ki môte nâ pâyòl apre u, sa yo te ye pu u?
         The people who went to the Dominican Republic after you, how are they related to you?

    30b. Eske u jâm kôtre avè yo nâ pâyòl?
         Did you ever meet up with them in the Dominican Republic?

31.   Ân'Ayiti, eske u jâm kite zòn kote u te rete–a pu u al chache travay ô lòt kote ân'Ayiti mêm?
       Have you ever left the area where you lived to go look for work elsewhere within Haiti?

       ⌐ wi
       │ yes
       │ nô
       └→ no

       31a.   Ki kote u kôn al chache travay ân'Ayiti?
               Where have you looked for work in Haiti?

       31b.   Ki lè u te travay la?
               When did you work there?

       31c.   Ki travay u te fè la?
               What work did you do there?

       31d.   Nâ travay–sa, kôbê kòb kôsa u te kôn tuche pa kêzên?
               In that work, about how much money did you earn semi-monthly?

32.   Ân'Ayiti, eske u kôn rete lavil deja?
       In Haiti, have you ever lived in a city?

       ⌐ wi
       │ yes
       │ nô
       └→ no

       32a.   Pòtoprês ubyê lòt vil pwovês?
               In Port–au–Prince or another city?

       32b.   Ki lè u te rete la?
               When did you live there?

       32c.   Ki travay u te fè la?
               What work did you do there?

       32d.   Nâ travay–sa, kôbê kòb kôsa u te kôn tuche pa kêzên?
               In that work, about how much money did you earn semi-monthly?

33.   Eske u gê tâ fè pitit deja?
       Have you had children?
       wi
       yes
       nô (GO TO Q.38)
       no

34. Depi u ap viv su latè, kôbê pitit u gê tâ fè âtut, ni sa'k la ni sa'k muri?
     In your life, how many children have you had in all, including those
     who are living and those who are dead?
     34a. Kôbê ki la? Kôbê ki muri?
           How many are living? How many are dead?

(REPEAT QQ.35–37 FOR EACH CHILD, LIVING OR DEAD. IF ALL
CHILDREN ARE LIVING, SKIP Q.35)

35. N° pitit u fè–a, eske li la?
     Your *n*th child, is s/he living?
     wi
     yes
     nô
     no
     35a. Nâ ki ane li muri?
           In what year did s/he die?
     35b. Su ki laj li muri?
           At what age did s/he die?

36. Nâ ki ane premye pitit–u te fèt?
     In what year was your first child born?
     p.k.
     n.k.
     36a. Ki laj u te gêyê lè'l te fèt?
           What age were you when s/he was born?
           p.k.
           n.k.
           36b. Su ki prezidâ n° pitit–u te fèt?
                 Under what president was your *n*th child born?

37. Lè'l te fèt, ki kote mâmâ–ni/u te rete?
     When s/he was born, where did her/his mother/you live?
(REPEAT QQ.35–37 FOR NEXT CHILD.)

38. Eske u gê madâm/mari kuniyea?
     Do you have a wife/husband now?
     wi
     yes
     nô
     no
     38a. Depi ki ane nu âsâm?
           Since what year have you been together?

39.   Eske u plase plizyè fwa ubyê ô sèl fwa?
       Have you been in conjugal union more than once or just once?

         plizyè fwa
         more than once
         ô sèl fwa
         just once
    └─> 39a.   Kôbê madâm/mari u gê tâ pase kôsa, ni sa'k fè pitit avèk u ni
               sa'k pa fè pitit avèk u?
               How many wives/husbands have you had, including those
               who had children with you and those who did not?

40.   Ak kôbê mâmâ/papa u fè pitit?
       With how many mothers/fathers have you had children?

(REPEAT QQ.41–45 FOR EACH MA/PA)
41.   Nâ ki ane u te komâse ak n° mâmâ–/papa–pitit–u?
       In what year did you take up with the nth mother/father of your
       children?

42.   Eske u te gê tâ rete nâ mêm kay avè li?
       Did you ever share the same dwelling with her/him?

         wi
         yes
         nô
         no
    └─> 42a.   Ki kote nu te rete âsâm?
               Where did you live together?

                 ân'Ayiti
                 in Haiti
                 nâ pâyòl
                 in the Dominican Republic
            └─> 42b.   Eske u/li te gê tâ bati kay pu li/u?
                       Did you/he build a house for her/you?

                         wi
                         yes
                         nô
                         no
                    └─> 42c.   Plasmâ kote u/li te bati kay–la, su ki dwa li te ye?
                               The site where you/he built the house, under what
                               terms did you occupy it?
                        42d.   Ki jâ u/li te fè pu u/li te kab bati kay–la?
                               How were you/was he able to afford to build the
                               house?

(IF NTH WIFE/HUSBAND IS PRESENT SPOUSE, SKIP QQ.43–45)

43.　U–mêm ak n° mâmâ–/papa–pitit–u, kite nu kite ubyê muri li muri?
　　Did you and the *n*th mother/father of your children split, or did s/
　　he die?

　　43a.　Nâ ki ane nu kite/li muri?
　　　　　In what year did you split/s/he die?

44.　Apre sa, eske u te pu kôt–u?
　　After that, were you on your own?

┌─　wi
│　yes
│　nô
│　no
└→　44a.　Kôbê tâ u te pase pu kôt–u âvâ u plase âkò?
　　　　　How long were you on your own before you entered another
　　　　　union?

45.　Eske u te retunê ak mêm mâmâ/papa âkò ubyê u te prâ ô lòt dâm/
　　mesye?
　　Did you return to the same mother/father, or did you take another
　　woman/man?

(REPEAT QQ.41–45 FOR THE NEXT MA/PA)

46.　Eske u jâm fè afè avèk ô fi/gasô ki <u>pa't</u> fè pitit avèk u?
　　Have you ever been in union with a woman/man with whom you
　　did not have children?

┌─　wi
│　yes
│　nô
│　no
└→　46a.　Kôbê madâm/mari u gê tâ pase ki pa't fè pitit avèk u?
　　　　　How many wives/husbands have you had with whom you did
　　　　　not have children?

(FOR EACH CHILDLESS UNION, REPEAT QQ.41–45)

47.   Pâdâ tut lavi–u, eske sila se sèl kay u gê tâ bati ubyê u gê tâ bati lòt
        kay âkò?
        In your entire life, is this the only house that you have built, or
        have you built others?
        sèl kay–la
        the only house
        lòt âkò
        others
→   47a. Kôbê lòt kay âkò?
              How many other houses?
        47b. N° kay–la, nâ ki ane u te bati li?
              The nth house, in what year did you build it?
        47c. Plasmâ kote u te bati li, su ki dwa li te ye?
              Under what terms did you occupy the site where you built it?
        47d. Ki jâ u te fè pu u te kab bati n° kay–la?
              How were you able to afford to build the nth house?

48.   Eske u kôn achte tè?
        Have you ever bought land?
        wi
        yes
        nô
        no
→   48a. Kôbê moso tè u gê tâ achte kôsa, ni sa'k nâ mê–u tuju ni sa u
              achte u revân deja?
              How many parcels of land have you bought, including those
              still in your hands and those you have bought and sold already?
        48b. Ki valè tè kôsa u gê tâ achte âtut, ni sa'k nâ mê–u tuju ni sa u
              achte u revân?
              Approximately how much land have you bought in total, in-
              cluding what is still in your hands and what you have bought
              and sold?
        48c. Eske u kab sôje ki lè kôsa u te achte chak moso tè?
              Can you remember more or less when you bought each parcel
              of land?
        48d. Tè sa(–yo), se nâ mê fâmiy–u u te achte li ubyê nâ mê etranjè?
              Was it from relatives that you bought the land or from
              nonrelatives?
        48e. Ki jâ u te fè pu u te kab achte tè sa(–yo)?
              How were you able to afford to buy that land?

49. Eske u gê eritaj bò papa–u? Bò mâmâ–u?
    Have you received inheritance from your father? From your mother?

     wi
     yes
     nô
     no

   49a. Kôbê moso tè u eritye, ât bò papa–u ak bò mâmâ–u?
       How many parcels of land have you inherited, between your
       father's side and your mother's side?

   49b. Ki valè tè kôsa u eritye deja?
       About how much land have you inherited already?

   49c. Depi ki lè kôsa u resevwa eritaj–la?
       When did you receive the inheritance?

50. Eske u kôn vân ubyê revân tè?
    Have you ever sold or resold land?

     wi
     yes
     nô
     no

   50a. Kôbê moso tè kôsa u te kab vân deja?
       How many parcels of land have you sold?

   50b. Ki valè tè kôsa u te kab vân deja?
       About how much land have you sold?

   50c. Eske u sôje ki lè kôsa u te vân chak moso tè sa(–yo)?
       Do you remember approximately when you sold that parcel/
       those parcels?

   50d. Splike'm, silvuple, pu ki sa u te vân moso tè sa(–yo).
       Explain to me, please, why you sold that parcel/those parcels.

Appendix B. Schematized Migration Histories of Twenty Men

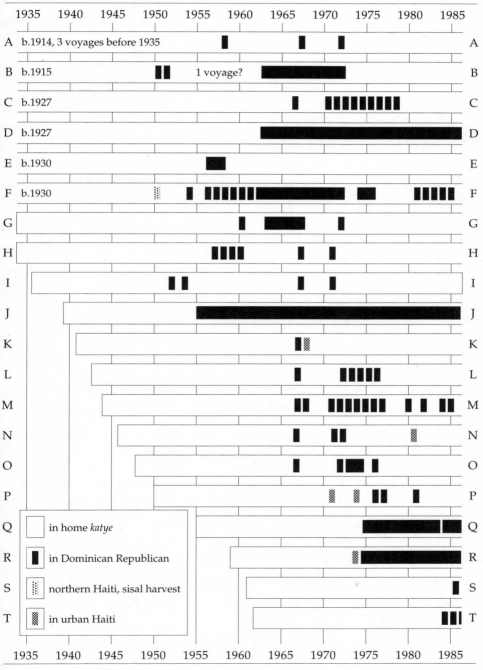

Each bar, A–T, spans life of one individual.

Notes

INTRODUCTION

1. As is common in migration studies, scholarly debates concerning the Haitian presence in the Dominican Republic have taken shape in a medium of political partisanship. On both sides of the island, the migratory labor system has long been a political football. Each country's government and its opponents have taken up the issue to score points against domestic and international adversaries—including, at times, U.S. corporations and military occupiers—only to drop it as its political expediency has worn thin. The most influential voices in Dominican dialogues concerning Haitian immigration have been those propagandists who warn that contact with Haitians places the Dominican people in danger of "progressive ethnic degradation" (Balaguer 1985, 45, my trans.; also Díaz-Ordóñez 1938; Peña Batlle 1943; Cornielle 1980). Recently, journalists and human rights investigators have altered the terms of debate somewhat in the immigrants' favor. They have alleged that the employment of Haitian labor on the Dominican sugar estates is like plantation slavery, given the severity of the constraints that cane growers and Dominican law enforcement authorities place on workers' freedoms (World Council of Churches 1978 and 1982; Anti-Slavery Society 1979; CIMADE 1979; ILO 1983; Veras 1983; Lemoine 1985; Madruga 1986; Plant 1987; Americas Watch 1989 and 1990; Lawyers Committee 1991a).

2. Since the rebirth of independent social research in the Dominican Republic in the late 1960s, several scholars, mainly Dominicans, have pursued an interest in the historical and present-day employment of immigrant labor in the Dominican Republic's sugar industry (Hernández 1973; Corten 1974, 1981, and 1986; Díaz-Santana 1974; Corten et al. 1976; Hernández et al. 1976; Lozano 1976 and 1980; Báez Evertsz 1978 and 1986; Castillo 1978, 1980, 1981a, 1981b, and 1985; Duarte 1980; Carreño 1984; Bryan 1985; Moya Pons et al. 1986; Hoetink 1988; Murphy 1986 and 1991; Baud

1992). More recently, several authors have examined the migration of Haitian men to the sugar estates of the Dominican Republic as a test case for theories of labor circulation in the world economy (Glaessel-Brown 1979; Vargas G. 1981; Grasmuck 1982 and 1983; Lundahl 1983; Perusek 1984). The migratory labor system has been studied considerably less on the Haitian side of the border than on the Dominican side (but see Price-Mars 1953; Legros 1955; Moral 1959, 40–41, and 1961, 69–71; Castor 1983; Corten 1986).

3. Definitions of the key terms "peasant" and "migration" are in order. "Peasant livelihood" here denotes life-styles that revolve around the production, for home consumption and sale in the marketplace, of subsistence and export staples on a small scale with capital managed, if not always owned, by the producer. "Migration" I define as any absence of one month or longer from the migrant's place of origin. As in Bedford's (1985, 338) study of population mobility in eastern Fiji, my primary concern was with "movements which necessitated a substantial restructuring of the round of social and economic activities of those involved. Absences from home for a few hours or days were thus not considered relevant whereas a period of at least four weeks generally did result in a locational shift in the primary activities of an individual mover."

4. Haitian Creole words are transcribed in this study in a modified Laubach Haitian Creole orthography. This, with the exception of a few signs, is identical to the International Phonetic Alphabet. The circumflex (^) indicates nasals. The letters *è, ò, y, ch, tch, j,* and *r* are pronounced approximately as in French. The single quotation mark denotes a liaison between words, and the hyphen links the definite article or a possessive particle as a suffix to a noun.

5. Carlos Dore's continuing study of second- and third-generation Haitians in the Dominican Republic promises to shed light on these and other unanswered questions about the Haitian population off the sugar estates. His preliminary research among ethnic Haitians in one neighborhood on the outskirts of the capital city of Santo Domingo reveals a large proportion of people who trace their origins back to *bateyes* of the Barahona estate in the southwestern part of the country (Dore Cabral 1987, 64). More fieldwork of this kind must be done in other low-income neighborhoods of the capital before firm conclusions can be drawn about the origins of the Haitian population of the city.

6. For many years, the CEA transported *âba fil* entrants in the same open flatbed trucks used to haul cane on its sugar estates. In a nightmarish road accident on 27 January 1989, a truck flipped while it was carrying Haitians from the frontier town of Dajabón to the Central Haina estate, killing forty-seven. Americas Watch (1990, 5–6) reports that *âba fil* entrants are now transported by bus.

7. Company bosses at times keep forcibly recruited workers under lock at night or confiscate workers' belongings in order to prevent their escape (Betances 1985, 80; Americas Watch 1989, 21, and 1990, 35). When I did fieldwork in Yerba Buena and its surrounding *bateyes* in 1985–86 and visited there briefly in 1987, I neither observed these practices nor was told of their existence by cane workers. These measures were allegedly used during the Balaguer governments of 1966 to 1978 (Plant 1987, 80), and

may have become the rule again after President Balaguer's return to power in 1986. Even so, a large body of evidence confirms that official restrictions on Haitians' movements in the Dominican Republic are neither constant nor impermeable. The personal histories of veteran *braceros*, for instance, reveal a high rate of internal mobility in the Dominican Republic. One reason why the CEA implemented its "incentive" system of forced savings (see chapter 4) was to encourage *braceros* to remain on the estates to which the company assigned them (ILO 1983, 69). Some CEA properties are notorious for losing Haitian laborers almost as rapidly as they can be replaced. This is especially true of certain areas of the massive Río Haina estate, which are known for their low yield of cane per hectare. These areas have to be replenished more or less constantly with recruits just to have enough hands to keep the harvest going.

8. Two of the recruits I interviewed may have been victims of fraud. They were separately persuaded to go to the Dominican Republic by strangers who upon crossing the border handed them over to the Dominican authorities.

CHAPTER 1. THE ORIGINS OF DEMAND

1. The idea that the use of slave labor in industrial agriculture arose in response to the existence of "open resources" in host territories can be traced largely to Nieboer. He wrote, "All of the peoples of the earth . . . may be divided into two categories. Among the peoples of the first category the means of subsistence are open to all; everyone who is able-bodied and not defective in mind can provide for himself independently of any capitalist or landlord. . . . Among the peoples of the other category subsistence depends on resources of which the supply is limited, and therefore people destitute of these resources are dependent on the owners. . . . [T]he relations between the social classes differ largely, according as resources are open or closed: only among people of open resources can slavery and serfdom exist, whereas free laborers dependent on wages are only found among peoples with closed resources" (Nieboer 1910, 385). Debate about the social effects of the land/labor ratio began long before Nieboer formulated his concept of open and closed resources. It dates back at least as far as Merivale, Wakefield, and Marx. And, of course, discussion of this topic has continued long after Nieboer's time. Mintz's (1977, 257 and 268, n. 15) deft outline provides as good a starting point as any for those who wish to know more about this issue. He observes, "Today, more and more students seem to be turning back to political factors in attempting to explain why abundant land plus scarce labor do not automatically result in slavery, but nonetheless often appear to 'generate' it" (ibid., 268, n. 15).

2. Castillo (1978, 49–50) has documented that 39,090 West Indian *braceros* entered the Dominican Republic between 1912 and 1920 under the sponsorship of the sugar companies. Between 1921 and 1928, another 40,668 entered. These figures do not include people who entered without official approval, of whom there were many, it seems. The official data indicates that West Indian migration reached its peak during the sugar boom years between 1916 and 1920. The magnitude of West Indian migration to the Dominican Republic can also be gauged according to its effects on the migrants' islands of origin. Bryan (1985, 241) observes that in some years, "About

90 percent of the male population of Anguilla . . . migrated on a seasonal basis to the plantations of the Dominican Republic." In 1926, on the same island, a British colonial officer remarked that there were "hardly a dozen young men in the place, because of the 6,000 inhabitants every available man had gone off as usual to work for the four- or five-month season on the sugarcane estates in the semi-Spanish territory of Santo Domingo." The same source added, "*mirabile dictu,* [they brought] back the money each year and with it they built houses or employed it in other useful ways at home" (quoted in Bryan 1985, 241). Similarly, Richardson (1983, 111) observes that "American dollars earned by men in the cane fields of Santo Domingo allowed parents, wives, and children on St. Kitts and Nevis to buy imported food, clothing, and building material." He adds that, in the mid-1930s, the "cutoff of emigration outlets for laborers from the smallest islands was a fundamental cause of West Indian unrest" (ibid., 142).

3. In 1983, Murphy (1991, 84) observed that the contract *braceros* received "professional and courteous" treatment as they passed through the CEA's immigration processing center at the Dominican-Haitian frontier. Veteran *braceros* report that, after 1978, contract workers were transported from the frontier to the estates in buses rather than, as before, on the open flatbed cargo holds of trucks. Prior to 1978, the only bedding the company would furnish for the *braceros* was an empty sugar sack and a length of rope, from which each man was expected to rig a makeshift hammock. Today, the company equips each room with two or three steel-frame bunk beds, and issues each *bracero* a thin foam mattress to cushion his bed frame. Since 1982, CEA weigh stations have given cane cutters receipts for the RD$0.60 per ton of cane that the company withholds from their pay, ostensibly until the end of the harvest as a form of forced savings. Previously, end-of-harvest bonuses either were not paid at all or were arbitrarily determined by the CEA. Company officials still sometimes refuse to honor these "incentive" receipts, or, more often, they delay in cashing them for weeks at harvest's end.

Chapter 2. Mobilizing Labor

1. Whether the poverty of rural Haiti is more properly explained as a product of forces "internal" to the nation's political economy or as an outcome of Haiti's relationship with the rest of world is a topic of lively academic debate. On the one hand, some prominent non-Haitian scholars (e.g., Rotberg 1971, and Lundahl 1979, 1982, and 1983) argue that Haitian farm incomes have fallen mainly as a result of the damage done to the soil by intense cultivation of the country's mountainous terrain. They also blame the malfeasance and shortsighted approach of the Haitian government for policies unfair to small-scale agriculturalists. On the other hand, a group made up mostly of Haitian scholars (e.g., Joachim 1979; Trouillot 1980 and 1990; Girault 1981; Caprio 1982a and 1982b) suggests that obstacles to development as great as misgovernment and environmental deterioration lay in the global circumstances of Haiti's nationhood. Among these, they have included the racism of the great powers and Haiti's continuing dependence on the manufactures and finances of the industrialized world.

2. Castor (1971, 78) arrives at an estimate of the total land area expropriated by U.S. businesses that is almost *four times* greater than what Moral (1961, 63) and Moore (1972, 45) estimate it to have been (271,600 acres versus 70,200 acres versus "not quite 50,000 acres in all"). Castor errs by including in her figures all concessions awarded to U.S. firms, regardless of whether the land was actually taken over or not. For example, in her list of "expropriations," she includes 125,000 acres on which an American group was given a two-year option for irrigation in the Artibonite Valley. This group failed to raise enough capital to get the project beyond the exploratory phase. There is no evidence that the land was expropriated at all, let alone on the scale of 125,000 acres (Millspaugh 1931, 154–56). Nicholls (1985, 261–62, n. 3) points out similar errors in Castor's figures.

3. Pierre-Charles (1967, 184), on the other hand, contends that the chaotic state of Haitian land tenure was the biggest obstacle to the reintroduction of plantation agriculture under the U.S. occupation, and Castor (1971, 90) seconds this opinion. This hypothesis sits uncomfortably with Pierre-Charles's (1967, 67) own claim that "[state] latifundism . . . is the predominant form of agrarian property" in Haiti (my trans.). It also contradicts Castor's insistence, which seems closest to the truth, that land legislation under the U.S. occupation threw the door open for foreign investors to acquire land in Haiti. Thus, on the one hand, Pierre-Charles and Castor say occupation of the land by tens of thousands of smallholders was the main bulwark against the spread of latifundia. On the other hand, they imply that those same smallholders had only an insecure hold on their land (or were actually expropriated en masse). Even though it might be possible to find evidence in support of either contention, it is not, in my opinion, logically defensible to have it both ways. Pierre (1988, 122, 128) raises the intriguing possibility that "the [sugar] industry's growth [in Haiti] was held back because of rivalries between large international sugar corporations," but admits that "until further research is carried out this must remain only a hypothesis." Pierre's hypothesis is plausible, as far as it goes, but it does not explain why agricultural exports other than sugar also failed to take off in Haiti in the period between the world wars. As Dauphin showed, sugar was not the only plantation crop that could be grown profitably in Haiti.

CHAPTER 3. THE SETTING

1. People who are familiar with life in the *bateyes* will recognize that my use of the term "*viejo*," to denote those Haitian men who maintain permanent residence on the sugar estates, is to some degree specific to my analytical purpose here. As a category of person in the *bateyes*, "*viejo*" may be defined in several ways, depending on the context of speech. The essence of its meaning is that it is always semantically opposed to "*congó*" (which I use here synonymously with "seasonal migrant" but which likewise has various meanings). It can be observed that a man who would at one moment be called a *viejo* under the defining criterion of residence might at another time, and by other criteria, be termed a *congó*. If asked to define the term, migrants and returnees may say that a *viejo* is "a person who never returns to Haiti."

This is clearly an overly exclusive definition, because many men who return occasionally or permanently to Haiti are also referred to, in Haitian Creole, as *"vyeho."* It confirms, nonetheless, that, to rural Haitians, a man's residence history is generally of central concern in determining whether or not he is a *viejo*. In the Dominican Republic, on the other hand, both Haitians and Dominicans may understand the term to denote the *language capabilities* of the person in question. In this sense of the word, it is of no importance whether a man resides permanently in the Dominican Republic or only goes there for the cane harvest. What matters is whether he speaks Spanish fairly well or not. He who can understand and make himself understood in Spanish is a *viejo*. He who cannot is a *congó*. Similarly, in Haiti, *"congó"* at times denotes a lack of experience in the Dominican Republic, as when a man speaks of his first migrant voyage as "when I came *congó* to the Dominican Republic" (*"lè'm vini kôgo nâ pâyòl"*). A third pair of meanings of *"congó/viejo,"* therefore, is "first-time/veteran migrant." Yet, at times, *batey* residents also use these terms just as I do here. For instance, they refer to the seasonal migrants collectively as "the *congoses.*" This is in spite of the fact that some men among this group could be called *viejos* by virtue of their knowledge of Spanish and lengthy experience in the Dominican Republic. Murphy (1991), a long-time student of Dominican *batey* social organization, makes scant use of the terms *"viejo"* and *"congó,"* perhaps out of misgivings about the fuzziness of these terms. He instead divides Haitian migrants into two main categories, *braceros*, or legal contract workers, and *anba fil*, which he defines as those who enter without legal permit or who stay in the Dominican Republic past the term of their legal contract. In effect, Murphy places both nonreturning and seasonal migrants under the same heading of *anba fil*. This, unfortunately, diminishes the relevance to my concerns of his extensive survey data and firsthand observations.

2. As of March 1987, the combined population of the two *katye* was about 450 persons. Among adults (persons over age 15) there at that time, there were about 86 men per 100 women. Of 73 households in the two *katye*, 53 (about 73 percent) had an immediate family member who had been to the Dominican Republic, and only 26 (about 36 percent) had a member who had gone to live in a Haitian city or a country *lòt bò lâmè*. It may be that the lower prevalence of emigration to Haitian cities and *lòt bò lâmè* is a product of my having collected data only in *rural* neighborhoods and not in the town of Cayes-Jacmel. Throughout Haiti, town people are reputed to be more prone to emigrate cityward than people in surrounding rural areas. To my knowledge, no other migration data set from Haiti separates residents of provincial towns, such as Cayes-Jacmel, from people who live outside of town. Therefore, I have no basis to say whether emigration to Haitian cities and to countries "beyond the sea" is more or less common in Rocheteau and Cabrouette than in most other rural *katye* in Haiti.

3. This observation is in keeping with Stepick's (1984, 4) findings, based on a survey of Haitian immigrants in South Florida: "[T]he Haitians who have made it to the U.S. migrated both within their own country and to the U.S., but only one Krome Haitian and one Haitian Entrant had migrated to the Dominican Republic before coming to the U.S. Clearly, these are separate migrant streams from Haiti with little overlap between them."

4. I gathered rudimentary migration history data for nearly everyone over the age of 15 who resided in Rocheteau and Cabrouette at the time of fieldwork and for each respondent's absent or deceased siblings or offspring, in the following way. I obtained a three-generation genealogy of all participating families in the two *katye*. I then determined, if possible, (1) which individuals in the genealogy had ever lived in the *katye*, (2) the birth order and the approximate year of birth (and/or, if deceased, the age at death) of each respondent's siblings and offspring, (3) the present place of residence of each of these relatives, and (4) whether or not any of the absent or deceased had ever emigrated to the Dominican Republic. I took care to avoid counting the same person twice, and excluded from my sample any relatives who had never lived in the *katye*. Hill (1972, 97, and 1986, 125) questions the reliability of any method of determining the volume of emigration that depends on the recollections of migrants and their relatives. Yet my method is similar to that for which Houghton and Walton (1952, 114–15, 125–35) claim success in fieldwork in South Africa. Of course, my data is not complete. Interviewees often could not provide any information about their absent or deceased siblings and offspring, and it is likely that some neglected to mention kinfolk who had been gone for a long time. Even so, gathering basic data on absent kinfolk surely compensated for some of the locational bias that plagues statistical analyses of population movements for which census data is not available (i.e., data gathered in host area samples tends to overcount permanent emigrants, and data gathered in source area samples tends to overcount returned migrants). My data probably still overrepresents returnees but does so much less than it would have if, in computing the prevalence of emigration and return, I had counted only those people who were in Rocheteau and Cabrouette at the time of fieldwork.

5. Between 1955 and 1986, the median duration of migrant voyages was 0.9 year (10 to 11 months), a figure somewhat higher than the length of a "typical" voyage as the result of a very negatively skewed distribution of scores for this variable.

Chapter 4. Poverty, Labor Circulation, and the Reproduction of Rural Livelihoods

1. My fieldwork in Yerba Buena took place in the months leading up to and following the fall from power of Haiti's President Duvalier. This was a time when Haitians in the Dominican Republic were not only willing but eager to talk about abuses which they and others had suffered at the hands of the Tontons Macoutes. In the Dominican capital, Santo Domingo, I met several Haitians who did not hesitate to identify themselves as political refugees, even though they knew me much less well than people in Yerba Buena did. Murphy (1986, 232), based on interviews and observations in several Dominican *bateyes,* comes to the same conclusion as I: "political exile does not appear to be a primary motivating factor in . . . migration to the Dominican sugar industry."

2. There is reason to suspect that 3,000 calories might well be an underestimate of the cane cutter's daily needs. Using advanced scientific techniques of measuring energy expenditure, Spurr, Barac-Nieto and Maksud (1975 and 1977) find that a cane cutter or loader who works eight hours a day needs *more than 3,500* calories a day.

3. Between 1980 and 1987, consumer prices increased in the Dominican Republic at an annual rate of 16 percent (UNICEF 1990, 87), but the daily wage rate (i.e., minus incentive payment) of the cane cutter rose only by an average of 7 percent per year (from RD$1.83 to $2.95 per ton of cane).

4. Báez Evertsz (1986, 302–6) claims that, insufficient as it is, the nutrition of the Haitian *bracero* is better than that of the average Haitian. He compares the results of his survey of *braceros'* food intake with data from several nutritional surveys in Haiti. This comparison reveals that the average *bracero* consumes between 107 and 1,015 more calories per day than the average Haitian adult. Yet a simple comparison of the numbers of calories consumed, as revealed in these surveys, does not necessarily demonstrate that "the Haitian immigrant eats more and better" in the Dominican Republic than at home (ibid., 306, my trans.). This is because Báez's data is not strictly speaking comparable to the Haitian nutritional surveys. Whereas he only surveyed *men,* the Haitian data represents the average daily nutrition of *all adults,* male and female. It is well known that in agrarian societies worldwide men generally eat more and better than women. One must suspect that Haiti is not an exception to this rule and that the average Haitian man may therefore be somewhat better nourished than what the national survey data reveals.

5. This point has been partly anticipated by earlier observers of the problem. G. F. Murray (1977, 19) notes that "the vast majority" of seasonal migrants to the Dominican Republic "return and . . . eventually establish households in Kinanbwa," the Cul de Sac village where he did fieldwork. Similarly, Lowenthal (1987, 29) observes, with reference to the Fond-des-Nègres region in southern Haiti, "The migratory impulse—at least until the last decade or so—has always been fueled primarily by the explicit desire to amass sufficient resources elsewhere *in order* to return, and to engage more successfully in agriculture." Larose (1975, 487), in an article on Haitian family land and ritual, also draws a somewhat opaque link between emigration to the Dominican Republic and young men's "needs to achieve personal independence." Wingfield (1966, 96–101) notes that Dominican Republic savings are used for the purchase of certain target goods in Haiti—clothing, building materials, land, and especially livestock. Murphy (1986, 266–67) lists similar uses for migrant money, and adds that "75 percent [of the migrant's savings] is taken back to his home community." Corten (1976, 106) argues that the motivation of most Dominican Republic migrants is "*not to earn more [abroad], but rather to save a certain amount of money [for home]*" (my trans.). Based on his finding that one-half to two-thirds of the *braceros* he interviewed had access to their own or to their family's land in Haiti (the relations of tenancy and quantities of land involved were not specified), Corten (1976, 97 and 1985, 76) voices doubts that the immigration of Haitian cane workers can be characterized simply as a "migration of misery."

6. That many migrants return to Haiti without savings to speak of suggests a possible, previously undiscussed function of labor circulation: seasonal emigration might tailor household composition to fit available food supplies and purchasing power during yearly periods of scarcity. Emigration might enable people at home to cope better with scarcity by sending away the biggest consumers, able-bodied adult

males, to fend for themselves at that time of the year when their labor is relatively redundant locally and when food supplies are insufficient to feed all hungry mouths. As one veteran migrant explained in Yerba Buena (I paraphrase), "Even if you return without a penny, if you had a calf at home, growing bigger during the six months you were away, when you return, you will find it still there, and it might then sell for much more than when you left home. But if you had not gone [to the Dominican Republic], you, there, at home, a man, you would spend money. You would have to sell that calf regardless, just to eat. But if you are not at home, it stays unsold." Yet the timing of emigration itself suggests that Haitian men seek more in the Dominican Republic than simply surviving at minimal cost to their households of origin. Men generally do not restrict their absences from home to the hungry months that follow spring planting (March and April) but leave home between November and January, weeks before the hungry season. If households seasonally expelled men in order to cope better with hunger, it is likely that most men would not leave until spring planting was under way and food supplies neared crisis point.

7. My understandings of the peasant life cycle, of the institutions that govern transmission and exchange of property, and of the gender-based division of labor in rural Haiti are based mainly on my reading of G. F. Murray (1977) and Lowenthal (1987). It is to their works that readers who wish to know more about these issues should turn for details.

8. Little evidence points to the loss of filial labor as a reason why parents might regret to see their sons go. It may be that many of the young men who emigrate have already begun to assert their independence from parental authority by diminishing their unremunerated labor in their fathers' gardens. Yet there were at least two cases in Rocheteau and Cabrouette in which the sons of single mothers had alternated their voyages, relay-style, so that at least one would always be at home to work the fields.

Chapter 5. The Impact on the Home Area

1. Concerning land transactions in a northern Haitian village, Smucker (1982, 291) observes an "overwhelming incidence of purchase from relatives," and adds that "it is clearly the predominant form of land sale" there.

2. Goats, traditionally raised alongside pigs, reproduce themselves more slowly, and fetch a lower resale price than Haitian pigs did. Cattle raising has not taken the place of swine production, because of the high price of calves and scarcity of land for pasture. And, according to DeWind and Kinley (1988, 87), "the promotion of agro-industrial poultry production is blocking small farmers from being able to replace their lost income by producing poultry."

CHAPTER 6. MIGRANTS AND STAY-AT-HOMES:
WOMEN AND LABOR CIRCULATION

1. Moscoso Puello's *Cañas y bueyes,* Marrero Aristy's *Over,* and Mir's *Hay un país en el mundo* . . . are the best known works of creative literature set on the sugar estates of the Dominican Republic.

2. With the exception of one recent study (Jansen and Millán 1991, 98), this level of economic activity is the highest ever recorded among women in the *bateyes* (Moya Pons et al. 1986, 443; Báez Evertsz 1986, 311; and Bobea and Guzmán C. 1985, 126).

3. I follow White (1980, 1) in defining "domestic labor" as "that labor which maintains and reproduces the labor power that is consumed daily in obtaining a wage. It gives laborers whatever they are culturally disposed to need to be fit for the next day's work."

4. In Santo Domingo, I explored the possibility of carrying out a survey of Haitian international traders but concluded that this could not be done with the time and resources I had at hand.

5. D. I. Marshall (1979, 49–50) makes much the same observation concerning Haitian immigrants in the Bahamas. In her survey, she found, "Most [female] respondents actually initiated new relationships or unions in Carmichael [the Bahamas]." She concludes that Haitian women enter into conjugal union there out of necessity "because of the great difficulty which [they] experience in obtaining jobs in the Bahamas." She adds, "This need must be known and appreciated in the North-West [Haiti], and therefore this knowledge should act as a deterrent upon the migration of women who are partners in satisfying unions in Haiti. It seems reasonable to assume that their male partners would object to their migration, given this knowledge."

6. This is, more or less, the argument Pittin (1984) makes concerning Hausa women who emigrate from rural Nigeria to the city of Katsina and become *karuwai* ("courtesans"). According to her, when she asked Hausa *karuwai* directly about their reasons for leaving home, they would consistently represent their departure as having responded entirely to "the intractable problems which they faced, and their need to run from an untenable situation" (ibid., 1307). In contrast with what they state publicly, the truth, says Pittin, is that Hausa *karuwai* actively choose their livelihood as a better alternative to rural life. "For the individual Hausa woman, the life-style associated with *karuwanci* [courtesanship] offers scope for independence, self-assertion, and economic attainment greater than is available within the confines of marriage, or within the limited resources of rural society" (ibid., 1308). It is only because "a career in *karuwanci* is not an acceptable life for a Hausa woman . . . [that] this career option must be explained away as the consequence of other insupportable pressures and burdens" (ibid., 1307).

7. Migrant women take up union almost exclusively with fellow Haitians. Of the 38 unions I recorded in personal history interviews as having been established in the Dominican Republic, 35 were with Haitian nationals. The remaining three were with Haitian-Dominican men.

8. In my fieldwork, I considered each group of persons (or solitary individual) that set up its own cooking fire for the main meal of the day to be a separate household. Cooking arrangements may signify much to rural Haitians about the kind of relationship that exists between people who sleep under the same roof or in the same residential yard (*laku*). As Comhaire-Sylvain (1961, 195) observed in and around the mountain village of Kenscoff near Port-au-Prince, "When a grown-up daughter comes back to her parents' home through separation after some years of *plasaj*, she may prefer to have separate cooking facilities. If she does, . . . it is a separate household; she is considered by her parents and siblings as an independent person who has been offered a temporary shelter. If she consents to cook with or for her mother, . . . she falls back under parental authority and she is only an additional member of her parents' household." At the time of fieldwork, about 38 percent of *laku* in Rocheteau and Cabrouette (20 of 53) contained more than one dwelling. About 15 percent (8 of 53) contained compound households, in which residents of more than one dwelling "ate out of the same pot." Five of 85 dwellings (about 6 percent), on the other hand, contained two groups of people that made separate cooking arrangements. Only in two instances did a single "household" span two yards. In other words, people sharing the same dwelling comprised 53 of 73 households (about 71 percent). Almost always, at the core of these coresidential groups there stood a nuclear family or a segment of one. Households headed by single women were also common. About 22 percent of all households (16 of 73) were headed by women who were not in conjugal union.

9. The belated entry of thousands of migrants in March through May counteracts the shortage of cane cutters that confronts the sugar companies each year once the midpoint of the harvest has passed. In the last years of contract labor recruitment, the CEA and the Haitian government arranged for a supplementary shipment of 4,000 to 5,000 *braceros* each April (Murphy 1986). This shortage of labor probably develops gradually each year, throughout the harvest, as migrants abandon government sugar estates in search of better pay on private estates, on farms, and in urban areas.

10. My thanks to Sidney Mintz for comments on this point.

CHAPTER 7. *VIEJOS AND CONGOSES*

1. Graves and Graves (1974, 128–29) define "*individualistic* strategies" as those "where a migrant relies essentially on his own resources or his own initiative for a solution. . . . By contrast, in *group-oriented* strategies the migrant turns for help to other people, usually kinsmen, fellow villagers, or migrants from his own ethnic group. Although such strategies tap a larger pool of resources than those possessed by the migrant himself, these are shared within a framework of reciprocity norms that require him to contribute his own resources to swell the adaptive potential of the group as a whole. Such strategies constitute the typical adaptive mode of many cooperative, kin-based societies described by anthropologists, and contrast with the individualistic strategies more common within Western society."

2. Some unresolved questions surround the role of migration decision maker, which Laguerre (1984, 34–38), Fjellman and Gladwin (1985), and Saint-Louis (1988) attribute to the Haitian family. What happens, for instance, if an individual deemed unfit to emigrate refuses to accept the family's judgment and persists in his or her efforts to go? Even stickier, how does the family resolve competing claims for its support? Haitian families (*fâmi*) are highly extensive (Herskovits 1937, 122–25; Simpson 1942, 661; Bastien 1961, 489) and may easily contain several individuals who stand a good chance of success in migration. Perhaps more importantly, it is unclear what unit these authors refer to when they say that "the family" decides whether or not an individual should emigrate. The Haitian *fâmi* differs from the North American family in that it is not a *group* but an extensive—in theory, unbounded—personal *network*. What Haitians call "*fâmi*" bears a closer formal resemblance to the *kindred*, as Freeman (1961 and 1970, 66–67) describes it among the Iban people of Borneo (also Davenport 1961 on Jamaica), than to the North American family, in either its nuclear or extended forms (Lowenthal 1987, chap. 5). It may therefore be misleading to assume that the Haitian *fâmi*, or even one restricted branch of it, makes decisions in the same way as the white, mainstream North American family (whatever that may be). Saint-Louis (1988, 351–52) goes further than any previous author toward defining who makes up the Haitian "family group" (her term) that makes decisions about migration. Yet more precise description is needed about who is approached, with what questions, concerning a relative's migration plans.

3. The *chef de section* is the top law enforcement officer of Haiti's lowest administrative unit, the *section*, and is usually a man of great influence locally.

4. A Haitian man may be rewarded with a meager salary during the cane harvest if he recruits a fairly large number of workers for his *batey*. In the CEA estates, the post with which the recruiter is most often rewarded is that of *capataz de braceros*. Dominican men are also assigned this post through the patronage of company administrators.

5. Báez finds considerable regional variation in internal mobility among Haitian residents of the sugar estates. This rate varied from a high of 47.7 percent in the Barahona estate to a low of 10.6 percent in the eastern estates around the city of San Pedro de Macorís.

6. Similarly, on the basis of fieldwork in rural northern Haiti, Ahlers (1979, 51) reports that "few . . . origin households maintain contact with out-migrants in the Dominican Republic."

7. To date, only one set of survey data, that of Báez Evertsz (1986, 39, and 1992, 117), has been analyzed with the purpose of periodizing permanent emigration. In his sample, taken in 1983, he finds that 37 percent of *viejos* entered the country between 1956 and 1965, and 40 percent entered between 1971 and 1980.

Postscript

1. I owe my phrasing here to P. Richards's (1983, 12) discussion of the evidence concerning the existence of a "hungry season" in sub-Saharan Africa: "talk of food shortages may constitute an idiom for the pursuit of political and economic disagreements, rather than evidence of nutritional deprivation."

References

Abbott, Susan. 1976. "Full-Time Farmers and Week-End Wives: An Analysis of Altering Conjugal Roles." *Journal of Marriage and the Family* 38 (1): 165–74.

Ahlers, Theodore H. 1979. "A Micro-Economic Analysis of Rural-Urban Migration in Haiti." Ph.D. dissertation, Fletcher School of Law and Diplomacy, Tufts University.

Allman, James, and Karen Richman. 1985. "Migration Decision Making and Policy: The Case of Haitian International Migration, 1971–1984." Paper presented at the Population Association of America meetings, Boston, March 28–30, 1985.

Americas Watch. 1989. *Haitian Sugar-Cane Cutters in the Dominican Republic.* New York: Americas Watch.

———. 1990. *Harvesting Oppression: Forced Haitian Labor in the Dominican Sugar Industry.* New York: Americas Watch.

Amersfoort, J. M. M. van. 1978. "Migrant Workers, Circular Migration and Development." *Tijdschrift voor Economische en Sociale Geografie* 69 (1/2): 17–26.

Ángeles Crummett, María de los. 1985. "Class, Household Structure, and Migration: A Case Study from Rural Mexico." Women in International Development, Working Paper no. 92. East Lansing: Michigan State University.

Anti-Slavery Society. 1979. "Migrant Workers in the Dominican Republic." *The Anti-Slavery Reporter and Aborigines' Friend (Series VI)* 12 (6): 11–14.

Aubin, Eugène (Descos, Louis Eugène Aubin Coullard). 1910. *En Haïti: Planteurs d'autrefois, nègres d'aujourd'hui.* Paris: Armand Colin.

Báez Evertsz, Franc. 1978. *Azúcar y dependencia en la República Dominicana.* Santo Domingo: Editora de la Universidad Autónoma de Santo Domingo.

———. 1986. *Braceros haitianos en la República Dominicana.* 2d ed. Santo Domingo: Taller.

———. 1992. "Explotación en los bateyes." In *Ayiti—República Dominicana: En el umbral de los años 90*, 109–25. Port-au-Prince: CIPROS.

Balaguer, Joaquín. 1985. *La isla al revés: Haití y el destino dominicano.* 3d ed. Santo Domingo: Librería Dominicana, S.A.

Balán, Jorge, Harley L. Browning, Elizabeth Jelin, and Lee Litzler. 1969. "A Computerized Approach to the Processing and Analysis of Life Histories Obtained in Sample Surveys." *Behavioral Science* 14 (1): 105–20.

Balch, Emily Greene, ed. 1927. *Occupied Haiti*. New York: Writers.

Bastien, Remy. 1951. *La familia rural haitiana: Valle de Marbial*. Mexico City: Libra.

———. 1961. "Haitian Rural Family Organization." *Social and Economic Studies* 10 (4): 478–510.

Bathgate, Murray A. 1985. "Movement Processes from Precontact to Contemporary Times: The Ndi-Nggai, West Guadalcanal, Solomon Islands." In *Circulation in Population Movement: Substance and Concepts from the Melanesian Case*, edited by Murray Chapman and R. Mansell Prothero, 83–118. London: Routledge and Kegan Paul.

Baud, Michiel. 1992. "Sugar and Unfree Labour: Reflections on Labour Control in the Dominican Republic, 1870–1935." *Journal of Peasant Studies* 19 (2): 301–25.

Beck, Jane C. 1979. *To Windward of the Land: The Occult World of Alexander Charles*. Bloomington: Indiana University Press.

Bedford, Richard. 1985. "Population Movement in a Small Island Periphery: The Case of Eastern Fiji." In *Circulation in Population Movement: Substance and Concepts from the Melanesian Case*, edited by Murray Chapman and R. Mansell Prothero, 333–59. London: Routledge and Kegan Paul.

Berg, Elliot J. 1961. "Backward-Sloping Labor Supply Functions in Dual Economies—The Africa Case." *Quarterly Journal of Economics* 75 (3): 468–92.

Bernstein, Hilda. 1985. *For Their Triumphs and for Their Tears: Women in Apartheid in South Africa*. 2d ed. London: International Defence and Aid Fund for Southern Africa.

Bertrand, Jean Wilfrid. 1973. "Le Phénomène migratoire dans la commune de Jacmel de 1957 à 1971." *Cahiers du CHISS* (Centre Haïtien d'Investigation en Sciences Sociales, Port- au-Prince) 7 (9): 42–60.

Betances, Ramón. 1985. "Una experiencia con los congoses." *Estudios Sociales* 18 (59): 77–81.

Bobea, Lilian, and Ana Rita Guzmán C. 1985. "Reproducción de la fuerza de trabajo familiar: Bateyes Lechería y Enriquillo." Tesis de licenciatura, Universidad Autónoma de Santo Domingo.

Breman, Jan. 1978. "Seasonal Migration and Co-operative Capitalism: The Crushing of Cane and of Labour by the Sugar Factories of Bardoli, South Gujarat—Part 1." *Journal of Peasant Studies* 6 (1): 41–70.

———. 1979. "Seasonal Migration and Co-operative Capitalism: The Crushing of Cane and of Labour by the Sugar Factories of Bardoli, South Gujarat—Part 2." *Journal of Peasant Studies* 6 (2): 168–209.

———. 1990. *Labour Migration and Rural Transformation in Colonial Asia*. Amsterdam: Free University Press.

Brookfield, Harold C. 1970. "Dualism, and the Geography of Developing Countries." Presidential address delivered to Section 21 (Geographical Sciences), Australian and New Zealand Association for the Advancement of Science, Port Moresby, Papua New Guinea, August 1970.

Brown, Barbara B. 1983. "The Impact of Male Labour Migration on Women in Botswana." *African Affairs* 82 (328): 367–88.

Bryan, Patrick E. 1985. "The Question of Labor in the Sugar Industry of the Dominican Republic in the Late Nineteenth and Early Twentieth Centuries." In *Between Slavery and Free Labor: The Spanish-Speaking Caribbean in the Nineteenth Century,* edited by Manuel Moreno Fraginals, Frank Moya Pons, and Stanley L. Engerman, 235–51. Baltimore: Johns Hopkins University Press.

Buchanan, Susan Huelsebusch. 1979. "Haitian Women in New York City." *Migration Today* 7 (4): 19–25, 39.

———. 1980. "Scattered Seeds: The Meaning of the Migration for Haitians in New York City." Ph.D. dissertation, New York University.

———. 1981. "Haitian Emigration: The Perspective from South Florida and Haiti." U.S. Agency for International Development, Port-au-Prince. Photocopy.

Burawoy, Michael. 1976. "The Functions and Reproduction of Migrant Labor: Comparative Material from Southern Africa and the United States." *American Journal of Sociology* 81 (5): 1050–87.

Calder, Bruce J. 1981. "The Dominican Turn toward Sugar." *Caribbean Review* 10 (3): 18–21, 44–45.

———. 1984. *The Impact of Intervention: The Dominican Republic during the U.S. Occupation of 1916–1924.* Austin: University of Texas Press.

Caprio, Giovanni. 1982a. "Un Livre de Mats Lundahl: 'Les Paysans et la pauvreté, une étude sur Haïti'." *Conjonction* 152: 61–69.

———. 1982b. "Réponse à Mats Lundahl." *Conjonction* 152: 87–97.

———. 1985. "De l'Indépendance à l'occupation américaine." In *Atlas d'Haïti.* Talence: CEGET.

Caroit, Jean-Michel. 1992. "El peso de la economía." In *Ayiti—República Dominicana: En el umbral de los años 90,* 71–85. Port-au-Prince: CIPROS.

Carreño, Nelson. 1984. "El sistema de explotación agrícola: La organización técnico-económica de la producción azucarera en la República Dominicana, 1875–1925." *Revista Estudios Dominicanos* 1: 109–35.

Casimir, Jean. 1964. "Aperçu sur la structure économique d'Haïti." *América Latina* 7 (3): 37–56.

Castells, Manuel. 1975. "Immigrant Workers and Class Struggles in Advanced Capitalism: The Western European Experience." *Politics & Society* 5 (1): 33–66.

Castillo, José del. 1978. *La inmigración de braceros azucareros en la República Dominicana, 1900–1930.* Santo Domingo: CENDIA.

———. 1979. "Las emigraciones y su aporte a la cultura dominicana (finales del siglo XIX y principios del siglo XX)." *eme eme, Estudios Dominicanos* 8 (45): 1–43.

———. 1980. "Problemas sociales en el sector azucarero (ponencia)." *Ciencia y Sociedad* 5 (2): 277–92.

———. 1981a. "Azúcar y braceros: Historia de un problema." *INAZUCAR* 6 (29): 37–48.

———. 1981b. *Ensayos de sociología dominicana.* Santo Domingo: Ediciones Siboney.

———. 1985. "The Formation of the Dominican Sugar Industry: From Competition to Monopoly, from National Semiproletariat to Foreign Proletariat." In *Between Slavery and Free Labor: The Spanish-Speaking Caribbean in the Nineteenth Century,* edited by Manuel Moreno Fraginals, Frank Moya Pons and Stanley L. Engerman, 215–34. Baltimore: Johns Hopkins University Press.

————, and Martin F. Murphy. 1987. "Migration, National Identity and Cultural Policy in the Dominican Republic." *Journal of Ethnic Studies* 15 (3): 49–69.

Castles, Stephen, and Godula Kosack. 1973. *Immigrant Workers and Class Structure in Western Europe.* London: Oxford University Press.

Castor, Suzy. 1971. *La ocupación norteamericana de Haití y sus consecuencias (1915–1934).* Mexico City: Siglo Veintiuno Editores.

————. 1974. "El impacto de la ocupación norteamericana en Haití (1915–1934) y en la República Dominicana (1916–1924)." In *Política y sociología en Haití y la República Dominicana.* Coloquio Domínico-Haitiano de Ciencias Sociales, México, July 1971, 42–64. Mexico City: Universidad Nacional Autónoma de México.

————. 1983. *Migraciones y relaciones internacionales (el caso haitiano-dominicano).* Mexico City: Facultad de Ciencias Políticas y Sociales, Universidad Nacional Autónoma de México and Centro de Estudios Latinoamericanos, CELA.

Cedeño Caroit, Amelia. 1992. "Aspectos jurídicos del 'problema haitiano'." In *Ayiti— República Dominicana: En el umbral de los años 90,* 87–107. Port-au-Prince: CIPROS.

Chapman, Murray. 1982. "Circulation." In *International Encyclopedia of Population, Vol. 1,* edited by John A. Ross, 93–98. New York: The Free Press.

————, and R. Mansell Prothero. 1985. "Themes on Circulation in the Third World." In *Circulation in Third World Countries,* edited by R. Mansell Prothero and Murray Chapman, 1–26. London: Routledge and Kegan Paul.

Charles, Carolle. 1990. "A Transnational Dialectic of Race, Class, and Ethnicity: Patterns of Identities and Forms of Consciousness among Haitian Migrants in New York City." Ph.D. dissertation, State University of New York, Binghampton.

CIMADE. 1979. *De Nouveaux esclaves dans les Caraïbes: Les Coupeurs de canne Haïtiens en République Dominicaine.* Paris: CIMADE.

Colfer, Carol. 1985. "On Circular Migration: From the Distaff Side." In *Labour Circulation and the Labour Process,* edited by Guy Standing, 219–51. London: Croom Helm.

Collins, Jane L. 1986. "The Household and Relations of Production in Southern Peru." *Comparative Studies in Society and History* 28 (4): 651–71.

————. 1988. *Unseasonal Migrations: The Effects of Rural Labor Scarcity in Peru.* Princeton: Princeton University Press.

Comhaire-Sylvain, S. 1961. "The Household in Kenscoff, Haiti." *Social and Economic Studies* 10 (2): 192–222.

Connell, John. 1985. "Copper, Cocoa, and Cash: Terminal, Temporary, and Circular Mobility in Siwai, North Solomons." In *Circulation in Population Movement: Substance and Concepts from the Melanesian Case,* edited by Murray Chapman and R. Mansell Prothero, 119–48. London: Routledge and Kegan Paul.

————, Biplab Dasgupta, Roy Laishley, and Michael Lipton. 1976. *Migration from Rural Areas: The Evidence from Village Studies.* Delhi: Oxford University Press.

Coote, Belinda. 1992. *The Trade Trap: Poverty and the Global Commodity Markets.* Oxford: OXFAM.

Cornielle, Carlos. 1980. *Proceso histórico domínico-haitiano: Una advertencia a la juventud dominicana.* Santo Domingo: Publicaciones América, S.A.

Corten, André. 1974. "Migraciones e intereses de clases." In *Política y sociología en Haití y la República Dominicana.* Coloquio Domínico-Haitiano de Ciencias Sociales, México, July 1971, 65–82. Mexico City: Universidad Nacional Autónoma de México.

———. 1976. "Haití: Estructura agraria y migración de trabajadores a los centrales azucareros dominicanos." In *Azúcar y política en la República Dominicana.* 2d ed., by André Corten, Carlos María Vilas, Mercedes Acosta and Isis Duarte, 85–114. Santo Domingo: Editora Taller.

———. 1981. "The Migration of Haitian Workers to Sugar Factories in the Dominican Republic." In *Contemporary Caribbean: A Sociological Reader,* edited by Susan Craig, 349–66. Maracas, Trinidad and Tobago: The College Press.

———. 1985. *Proletariado y procesos de proletarización en República Dominicana.* Santo Domingo: Editora Alfa and Omega.

———. 1986. *Port au Sucre: Prolétariat et prolétarisations, Haïti et république Dominicaine.* Montreal: Éditions du CIDIHCA.

———. 1992. "La Démocratie ou l'évasion: Les Réfugiés haïtiens à l'assaut de l'Amérique." *Le Monde diplomatique* no. 455: 15.

———, Mercedes Acosta, and Isis Duarte. 1976. "Las relaciones de producción en la economía azucarera dominicana." In *Azúcar y política en la República Dominicana.* 2d ed., by André Corten, Carlos María Vilas, Mercedes Acosta and Isis Duarte, 9–83. Santo Domingo: Editora Taller.

———, Carlos María Vilas, Mercedes Acosta, and Isis Duarte. 1976. *Azúcar y política en la República Dominicana.* 2d ed. Santo Domingo: Editora Taller.

Crassweller, Robert D. 1966. *Trujillo: The Life and Times of a Caribbean Dictator.* New York: Macmillan.

Dalencour, François. 1923. *Le Sauvetage national par le retour à la terre.* Port-au-Prince: Imprimerie V. Pierre-Noël.

Dartigue, Maurice. 1938. *Conditions rurales en Haïti: Quelques Données basées en partie sur l'étude de 884 familles.* République d'Haïti, Service National de la Production Agricole, Bulletin no. 13. Port-au-Prince: Imprimerie de l'État.

Davenport, William. 1961. "The Family System of Jamaica." *Social and Economic Studies* 10 (4): 420–54.

Davis, Kingsley. 1974. "The Migrations of Human Population." *Scientific American* 231 (3): 92–105.

Dejean, Paul. 1978. *Les Haïtiens au Québec.* Montreal: Presses de l'Université du Québec.

DeWind, Josh, and David H. Kinley. 1988. *Aiding Migration: The Impact of International Development Assistance on Haiti.* Boulder: Westview Press.

Díaz-Ordóñez, V. 1938. *El más antiguo y grave problema antillano.* Ciudad Trujillo: Imp. "La Opinión, C. por A."

Díaz-Santana, Arismendi. 1974. "Papel de los braceros haitianos en la producción de azúcar dominicano." Colección Conferencia no. 24, vol. 177. Santo Domingo: Publicaciones de la UASD.

Docker, Edward Wybergh. 1970. *The Blackbirders: The Recruiting of South Sea Labour for Queensland, 1863–1907.* Sydney: Angus and Robertson.

Dore Cabral, Carlos. 1987. "Los dominicanos de origen haitiano y la segregación social en la República Dominicana." *Estudios Sociales* 20 (68): 57–80.

Dorsinville, Max. 1953. "Accord sur l'embauchage en Haïti et l'entrée en République Dominicaine des journaliers temporaires haïtiens." *Revue du Travail* (Port-au-Prince) 3: 107–14.

Duarte, Isis. 1980. *Capitalismo y superpoblación en Santo Domingo: Mercado de trabajo rural y ejército de reserva urbano.* Santo Domingo: CODIA.

Dupuy, Alex. 1989. *Haiti in the World Economy: Class, Race, and Underdevelopment since 1700.* Boulder: Westview Press.

Dwyer, Daisy, and Judith Bruce, eds. 1988. *A Home Divided: Women and Income in the Third World.* Stanford, CA: Stanford University Press.

Elkan, Walter. 1959. "Migrant Labor in Africa: An Economist's Approach." *American Economic Review* 49 (2): 188–97.

Emmer, P. C., ed. 1986. *Colonialism and Migration: Indentured Labour before and after Slavery.* Dordrecht, Netherlands: Martinus Nijhoff.

Fan, Yiu-Kwan, and Alan Stretton. 1985. "Circular Migration in South-East Asia: Some Theoretical Explanations." In *Labour Circulation and the Labour Process,* edited by Guy Standing, 338–57. London: Croom Helm.

Ferguson, James. 1992. *The Dominican Republic: Beyond the Lighthouse.* London: Latin America Bureau.

Fjellman, Stephen M., and Hugh Gladwin. 1985. "Haitian Family Patterns of Migration to South Florida." *Human Organization* 44 (4): 301–12.

Flores, Miguela. 1984. "The Philippines: Temporary Household Heads." In *Women in the Villages, Men in the Towns,* 147–86. Paris: Unesco.

Fortes, M. 1949. *The Web of Kinship among the Tallensi.* London: Oxford University Press.

Frazer, Ian. 1985. "Circulation and the Growth of Urban Employment amongst the To'ambaita, Solomon Islands." In *Circulation in Population Movement: Substance and Concepts from the Melanesian Case,* edited by Murray Chapman and R. Mansell Prothero, 225–47. London: Routledge and Kegan Paul.

Freeman, Derek. 1970. *Report on the Iban.* London: Athlone.

Freeman, J. D. 1961. "On the Concept of the Kindred." *Journal of the Royal Anthropological Institute* 91 (2): 192–220.

Georges, Eugenia. 1990. *The Making of a Transnational Community: Migration, Development, and Cultural Change in the Dominican Republic.* New York: Columbia University Press.

Girault, Christian A. 1981. *Le Commerce du café en Haïti: Habitants, spéculateurs et exportateurs.* Mémoire du Centre d'Etudes de Géographie Tropicale (CEGET)-Bordeaux. Paris: Éditions du Centre National de la Recherche Scientifique.

Glaessel-Brown, Eleanor E. 1979. "Seasonal Labor Migration on Hispaniola: A Policy of Convenience." In *Patterns of Policy: Comparative and Longitudinal Studies of Population Events,* edited by John D. Montgomery, Harold D. Lasswell and Joel S. Migdal, 235–56. New Brunswick: Transaction Books.

Glick, Nina Barnett. 1975. "The Formation of a Haitian Ethnic Group." Ph.D. dissertation, Columbia University.

Glick-Schiller, Nina, and Georges Fouron. 1990. "'Everywhere We Go, We Are in Danger': Ti Manno and the Emergence of a Haitian Transnational Identity." *American Ethnologist* 17 (2): 329–47.

Gmelch, George. 1987. "Work, Innovation, and Investment: The Impact of Return Migrants in Barbados." *Human Organization* 46 (2): 131–40.

Gómez, Alcides J., and Luz Marina Díaz M. 1983. *La moderna esclavitud: Los indocumentados en Venezuela.* Bogota: Fines and Editorial La Oveja Negra.

González, Nancie L. Solien. 1969. *Black Carib Household Structure: A Study of Migration and Modernization.* Seattle: University of Washington Press.

González Canalda, María Filomena, and Rubén Silié. 1985. "La nación dominicana en la enseñanza de la historia a nivel primario." *eme eme, Estudios Dominicanos* 14 (79): 15–29.

Goody, Jack. 1958. "The Fission of Domestic Groups among the LoDagaba." In *The Developmental Cycle in Domestic Groups,* edited by Jack Goody, 53–91. Cambridge: Cambridge University Press.

Gordon, Elizabeth. 1981. "An Analysis of the Impact of Labour Migration on the Lives of Women in Lesotho." In *African Women in the Development Process,* edited by Nici Nelson, 59–76. London: Frank Cass.

Grasmuck, Sherri. 1982. "Migration within the Periphery: Haitian Labor in the Dominican Sugar and Coffee Industries." *International Migration Review* 16 (2): 365–77.

———. 1983. "International Stair-Step Migration: Dominican Labor in the United States and Haitian Labor in the Dominican Republic." *Research in the Sociology of Work* 2: 149–72.

———, and Patricia R. Pessar. 1991. *Between Two Islands: Dominican International Migration.* Berkeley: University of California Press.

Graves, Nancy B., and Theodore B. Graves. 1974. "Adaptive Strategies in Urban Migration." *Annual Review of Anthropology* 3: 117–51.

Greaves, I. C. 1935. *Modern Production among Backward Peoples.* London: George Allen and Unwin.

Greene, Duty D., and Terry L. Roe. 1989. *Trade, Exchange Rate, and Agricultural Pricing Policies in the Dominican Republic, Volume I: The Country Study.* Washington, D.C.: The World Bank.

Griffith, David C. 1985. "Women, Remittances, and Reproduction." *American Ethnologist* 12 (4): 676–90.

———. 1986. "Social Organizational Obstacles to Capital Accumulation among Returning Migrants: The British West Indies Temporary Alien Labor Program." *Human Organization* 45 (1): 34–42.

Griffiths, Stephen L. 1979. "Emigration and Entrepreneurship in a Philippine Peasant Village." *Papers in Anthropology* 20 (1): 127–43.

Guerra y Sánchez, Ramiro. 1964. *Sugar and Society in the Caribbean: An Economic History of Cuban Agriculture.* New Haven: Yale University Press.

Gulliver, P. H. 1957. "Nyakyusa Labour Migration." *Rhodes-Livingstone Journal* 21: 32–63.

Guyer, Jane I. 1981. "Household and Community in African Studies." *African Studies Review* 24 (2-3): 87–137.

Harris, Olivia. 1984. "Households as Natural Units." In *Of Marriage and the Market: Women's Subordination Internationally and Its Lessons.* 2d ed., edited by Kate Young, Carol Wolkowitz and Roslyn McCullagh, 136–55. London: Routledge and Kegan Paul.

Hay, Margaret Jean. 1976. "Luo Women and Economic Change during the Colonial Period." In *Women in Africa: Studies in Social and Economic Change,* edited by Nancy Hafkin and Edna Bay, 87–110. Stanford: Stanford University Press.

Hayano, David M. 1979. "Male Migrant Labour and Changing Sex Roles in a Papua New Guinea Highlands Society." *Oceania* 50 (1): 37–52.

Hazard, Samuel. 1873. *Santo Domingo, Past and Present, with a Glance at Hayti.* New York: Harper and Brothers.

Heinl, Robert Debs, Jr., and Nancy Gordon Heinl. 1978. *Written in Blood: The Story of the Haitian People, 1492–1971.* Boston: Houghton Mifflin.

Hernández, Frank Marino. 1973. *La inmigración haitiana.* Santo Domingo: Ediciones Sargazo.

———, André Corten, Manuel Cocco, and Isis Duarte. 1976. *Inmigración haitiana y producción azucarera en la República Dominicana.* Santo Domingo: Editora "Alfa y Omega."

Herskovits, Melville J. 1937. *Life in a Haitian Valley.* New York: Alfred A. Knopf.

Hill, Polly. 1972. *Rural Hausa: A Village and a Setting.* Cambridge: Cambridge University Press.

———. 1986. *Development Economics on Trial: The Anthropological Case for a Prosecution.* Cambridge: Cambridge University Press.

Hoetink, H. 1982. *The Dominican People, 1850–1900: Notes for a Historical Sociology,* translated by Stephen K. Ault. Baltimore: Johns Hopkins University Press.

———. 1988. "Labour 'Scarcity' and Immigration in the Dominican Republic c. 1875–c. 1930." In *Labour in the Caribbean: From Emancipation to Independence,* edited by Malcolm Cross and Gad Heuman, 160–75. London: Macmillan.

Holly, Daniel, Micheline Labelle, and Serge Larose. 1979. "Dossier, l'émigration haïtienne, un problème national." *Collectif Paroles* 2: 18–26.

Houghton, D. Hobart, and Edith M. Walton. 1952. *Keiskammahoek Rural Survey, Volume II: The Economy of a Native Reserve.* Pietermaritzburg: Shuter and Shooter.

Hunter, Monica. 1936. *Reaction to Conquest: Effects of Contact with Europeans on the Pondo of South Africa.* London: Oxford University Press.

ILO. 1983. "Report of the Commission of Inquiry Appointed under Article 26 of the Constitution of the International Labour Organisation to Examine the Observance of Certain International Labour Conventions by the Dominican Republic and Haiti with Respect to the Employment of Haitian Workers on the Sugar Plantations of the Dominican Republic." *International Labour Office, Official Bulletin, Special Supplement* 66 (Series B).

Ireland, Gordon. 1941. *Boundaries, Possessions, and Conflicts in Central and North America and the Caribbean.* Cambridge, MA: Harvard University Press.

Islam, Mahmuda, and Perveen Ahmad. 1984. "Bangladesh: Tradition Reinforced." In *Women in the Villages, Men in the Towns,* 21–74. Paris: Unesco.

Jansen, Senaida, and Cecilia Millán. 1991. *Género, trabajo y etnia en los bateyes dominicanos*. Santo Domingo: Instituto Tecnológico de Santo Domingo, Programa Estudios de la Mujer.

Jellinek, Lea. 1978. "Circular Migration and the *Pondok* Dwelling System: A Case Study of Ice-Cream Traders in Jakarta." In *Food, Shelter and Transport in Southeast Asia and the Pacific*, edited by P. J. Rimmer, D. W. Drakakis-Smith, and T. G. McGee, 135–54. Research School of Pacific Studies, Department of Human Geography Publication HG/12. Canberra: Australian National University.

Jetley, Surinder. 1984. "India: Eternal Waiting." In *Women in the Villages, Men in the Towns*, 75–146. Paris: Unesco.

Joachim, Benoit. 1979. *Les Racines du sous-développement en Haïti*. Port-au-Prince: Imprimerie H. Deschamps.

Kayser, Bernard. 1972. *Cyclically-Determined Homeward Flows of Migrant Workers*. Paris: Organisation for Economic Co-operation and Development.

Kemper, Robert V. 1979. "Frontiers in Migration: From Culturalism to Historical Structuralism in the Study of Mexico–U.S. Migration." In *Migration across Frontiers: Mexico and the United States*, edited by Fernando Camara and Robert Van Kemper, 9–21. Albany: Institute for Mesoamerican Studies, State University of New York at Albany.

Kermel-Torrès, Doryane, and Pierre-Jean Roca. 1991. "Autosuffisance alimentaire: L'Avenir d'une utopie." *la lettre de Solagral, mensuel des solidarités agricoles et alimentaires* 103: 10–12.

King, Russell, and Alan Strachan. 1980. "The Effects of Return Migration on a Gozitan Village." *Human Organization* 39 (2): 175–79.

Knight, Melvin M. 1928. *The Americans in Santo Domingo*. New York: Vanguard Press.

Kubat, Daniel, ed. 1984. *The Politics of Return: International Return Migration in Europe*. Proceedings of the First European Conference on International Return Migration, Rome, November 11–14, 1981. Rome and New York: Centro Studi Emigrazione and Center for Migration Studies.

Labelle, Micheline, Serge Larose, and Victor Piché. 1983. "Emigration et immigration: Les Haïtiens au Québec." *Sociologie et Sociétés* 15 (2): 73–88.

Laguerre, Michel S. 1978. "The Impact of Migration on the Haitian Family and Household Organization." In *Family and Kinship in Middle America and the Caribbean*, edited by Arnaud F. Marks and René A. Römer, 446–81. Leiden: Institute of Higher Studies, Curaçao and Department of Caribbean Studies of the Royal Institute of Linguistics and Anthropology.

———. 1984. *American Odyssey: Haitians in New York City*. Ithaca: Cornell University Press.

Larose, Serge. 1975. "The Haitian Lakou, Land, Family and Ritual." In *Family and Kinship in Middle America and the Caribbean*, edited by Arnaud F. Marks and René A. Römer, 482–512. Leiden: Institute of Higher Studies, Curaçao and Department of Caribbean Studies of the Royal Institute of Linguistics and Anthropology.

Latortue, Paul R. 1985. "La migración haitiana a Santo Domingo." *Estudios Sociales* 18 (59): 43–59.

Laville, Lélio. 1933. *La Traite des nègres au XXème siècle, ou le dessous de l'émigration haïtienne à Cuba.* Port-au-Prince: Imprimerie Nouvelle.

Lawyers Committee for Human Rights. 1991a. *A Childhood Abducted: Children Cutting Sugar Cane in the Dominican Republic.* New York: Lawyers Committee for Human Rights.

————. 1991b. "Petition to the Inter-American Commission on Human Rights concerning the Situation of Haitians and Dominico-Haitians in the Dominican Republic." New York: Lawyers Committee for Human Rights.

Legassick, Martin. 1974. "South Africa: Capital Accumulation and Violence." *Economy and Society* 3 (3): 253–91.

Legros, Émile. 1955. "Résultats de l'enquête menée à Malpasse auprès des journaliers haïtiens revenant de la République Dominicaine en vue de recueillir des renseignements relatifs à leurs conditions de vie et de travail en ce pays." *Revue du Travail* (Port-au-Prince) 5: 67–76.

Lemoine, Maurice. 1985. *Bitter Sugar: Slaves Today in the Caribbean,* translated by Andrea Johnston. Chicago: Banner Press.

Lentz, Carola. 1986. "Los 'pilamungas' en San Carlos: Un estudio de caso sobre la inserción de migrantes serranos como trabajadores eventuales en un ingenio azucarero de la costa ecuatoriana." *HISLA: Revista Latinoamericana de Historia Económica y Social* 7: 45–63.

Lepkowski, Tadeusz. 1968. *Haití.* Havana: Casa de las Américas.

Lewis, W. Arthur. 1978. *The Evolution of the International Economic Order.* Princeton: Princeton University Press.

Leyburn, James G. 1966. *The Haitian People.* New Haven: Yale University Press.

Lipton, Michael. 1980. "Migration from Rural Areas of Poor Countries: The Impact on Rural Productivity and Income Distribution." *World Development* 8 (1): 1–24.

Locher, Huldrych C. 1978. "The Fate of Migrants in Urban Haiti—a Survey of Three Port-au-Prince Neighborhoods." Ph.D. dissertation, Yale University.

Locher, Uli. 1984. "Migration in Haiti." In *Haiti—Today and Tomorrow: An Interdisciplinary Study,* edited by Charles R. Foster and Albert Valdman, 325–36. Lanham, MD: University Press of America.

Logan, Rayford W. 1968. *Haiti and the Dominican Republic.* New York: Oxford University Press.

Lomnitz, Larissa. 1977. *Networks and Marginality: Life in a Mexican Shantytown,* translated by Cinna Lomnitz. New York: Academic Press.

Look Lai, Walton, 1993. *Indentured Labor, Caribbean Sugar: Chinese and Indian Migrants to the British West Indies, 1838–1918.* Baltimore: Johns Hopkins University Press.

Lowenthal, Ira P. 1984. "Labor, Sexuality and the Conjugal Contract in Rural Haiti." In *Haiti—Today and Tomorrow: An Interdisciplinary Study,* edited by Charles R. Foster and Albert Valdman, 15–33. Lanham, MD: University Press of America.

————. 1987. "'Marriage Is 20, Children Are 21': The Cultural Construction of Conjugality and the Family in Rural Haiti." Ph.D. dissertation, Johns Hopkins University.

Lozano, Wilfredo. 1976. *La dominación imperialista en la República Dominicana.* Santo Domingo: Editora de la Universidad Autónoma de Santo Domingo.

————. 1980. "Azúcar, fuerza de trabajo y desarrollo en República Dominicana (comentario)." *Ciencia y Sociedad* 5 (2): 293–300.

Lundahl, Mats. 1979. *Peasants and Poverty: A Study of Haiti.* New York: St. Martin's Press.

————. 1982. "Deux Interprétations de la réalité haïtienne: Critique d'une critique." *Conjonction* 152: 73–82.

————. 1983. *The Haitian Economy: Man, Land and Markets.* New York: St. Martin's Press.

Lwoga, Christopher. 1985. "Seasonal Migration in Tanzania: The Case of Ludewa District." In *Labour Circulation and the Labour Process,* edited by Guy Standing, 120–54. London: Croom Helm.

Madruga, José Manuel. 1986. *Azúcar y haitianos en la República Dominicana.* Santo Domingo: Ediciones MSC.

Marshall, Dawn I. 1979. *'The Haitian Problem': Illegal Migration to the Bahamas.* Kingston: Institute of Social and Economic Research, University of the West Indies.

————. 1982. "The History of Caribbean Migrations: The Case of the West Indies." *Caribbean Review* 11 (1): 6–9, 51–53.

Marshall, Woodville K. 1968. "Notes on Peasant Development in the West Indies since 1838." *Social and Economic Studies* 17 (3): 252–63.

Massey, Douglas S. 1987. "The Ethnosurvey in Theory and Practice." *International Migration Review* 21 (4): 1498–1522.

————. 1988. "Economic Development and International Migration in Comparative Perspective." *Population and Development Review* 14 (3): 383–413.

————, Rafael Alarcón, Jorge Durand, and Humberto González. 1987. *Return to Aztlán: The Social Process of International Migration from Western Mexico.* Berkeley: University of California Press.

McArthur, Harold J. 1979. "The Effects of Overseas Work on Return Migrants and Their Home Communities: A Philippine Case." *Papers in Anthropology* 20 (1): 85–104.

Meillassoux, Claude. 1981. *Maidens, Meal and Money: Capitalism and the Domestic Community.* Cambridge: Cambridge University Press.

Métraux, Alfred. 1951. *Making a Living in the Marbial Valley (Haïti).* Paris: Unesco.

Métraux, Rhoda. 1952. "Affiliations through Work in Marbial, Haiti." *Primitive Man* 25 (1/2): 1–22.

Millet, Kethly. 1978. *Les Paysans haïtiens et l'occupation Américaine, 1915–1930.* La Salle, Canada: Collectif Paroles.

Millspaugh, Arthur C. 1931. *Haiti under American Control.* Boston: World Peace Foundation.

Mines, Richard. 1981. *Developing a Community Tradition of Migration to the United States: A Field Study in Rural Zacatecas, Mexico, and California Settlement Areas.* Monographs in U.S.-Mexican Studies, 3. La Jolla: Program in United States-Mexican Studies, University of California, San Diego.

Mintz, Sidney W. 1959. "The Plantation as a Socio-Cultural Type." In *Plantation Systems of the New World,* edited by Vera Rubin, 42–49. Washington, D.C.: Pan American Union.

————. 1964. "The Employment of Capital by Market Women in Haiti." In *Capital, Savings and Credit in Peasant Societies,* edited by Raymond Firth and Basil S. Yamey, 256–86. Chicago: Aldine.

————. 1966. "The Caribbean as a Socio-Cultural Area." *Cahiers d'Histoire Mondiale* 9 (4): 912–37.

————. 1977. "The So-Called World System: Local Initiative and Local Response." *Dialectical Anthropology* 2 (4): 253–70.

————. 1979. "Slavery and the Rise of Peasantries." *Historical Reflections* 6 (1): 213–42.

————. 1985. *Sweetness and Power: The Place of Sugar in Modern History*. New York: Viking.

————. 1987. "Labor and Ethnicity: The Caribbean Conjuncture." In *Crises in the Caribbean Basin*, edited by Richard Tardanico, 47-57. Newbury Park, CA: Sage.

————. 1989. *Caribbean Transformations*. New York: Columbia University Press.

Mitchell, J. Clyde. 1959. "The Causes of Labour Migration." *Bulletin of the Inter-African Labour Institute* 6 (1): 12–46.

Moore, O. Ernest. 1972. *Haiti: Its Stagnant Society and Shackled Economy*. New York: Exposition Press.

Moral, Paul. 1959. *L'Économie haïtienne*. Port-au-Prince: Imprimerie de l'État.

————. 1961. *Le Paysan haïtien (étude sur la vie rurale en Haïti)*. Paris: G. P. Maisonneuve and Larose.

Moreno Fraginals, Manuel. 1985. "Plantations in the Caribbean: Cuba, Puerto Rico, and the Dominican Republic in the Late Nineteenth Century." In *Between Slavery and Free Labor: The Spanish-Speaking Caribbean in the Nineteenth Century*, edited by Manuel Moreno Fraginals, Frank Moya Pons, and Stanley L. Engerman, 3–21. Baltimore: Johns Hopkins University Press.

Morokvasic, Mirjana. 1984. "Birds of Passage Are Also Women . . . ." *International Migration Review* 18 (4): 886–907.

Moses, Yolanda T. 1977. "Female Status, the Family, and Male Domination in a West Indian Community." *Signs* 3 (1): 142–53.

Moya Pons, Frank. 1978. *Manual de historia dominicana*. Santiago de los Caballeros: Universidad Católica Madre y Maestra.

————, et al. 1986. *El batey: Estudio socioeconómico de los bateyes del Consejo Estatal del Azúcar*. Santo Domingo: Fondo para el Avance de las Ciencias Sociales.

Mueller, Martha. 1977. "Women and Men, Power and Powerlessness in Lesotho." *Signs* 3 (1): 154–66.

Murphy, Martin Francis. 1986. "Historical and Contemporary Labor Utilization Practices in the Sugar Industries of the Dominican Republic." Ph.D. dissertation, Columbia University.

————. 1991. *Dominican Sugar Plantations: Production and Foreign Labor Integration*. New York: Praeger.

Murray, Colin. 1981. *Families Divided: The Impact of Migrant Labour in Lesotho*. Johannesburg: Ravan.

Murray, Gerald Francis. 1977. "The Evolution of Haitian Peasant Land Tenure: A Case Study in Agrarian Adaptation to Population Growth." 2 vols. Ph.D. dissertation, Columbia University.

————, and María D. Álvarez. 1975. "Haitian Bean Circuits: Cropping and Trading Maneuvers among a Cash-Oriented Peasantry." In *Working Papers in Haitian Society and Culture*, edited by Sidney W. Mintz, 85–126. Occasional Papers 4. New Haven: Antilles Research Program.

Mutto, Paul. 1974. "Desarrollo de la economía de exportación Dominicana, 1900–1930." *eme eme, Estudios Dominicanos* 3 (15): 67–110.

Newton, James R. 1980. "The People of Batey Mosquitisol: Workers on a Sugar Cane Plantation in the Dominican Republic." Ph.D. dissertation, New School for Social Research.

Nicholls, David. 1979. *From Dessalines to Duvalier: Race, Colour and National Independence in Haiti.* Cambridge: Cambridge University Press.

———. 1985. *Haiti in Caribbean Context: Ethnicity, Economy and Revolt.* New York: St. Martin's Press.

Nieboer, H. J. 1910. *Slavery as an Industrial System.* The Hague: Martinus Nijhoff.

ONAPLAN. 1981a. *Empleo en la zafra azucarera dominicana.* Santo Domingo: Secretariado Técnico de la Presidencia, Oficina Nacional de Planificación.

———. 1981b. *Participación de la mano de obra haitiana en el mercado laboral: Los casos de la caña y el café.* Santo Domingo: Secretariado Técnico de la Presidencia, Oficina Nacional de Planificación.

Orbe, Justino José del. 1981. *Mauricio Báez y la clase obrera.* Santo Domingo: Taller.

Palmer, Ernest Charles. 1976. "Land Use and Landscape Change among the Dominican–Haitian Borderlands." Ph.D. dissertation, University of Florida.

Paranakian, Kanda. 1984. "Thailand: Continuing Hardship." In *Women in the Villages, Men in the Towns,* 247–89. Paris: Unesco.

Peña Batlle, Manuel A. 1943. *El sentido de una política.* Ciudad Trujillo: La Nación, C. por A.

Pérez de la Riva, Juan. 1979. "Cuba y la migración antillana, 1900–1931." In *Anuario de Estudios Cubanos 2: La República neocolonial,* Juan Pérez de la Riva, et al., 1–75. Havana: Editorial de Ciencias Sociales.

Perusek, Glenn. 1984. "Haitian Emigration in the Early Twentieth Century." *International Migration Review* 18 (1): 4–18.

Pessar, Patricia. 1982. "The Role of Households in International Migration and the Case of U.S.-Bound Migration from the Dominican Republic." *International Migration Review* 16 (2): 342–63.

Philpott, Stuart B. 1973. *West Indian Migration: The Montserrat Case.* London: Athlone.

Pierre, Guy. 1988. "The Frustrated Development of the Haitian Sugar Industry between 1915/18 and 1938/39: International Financial and Commercial Rivalries." In *The World Sugar Economy in War and Depression, 1914–40,* edited by Bill Albert and Adrian Graves, 121–30. London: Routledge.

Pierre-Charles, Gérard. 1967. *L'Économie haïtienne et sa voie de développement.* Paris: Editions G.-P. Maisonneuve and Larose.

Piore, Michael J. 1979. *Birds of Passage: Migrant Labor and Industrial Societies.* Cambridge: Cambridge University Press.

Pittin, Renée. 1984. "Migration of Women in Nigeria: The Hausa Case." *International Migration Review* 18 (4): 1293–1314.

Plant, Roger. 1987. *Sugar and Modern Slavery: A Tale of Two Countries.* London: Zed Books.

Plummer, Brenda Gayle. 1988. *Haiti and the Great Powers, 1902–1915.* Baton Rouge: Louisiana State University Press.

Portes, Alejandro. 1981. "Modes of Structural Incorporation and Present Theories of Labor Immigration." In *Global Trends in Migration: Theory and Research on International Population Movements,* edited by Mary M. Kritz, Charles B. Keely and Silvano M. Tomasi, 279–97. Staten Island: Center for Migration Studies.

———, and Robert L. Bach. 1985. *Latin Journey: Cuban and Mexican Immigrants in the United States.* Berkeley: University of California Press.

———, and John Walton. 1981. *Labor, Class, and the International System.* New York: Academic Press.

Price, Richard. 1971. "Studies of Caribbean Family Organization: Problems and Prospects." *Dédalo* 14: 23–59.

Price-Mars, Jean. 1953. *La República de Haití y la República Dominicana: Diversos aspectos de un problema histórico, geográfico y etnológico.* 3 vols. Translated by Martín Aldao and José Luis Muñoz Azpiri. Port-au-Prince: Colección del Tercer Cincuentenario de la Independencia de Haití.

Prothero, R. Mansell. 1957. "Migratory Labour from North-Western Nigeria." *Africa* 27 (3): 251–61.

Radcliffe, Sarah A. 1990. "Between Hearth and Labor Market: The Recruitment of Peasant Women in the Andes." *International Migration Review* 24 (2): 229–49.

Ratekin, Mervyn. 1954. "The Early Sugar Industry in Española." *Hispanic American Historical Review* 34 (1): 1–19.

Reichert, Joshua S. 1981. "The Migrant Syndrome: Seasonal U.S. Wage Labor and Rural Development in Central Mexico." *Human Organization* 40 (1): 56–66.

Renaud, Raymond. 1934. *Le Régime foncier en Haïti.* Paris: F. Loviton and Cie.

Rhoades, Robert E. 1978. "Intra-European Return Migration and Rural Development: Lessons from the Spanish Case." *Human Organization* 37 (2): 136–47.

Richards, Audrey I. 1939. *Land, Labour and Diet in Northern Rhodesia: An Economic Study of the Bemba Tribe.* London: Oxford University Press.

———. 1954. "The Travel Routes and the Travellers." In *Economic Development and Tribal Change: A Study of Immigrant Labour in Buganda,* edited by Audrey I. Richards, 52–76. Cambridge: W. Heffer and Sons Ltd.

Richards, Paul. 1983. "Farming Systems and Agrarian Change in West Africa." *Progress in Human Geography* 7 (1): 1–39.

Richardson, Bonham C. 1983. *Caribbean Migrants: Environment and Human Survival on St. Kitts and Nevis.* Knoxville: University of Tennessee Press.

Richman, Karen. 1990. "Guarantying Migrants in the Core: Commissions of Gods, Descent Groups, and Ritual Leaders in a Transnational Haitian Community." *Cimarrón: New Perspectives on the Caribbean* 2 (3): 114–28.

Rigaud, Candelon. 1930. *Promenades dans les campagnes d'Haïti, agriculture, industrie, légendes, religions, superstitions: La Plaine de la Croix des Bouquets dite 'Cul de Sac', 1789–1928.* Paris: L'Édition Française Universelle.

Rigg, Jonathan. 1988. "Perspectives on Migrant Labouring and the Village Economy in Developing Countries: The Asian Experience in World Context." *Progress in Human Geography* 12 (1): 66–86.

Rodriguez, Adrian, and Deborah Huntington. 1982. "Dominican Republic: The Launching of Democracy?" *NACLA Report on the Americas* 16 (6): 2–35.

Romain, J. B. 1959. *Quelques Moeurs et coutumes des paysans haïtiens*. Port-au-Prince: Imprimerie de l'État.

RONCO. 1987. *Agricultural Sector Assessment: Haiti*. Washington, D.C.: RONCO Consulting Corporation.

Root, Brenda Davis. 1987. "A Family Migration Model: Development and Empirical Application in the Philippines." Ph.D. dissertation, Pennsylvania State University.

Rotberg, Robert I. 1971. *Haiti: The Politics of Squalor*. Boston: Houghton Mifflin.

Rubenstein, Hymie. 1983. "Remittances and Rural Underdevelopment in the English-Speaking Caribbean." *Human Organization* 42 (4): 295–306.

Sabbagh Khoury, Yvette Teresa, and Dinorah Tavárez García. 1983. "La reproducción social de la fuerza de trabajo azucarera: Caso del Ingenio Barahona." Tesis de licenciatura, Universidad Autónoma de Santo Domingo.

St. John, Sir Spenser. 1971. *Hayti, or the Black Republic*. London: Frank Cass.

Saint-Louis, Loretta Jane Prichard. 1988. "Migration Evolves: The Political Economy of Network Process and Form in Haiti, the U.S., and Canada." Ph.D. dissertation, Boston University.

Sánchez, Juan J. 1976. *La caña en Santo Domingo*. Santo Domingo: Ediciones Taller.

Sanjek, Roger. 1982. "The Organization of Households in Adabraka: Toward a Wider Comparative Perspective." *Comparative Studies in Society and History* 24 (1): 57–103.

Sassen-Koob, Saskia. 1978. "The International Circulation of Resources and Development: The Case of Migrant Labour." *Development and Change* 9 (4): 509–45.

Savané, Marie Angelique. 1986. "The Effects of Social and Economic Changes on the Role and Status of Women in Sub-Saharan Africa." In *Understanding Africa's Rural Households and Farming Systems*, edited by Joyce Lewinger Moock, 124–32. Boulder: Westview Press.

Schapera, I. 1941. *Married Life in an African Tribe*. New York: Sheridan House.

Schmidt, Hans. 1971. *The United States Occupation of Haiti, 1915–1934*. New Brunswick: Rutgers University Press.

Schnakenbourg, Christian. 1984. "From Sugar Estate to Central Factory: The Industrial Revolution in the Caribbean (1840–1905)." In *Crisis and Change in the International Sugar Economy, 1869–1914*, edited by Bill Albert and Adrian Graves, 83-93. Norwich: ISC Press.

Sharp, John. 1987. "Relocation, Labour Migration, and the Domestic Predicament: Qwaqwa in the 1980s." In *Migrants, Workers, and the Social Order*, edited by Jeremy Eades, 130–47. ASA Monographs 26. London: Tavistock.

———, and Andrew Spiegel. 1990. "Women and Wages: Gender and the Control of Income in Farm and Bantustan Households." *Journal of Southern African Studies* 16 (3): 527–49.

Sibisi, Harriet. 1977. "How African Women Cope with Migrant Labor in South Africa." *Signs* 3 (1): 167–77.

Simmons, Alan B. 1984. "Migration and Rural Development: Conceptual Approaches, Research Findings and Policy Issues." In *Population Distribution, Migration and Development*. Proceedings of the Expert Group on Population Distribution, Migration and Development, Hammamet, Tunisia, 21–25 March 1983, edited by UN, Department of International Economic and Social Affairs, 156–92. New York: United Nations.

———, Sergio Diaz-Briquets, and Aprodicio A. Laquian. 1977. *Social Change and Internal Migration: A Review of Research Findings from Africa, Asia, and Latin America.* Ottawa: International Development Research Centre.

Simpson, George Eaton. 1942. "Sexual and Familial Institutions in Northern Haiti." *American Anthropologist* 44 (4): 655–74.

Skeldon, Ronald. 1985. "Circulation: A Transition in Mobility in Peru." In *Circulation in Third World Countries*, edited by R. Mansell Prothero and Murray Chapman, 100–20. London: Routledge and Kegan Paul.

Skinner, Elliott P. 1960. "Labour Migration and Its Relationship to Socio-Cultural Change in Mossi Society." *Africa* 30 (4): 375–401.

Smith, M. G. 1962. *Kinship and Community in Carriacou.* New Haven: Yale University Press.

Smith, Raymond T. 1956. *The Negro Family in British Guiana: Family Structure and Social Status in the Villages.* London: Routledge and Kegan Paul.

Smucker, Glenn R. 1982. "Peasants and Development Politics: A Study in Haitian Class and Culture." Ph.D. dissertation, New School for Social Research.

Solien, Nancie L. 1960. "Household and Family in the Caribbean: Some Definitions and Concepts." *Social and Economic Studies* 9 (1): 101–6.

Spiegel, Andrew D. 1980. "Rural Differentiation and the Diffusion of Migrant Labour Remittances in Lesotho." In *Black Villagers in an Industrial Society: Anthropological Perspectives on Labour Migration in South Africa*, edited by Philip Mayer, 109–68. Cape Town: Oxford University Press.

———. 1987. "Dispersing Dependents: A Response to the Exigencies of Labour Migration in Rural Transkei." In *Migrants, Workers, and the Social Order*, edited by Jeremy Eades, 113–29. ASA Monographs 26. London: Tavistock.

Spindel, Cheywa R. 1985. "Temporary Work in Brazilian Agriculture: 'Boia-Fria'—A Category under Investigation." In *Labour Circulation and the Labour Process*, edited by Guy Standing, 313–37. London: Croom Helm.

Spurr, G. B., M. Barac-Nieto, and M. G. Maksud. 1975. "Energy Expenditure Cutting Sugar Cane." *Journal of Applied Physiology* 39 (6): 990–96.

Spurr, G. B., M. G. Maksud, and M. Barac-Nieto. 1977. "Energy Expenditure, Productivity, and Physical Work Capacity of Sugarcane Loaders." *American Journal of Clinical Nutrition* 30 (10): 1740–46.

Stahl, Charles W., and Fred Arnold. 1986. "Overseas Workers' Remittances in Asian Development." *International Migration Review* 20 (4): 899–925.

Stepick, Alex. 1982a. "Haitian Boat People: A Study in the Conflicting Forces Shaping U.S. Refugee Policy." *Law and Contemporary Problems* (Duke University Law Journal) 45 (2): 163–96.

———. 1982b. "The New Haitian Exodus: The Flight from Terror and Poverty." *Caribbean Review* 11 (1): 14–17, 55–57.

———. 1984. *Haitians Released from Krome: Their Prospects for Adaptation and Integration in South Florida*. Occasional Papers Series, Dialogues, no. 24. Miami: Latin American and Caribbean Center, Florida International University.

———, and Alejandro Portes. 1986. "Flight into Despair: A Profile of Recent Haitian Refugees in South Florida." *International Migration Review* 20 (2): 329–50.

Stichter, Sharon. 1985. *Migrant Laborers*. Cambridge: Cambridge University Press.

Stretton, Alan. 1985. "Circular Migration, Segmented Labour Markets and Efficiency." In *Labour Circulation and the Labour Process*, edited by Guy Standing, 290–312. London: Croom Helm.

Sudarkasa, Niara. 1977. "Women and Migration in Contemporary West Africa." *Signs* 3 (1): 178–89.

Tanzi, Vito. 1976. "Export Taxation in Developing Countries: Taxation of Coffee in Haiti." *Social and Economic Studies* 25 (1): 66–76.

Taylor, Elizabeth. 1984. "Egyptian Migration and Peasant Wives." *MERIP Report* no. 124: 3–10.

Thomas, Hugh. 1971. *Cuba: The Pursuit of Freedom*. New York: Harper and Row.

Thomas-Hope, Elizabeth M. 1978. "The Establishment of a Migration Tradition: British West Indian Movements to the Hispanic Caribbean in the Century after Emancipation." In *Caribbean Social Relations*, edited by Colin G. Clarke, 66–81. Monograph Series no. 8. Liverpool: Centre for Latin American Studies, University of Liverpool.

Tilly, Charles, and C. Harold Brown. 1967. "On Uprooting, Kinship, and the Auspices of Migration." *International Journal of Comparative Sociology* 8 (2): 139–64.

Trager, Lillian. 1988. *The City Connection: Migration and Family Interdependence in the Philippines*. Ann Arbor: University of Michigan Press.

Trouillot, Michel-Rolph. 1980. Review of *Peasants and Poverty: A Study of Haiti*, by Mats Lundahl. *Journal of Peasant Studies* 8 (1): 112–16.

———. 1985. "Nation, State, and Society in Haiti, 1804–1984." Washington, D.C.: Latin America Program, The Woodrow Wilson International Center for Scholars.

———. 1990. *Haiti, State against the Nation: The Origins and Legacy of Duvalierism*. New York: Monthly Review Press.

UNDP. 1992. *Human Development Report 1992*. New York: Oxford University Press.

Unesco. 1985. *Femmes au pays: Effets de la migration sur les femmes dans les cultures méditerranéennes*. Paris: Unesco.

UNICEF. 1990. *The State of the World's Children, 1990*. Oxford: Oxford University Press.

Union Nationaliste. 1930. *Dépossessions: «le latifundia américain contre la petite propriété d'Haïti»*. Tome 1er. Port-au-Prince: Imprimerie de «La Presse».

Vargas G., Rosemary. 1981. "Unemployment, Underemployment, and Labor Imports in the Dominican Republic: A Sketch of Some of the Problems." *Ibero Americana, Nordic Journal of Latin American Studies* 10 (1/2): 39–61.

Veras, Ramón Antonio. 1983. *Inmigración-haitianos-esclavitud*. Santo Domingo: Ediciones de Taller.

Vidal, L. F. 1926. *Apuntes sobre inmigración*. Santo Domingo: Imprenta Montalvo.

WGBH. 1993. *Americas, Part 4—Mirrors of the Heart: Race and Identity*. Lourdes Portillo, executive producer. Boston: WGBH and Central Television Enterprises for Channel 4, UK.

White, Luise. 1980. "Women's Domestic Labor in Colonial Kenya: Prostitution in Nairobi, 1900–1950." Working Paper no. 30. Boston: African Studies Center, Boston University.

Whiteford, Scott. 1981. *Workers from the North: Plantations, Bolivian Labor, and the City in Northwest Argentina*. Austin: University of Texas Press.

Williams, Eric. 1944. *Capitalism and Slavery*. Chapel Hill: University of North Carolina Press.

Wilson, Godfrey. 1941–42. *An Essay on the Economics of Detribalization in Northern Rhodesia, Parts I and II*. Rhodes-Livingstone Papers, nos. 5 and 6. Livingstone, Northern Rhodesia: The Rhodes-Livingstone Institute.

Wingfield, Roland. 1966. "Haiti: A Case Study of an Underdeveloped Area." Ph.D. dissertation, Louisiana State University.

Woldemikael, Teklemariam. 1980. "Maintenance and Change of Status in a Migrant Community: Haitians in Evanston, Illinois." Ph.D. dissertation, Northwestern University.

Wolf, Eric R. 1982. *Europe and the People without History*. Berkeley: University of California Press.

Wolpe, Harold. 1972. "Capitalism and Cheap Labour-Power in South Africa: From Segregation to Apartheid." *Economy and Society* 1 (4): 425–56.

Wong, Diana. 1984. "The Limits of Using the Household as a Unit of Analysis." In *Households and the World-Economy*, edited by Joan Smith, Immanuel Wallerstein and Hans-Dieter Evers, 56–63. Beverly Hills: Sage.

Wood, Charles H. 1981. "Structural Changes and Household Strategies: A Conceptual Framework for the Study of Rural Migration." *Human Organization* 40 (4): 338–44.

———. 1982. "Equilibrium and Historical-Structural Perspectives on Migration." *International Migration Review* 16 (2): 298–319.

Woodson, Drexel G. 1990. "Tout Mounn se Mounn men Tout Mounn pa Menm: Microlevel Sociocultural Aspects of Land Tenure in a Northern Haitian Locality." 3 vols. Ph.D. dissertation, University of Chicago.

World Council of Churches. 1978. *Migrant Workers in the Dominican Republic: A Case for Human Rights Action*. Geneva: World Council of Churches.

———. 1980. *'Sold like Cattle': Haitian Workers in the Dominican Republic*. Geneva: World Council of Churches.

Zegeye, Abebe, and Shubi Ishemo, eds. 1989. *Forced Labour and Migration: Patterns of Movement within Africa*. London: Hans Zell.

Zelinsky, Wilbur. 1971. "The Hypothesis of the Mobility Transition." *Geographical Review* 61 (2): 219–49.

———. 1979. "The Demographic Transition: Changing Patterns of Migration." In *Population Science in the Service of Mankind*, 165–89. Liège: International Union for the Scientific Study of Population.

Zuvekas, Clarence, Jr. 1979. "Land Tenure in Haiti and Its Policy Implications: A Survey of the Literature." *Social and Economic Studies* 28 (4): 1–30.

Index

housing: sugar estates, 69–70, 120, 122
(*see also batey/es*); rural Haiti, 63, 72–
73, 93–94, 97–100, 102–9, 112–25,
200n5; *see also* Haitian cane workers,
earnings, expenditure of
human rights organizations, 29, 162,
164–65, 167; *see also* Haitians in
Dominican Republic, legal status;
Lesser Antilles, migrants in Dominican Republic
Hurricane Ines (1966), 99

Immigration Society of Macorís, 38
individualism, methodological, 92
India, migrants from, 15
inflation, 37–38, 48, 51, 86, 114, 200n3
Ingenio Santa Ana (pseud., site of
author's fieldwork in Dominican
Republic), described, 66–72, 144–45

Jacmel, 72–73, 78–79, 112
Jamaicans in U.S., 167
Jorge Blanco, Salvador, 49–50

labor circulation: communication, home
and host areas, 23, 28; Haiti-
Dominican Republic, 6, 12–14, 32–
34, 40–52, 57–66, 72, 78–132, 137–65,
168, 198nn2, 3 (*see also* Haitian cane
workers; Haitians in Dominican
Republic; migration, from Haiti); in
Latin America, 17; modern history
of, 14–16; in southern and central
Africa, 16, 19, 21–22, 24; theories of,
16, 18–25, 159–60; Third World, 17–
18, 25; *see also* migrant labor;
migration
labor contract, Haiti-Dominican
Republic, 2, 8, 12–13, 46–49, 114,
161, 203n9; *see also* Haitian cane
workers, recruitment of
laku. *See* peasantry, Haiti, family and
household organization
land
—Dominican Republic, 5, 34, 37–38, 42–
43, 69

—Haiti, 57–59, 197nn2, 3: availability,
32–33, 54–55, 60–63, 200n5; rental
and sharecropping, 53, 62–63, 75,
87–88, 92, 111; tenure, 63–64, 75, 90,
93, 110–11, 116, 160; transactions, 54,
89, 98, 104, 109–10, 113–14, 201n1;
see also Haiti, politics and government, land titles and laws; peasantry, Haiti, social stratification
—Lesser Antilles, 31–32
—*see also* resources, theory of open/
closed
Lawyers Committee for Human Rights,
50, 164; *see also* human rights
organizations
Lemoine, Maurice, 48
Léogâne, 58, 78
Lesser Antilles, migrants in Dominican
Republic: discrimination and rights
abuses against, 39–40; recruitment
of, 31–32, 34, 37–41, 195n2; return
migration, 39–40
lòt bò lâmè. *See* Haitians in North America
lottery, 82, 153
L'Ouverture, Toussaint, 53
lwa (ancestral spirits). *See* Voodoo

Melanesians in Australia, 15–16
Mexicans in U.S., 26
migrant labor: benefits of, for employers, 2, 12, 23–24, 29, 39–40; discrimination against, 15–16; repatriation
of, 21–22, 28–29; social backgrounds
of, 26–27; social mobility of, 28, 40;
social reproduction of, 23–24; and
trade unions, 29; *see also* labor
circulation; migration
migration
—from Haiti, 55–62, 83–84, 142–43, 146–
47, 157–62, 198n2: clandestine, 8–9,
45, 47, 72, 79, 85, 106, 108, 115, 121,
194n6; impact, on Haiti, 76, 102,
111–12, 116–17, 134–40, 200n6,
201n8; personal histories, 63–64, 84,
91–99, 105, 171–75, 199n4; relay, 92
—theory: auspices of, 17, 27–29, 141,